WITNESS TO
MARGARET BOURKE-WHITE IN INDIA & PAKISTAN
LIFE AND FREEDOM

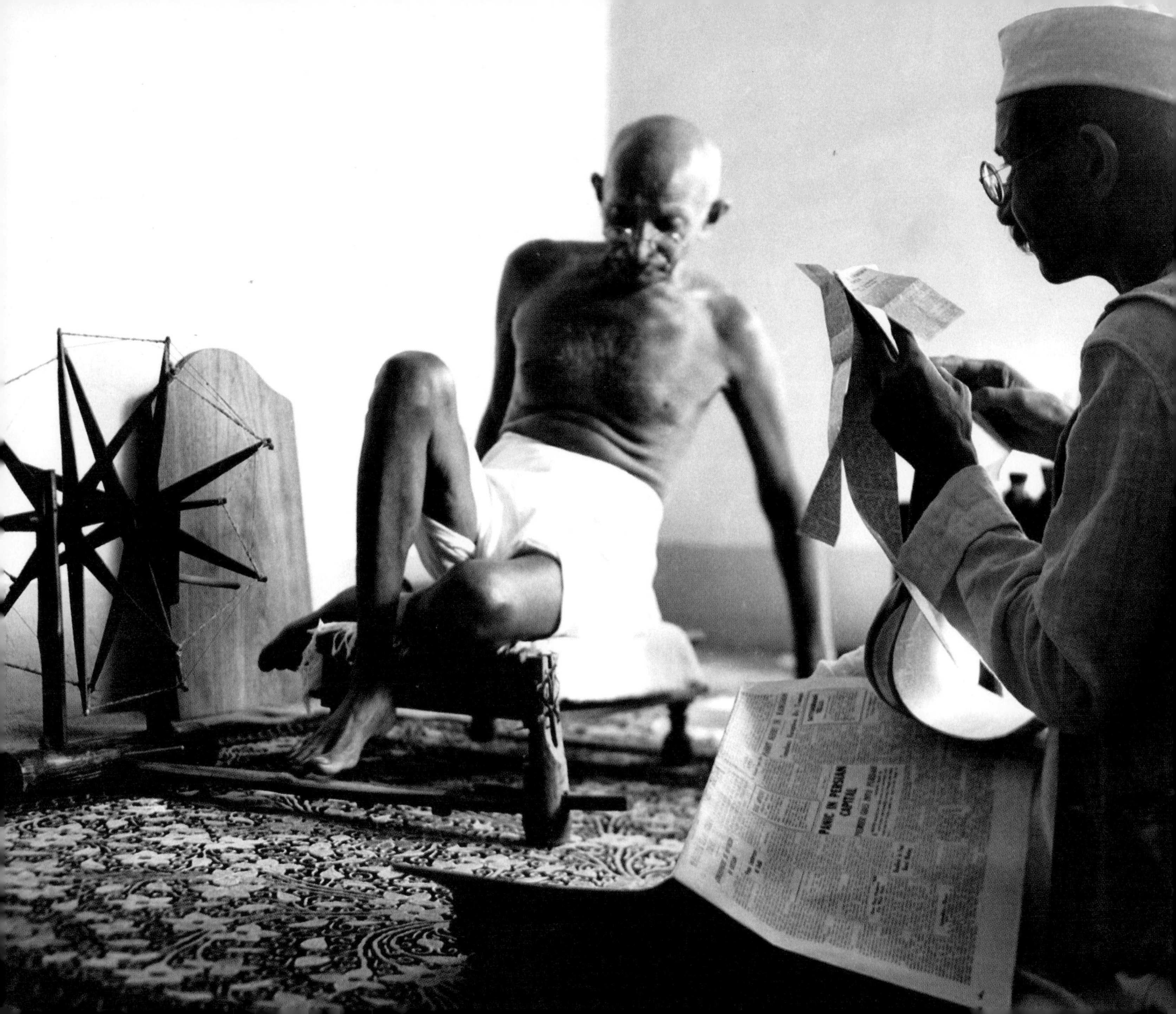
PANIC IN PERSIAN CAPITAL

WITNESS TO
MARGARET BOURKE-WHITE IN INDIA & PAKISTAN
LIFE AND FREEDOM

Concept, Text and Visuals
PRAMOD KAPOOR

Foreword
GOPALKRISHNA GANDHI

With an essay by
VICKI GOLDBERG

Lustre Press
Roli Books

The captions for the photographs of this book are taken from Margaret Bourke-White's original writings – *Halfway to Freedom: A Report on the New India in the Words and Photographs of Margaret Bourke-White* (Simon and Schuster, 1949); her autobiography *Portrait of Myself* (Collins, 1964); and from her biography by Vicki Goldberg, *Margaret Bourke-White: A Biography.* The captions in roman are excerpted from these writings.

'India a Pillar of Fire' taken from *Margaret Bourke-White: A Biography* by Vicki Goldberg, © 1986, Vicki Goldberg. Reprinted by permission.

Photo Credit: Getty Images

ISBN: 978-81-7436-699-3

Published in India by Roli Books in arrangement with Roli & Janssen BV
M-75 Greater Kailash II Market,
New Delhi-110 048, India
Ph: ++91-11-4068 2000; Fax: ++91-11-2921 7185
E-mail: info@rolibooks.com, Website: www.rolibooks.com

Layout Design: Naresh L. Mondal

Printed and bound in India.

Dedicated to you
who inspired me for forty years
through thick and thin.

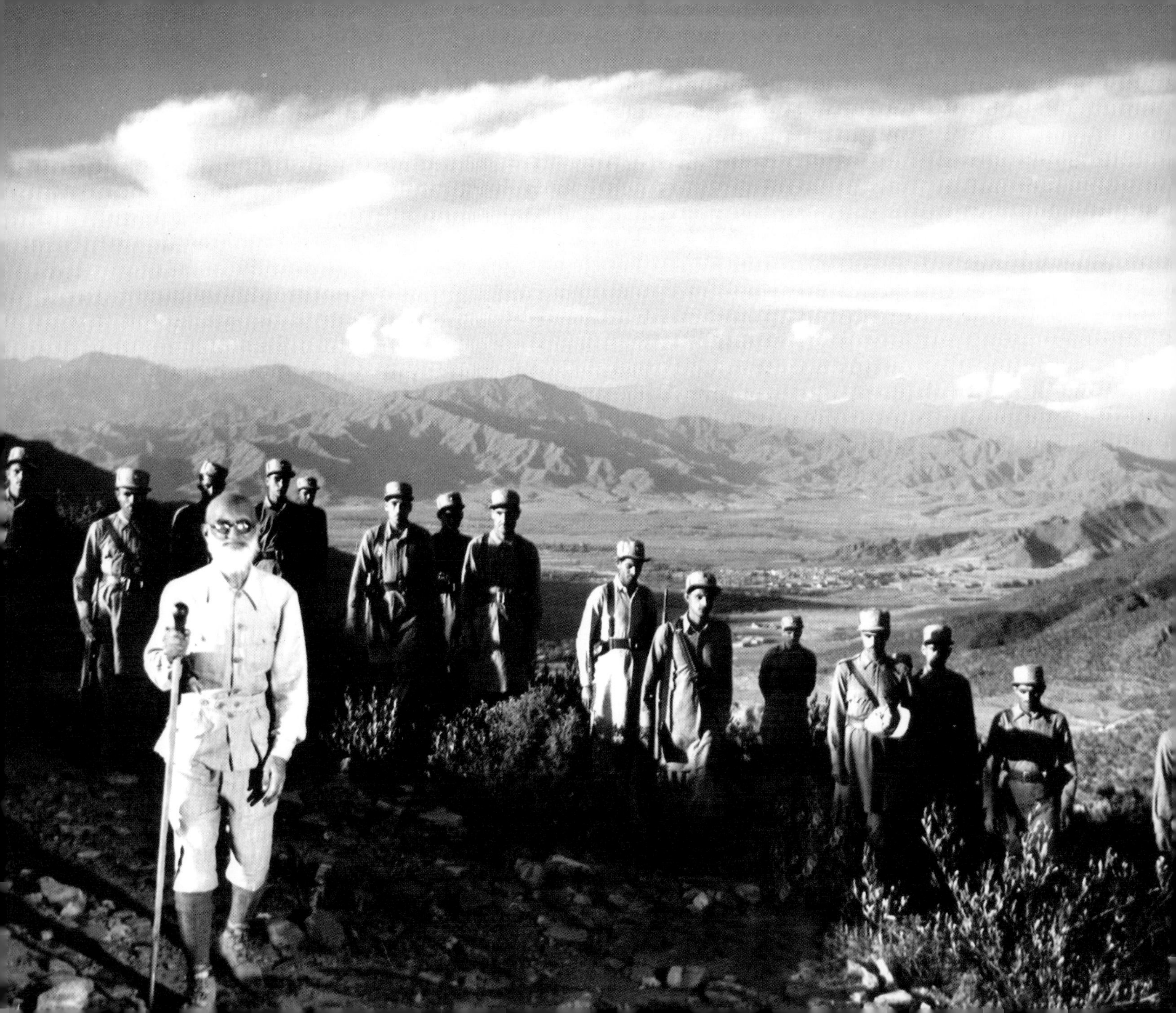

FOREWORD

Margaret Bourke-White's photographs reproduced in this volume were captured for *Life*. They are about Life and Time – India's, with its hour-hand reaching climactic moments, and the minute-hand touching, second by inexorable second, the day's grind or its rapture. The photographs observe without commenting, 'catch' without trapping. They 'frame'. Bit without decorating the scene for adulation or singling it out for sarcasm. As her flashbulbs turn, in a second's exposure, from clear glass to milky opacity, a moment is lifted as time's offspring from the sequence of its fleeting. It is then placed in the hammock of a rare photographer's art. We can see a laugh set free from the prison of preoccupation, a fear imprisoned by bars of silence. We see death handed by life through a stilled cartwheel. Equally, life perched atop its ending, among the branches of a self-renewing tree.

The great who walk on human feet and the simple who hold their heads high, come on to Margaret Bourke-White's stage from the past, which is so present in this curtain-call.

Gopalkrishna Gandhi

Facing Page: Miangul Abdul Wadud Wali of Swat with his bodyguards. When Margaret Bourke-White visited the State of Swat, a tiny principality on the snow-capped mountains near Islamabad, the Swati women were 'thorougly puzzled' by her costumes – 'It wears clothes like a man, but it has hair like a woman.' Though her interpreter could settle the 'sex question', he could not answer if she was a movie actress or a circus performer!

FROM POIGNANT TO POWERFUL

In the summer of 2005, while looking for material to commemorate sixty years of the partition of India, I stumbled upon unpublished photographs taken by Margaret Bourke-White of that cataclysmic event. Until then, I knew her largely through her persona enacted by Candice Bergen in the Richard Attenborough's 1982 Academy award-winning film, *Gandhi*. Around that time I had re-read Khushwant Singh's *Train to Pakistan*, and when I saw Bourke-White's photographs of the Partition, I felt they were made for each other. We subsequently published a special edition of this classic with photographs taken by her of those tumultuous days. My interest in her works led me to discover some of the stunning but unpublished images.

In a short period of time, from 1946 to 1948, she travelled the length and breadth of the country, and seemed to befriend the very spirit of India. This was reflected in the sheer range of her photographs, which extended from the poignant to the powerful. I was enchanted and moved, and decided to put together the best of her images taken in India and Pakistan into a book.

Margaret Bourke-White's India photographs in the archives of Getty Images went beyond the Partition. Getty was very supportive in letting me go through their archival images, especially Charles Merullo and Rick Mayston, who helped the project generously, for which I owe them a debt of gratitude. With the selected images, I approached Gopalkrishna Gandhi, former Governor of West Bengal and Mahatma Gandhi's grandson, who graciously agreed to write a foreword. His contribution adds great value to the book.

My interest in her life and her work in India led me to read Margaret Bourke-White's book on the experiences in India, *Halfway to Freedom*; her autobiography, *Portrait of Myself*, and an excellent and meticulously researched biography written by Vicki Goldberg, *Margaret Bourke-White: A Biography*. Goldberg very kindly gave us permission to include a chapter from this biography in our edition, for which we are indebted.

Special thanks are due to Hameed Haroon, Publisher, Dawn Group of Newspapers, for his time and effort in identifying pictures of his family members and various political leaders from Pakistan; and my friend Ganesh Saili for offering his valuable inputs.

My colleagues at Roli Books, Neelam Narula, Swati Chopra, Naresh Mondal and Jyoti Dey deserve special thanks for their support in putting the book together.

This is a humble homage to one of the greatest news photographer of our times.

Pramod Kapoor

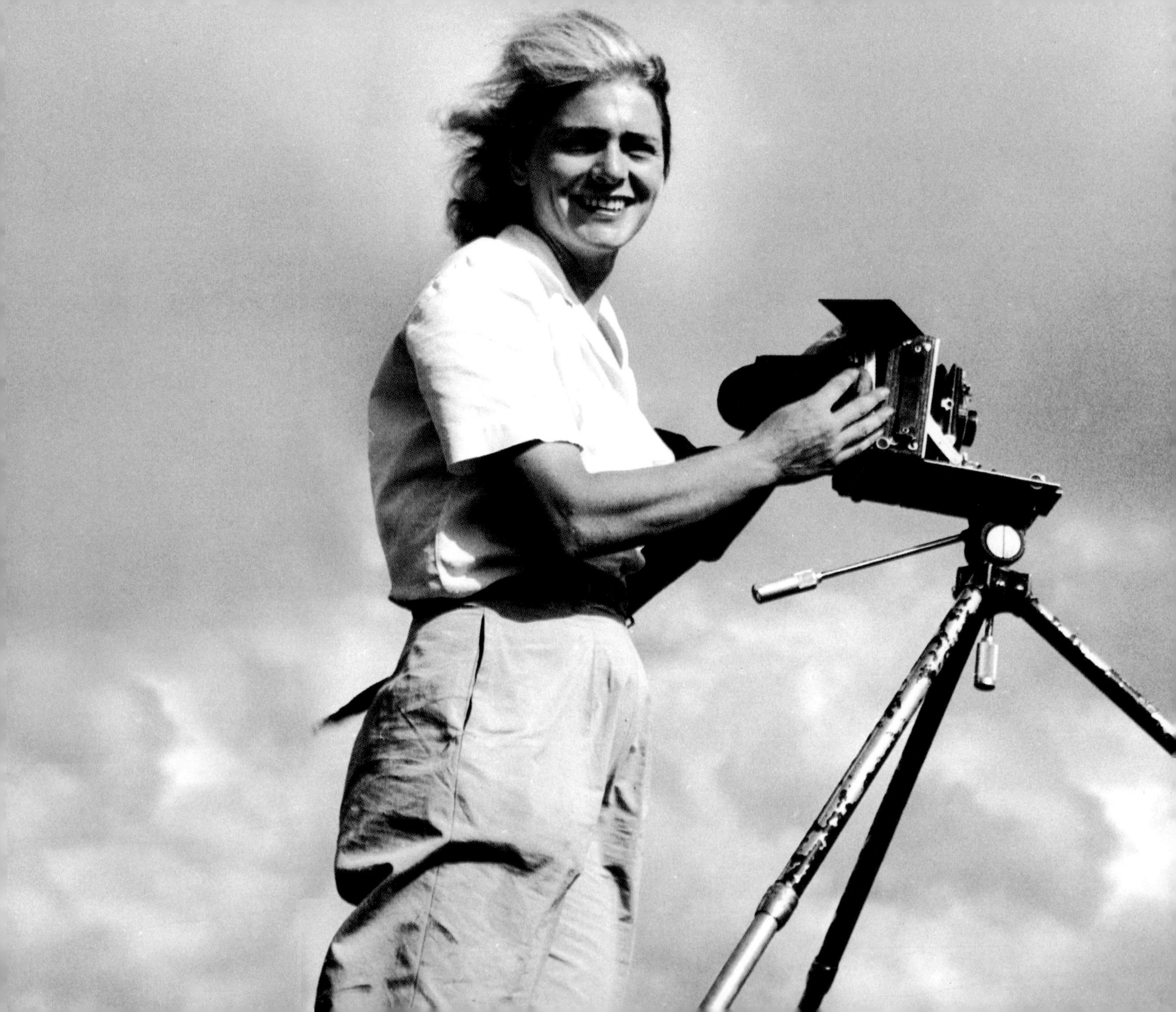

INTRODUCTION

'Margaret, you can always be proud that you were invited into the world,' said a mother to her daughter, who would live up to the 'invitation' by creating a truly remarkable life rich in adventure, depth and meaning. The little girl was Margaret Bourke-White, the celebrated photojournalist who documented some of the most cataclysmic and iconic moments of the twentieth century, events that forever changed the course of human history. She was truly one of a kind.

Margaret came into this world on 14 June 1904. Her father, Joseph White, a Polish immigrant of Jewish descent, was a trained printing engineer, while her mother, Minnie Bourke, was an Irish Orthodox Christian, whose father, a carpenter, had died after falling from scaffoldings that were used to build the first few skyscrapers in New York in the 1880s. Both Joseph and Minnie were nature lovers, and were afflicted by the 'bicycle mania' that hit America in the 1890s. On one such nature ride, Minnie's cycle broke down going uphill. Joseph, usually a quiet man, broke his silence atop the mountain and proposed to her. They were married on 14 June 1898.

Margaret was the second of their three children. Joseph and Minnie 'agreed while they were still engaged that they would have intercourse only when they wished to have a child'. Principled and meticulous, they decided that their second child, Margaret, would come into this world on a specific date. This invitation into the world had been set for 13 June, when her

Facing Page: Margaret Bourke-White (1904-71): 'I arrived in India in the early spring of 1946. The groundwork for independence was being laid, and I stayed for most of that year, traveling about the country. Then I came home, ... found I wanted to learn more about India, and returned to spend part of 47 and 48 there.'

mother, Minnie went into labour, but once the doctor learnt that the parents' anniversary was just a day away, he gently put Minnie back to bed and delayed things just long enough. Her friends would later joke that it was for this reason she was never on time, but her biographer Vicki Goldberg noted, 'yet she never once missed an important date with history'.

Given her parents' love for natural history, Margaret grew up in the midst of a variety of pets, ranging from caterpillars to snakes and turtles. She spoke well in class, joined the debating society, became editor of her school's year book, president of the dramatic society, and to top it all, would often turn up in school with a snake around her arm. She almost became a herpetologist, a zoologist who studies amphibians, but her father's love for photography, and his passion to improve photographing techniques, drew her to be his assistant, both in taking pictures and developing them artistically. He encouraged her to study the world of machines, which he thought was as charming as the world of nature.

Her father was also responsible for introducing Margaret to a work ethic that she would hold sacred all her life. 'His positive contribution was to build in me the deepest respect for work,' she wrote in her notes. 'Work is religion to me, the only religion I have.'

After her father's death, when Margaret returned to school, she simultaneously signed up for a two hours a week course with Clarence H. White, one of the first photographers of the time, not to learn photography but design and composition.

At one point Margaret wrote that she never considered becoming a professional photographer until her senior year in college, when she was hired as photography counselor at a camp near her home. She took some great pictures of the camp set against the mountain, often staying up the whole night to get that single picture at the crack of dawn. It was an image that sold in hundreds. A professional photographer was born. 'I am so proud of myself now,' she wrote in her diary. 'I feel as if I could make my living anywhere.'

That one picture had pushed her into a career that would see her at the most troubled spots through the best part of the twentieth century.

She attended the University of Michigan for a while where she began photographing for the *Michiganensian*, or '*Ensian*, the college yearbook. Joe Vlack, who also took pictures for the '*Ensian*, took her under his wing. He found her attractive and could always persuade her to spend time with him if photography was the object. He confirmed her notion that photography meant adventure. Together they photographed the clock tower from a window in a fourth-floor men's toilet; they thought for a while they'd got themselves locked in for the night. Another evening, Vlack told her that a perfect view lay on the other side of the engineering building's roof. They squeezed out a window and clambered up a rope to the pitched roof. (The first time, her arms weren't strong enough, but she worked on it incessantly in gym class.) They ran, slipping, to the roof, and then slid down the other side. Margaret was scared. She loved it.

In 1924, Margaret met and married a fellow student, Everett Chapman. When the marriage fell apart two years later, determined not to let its failure hamper her, she shifted to Cornell University and took up photography once more. Upon graduating in 1927, Margaret started a commercial photography studio where she began doing industrial and architectural photography. One of her first major clients was Otis Steel. Her photographs of the steel factory, done using a new style of lighting with magnesium flares, earned her national attention, including that of the legendary publisher, Henry Luce.

Luce, who was on the verge of starting a new business magazine, *Fortune*, saw the Otis Steel photographs in a Midwestern newspaper. He immediately cabled the as-yet-unknown photographer, saying, 'Harold Wagner has shown me your photographs stop would like to see you stop could you come to New York within a week at our expense please telegraph when – Henry R Luce Publisher Time the weekly newsmagazine'. When Margaret arrived to meet him, Luce immediately began talking about his plans for the magazine which would prioritize photographs much more than ordinary business journals. Would she care to join in the adventure?

Margaret jumped at the opportunity, which in six years' time would lead to another, even greater one. Luce had his pulse on the times and realized that America was ready for a magazine that documented the times through photographs. Thus was born the iconic journal, *Life*, and Margaret was the first photojournalist to be offered a berth. It is this job that would provide her the means and the opportunity to do some of her most celebrated work.

To Margaret, *Life* seemed like the perfect vehicle to put her work into alignment with her new social awareness. She had written just before *Life* began, 'People don't realize how serious conditions in this country are.... The new job (*Life*) will give me more opportunity to work with creative things like this... I am delighted to be able to turn my back on all advertising agencies and go on to life as it really is.'

She learnt very early in her career that if it's a picture one wanted, the number of images taken or the rolls used was of no consequence. If it wasn't worth a dollar, it was worth nothing. She never stopped after that; she took more photographs than anyone would have thought reasonable. Of course, one camera would never be enough, so she travelled ever after with at least five cameras in tow.

During the mid-1930s, she travelled extensively in the American south to photograph drought victims, and collaborated with the novelist Erskine

Caldwell on a book, *You Have Seen Their Faces*. Though Margaret insisted she wasn't looking for love, or marriage, and went through lovers rapidly, she agreed to marry a persistent Caldwell in 1939. The union was perhaps doomed from the start, ending in divorce three years later due to Caldwell's inability to handle his wife's frequent disappearances on missions abroad.

Margaret's interest in 'life as it really is' would see her travelling from one hotspot to another, becoming the first woman photographer to cover war during the Second World War, where she documented the concentration camp at Buchenwald when it was liberated. As the first American photographer to be allowed into the Soviet Union, Margaret wangled an entry into the Kremlin to photograph Joseph Stalin. Expecting a towering figure, in accordance with the hoardings she had seen all over the Soviet Union, Margaret was shocked to find a short, pockmarked man who wouldn't be drawn into conversation. As she set about photographing him, her flashbulbs fell out from her pocket and went bouncing all over the floor. As she and her interpreter raced after them, Stalin burst into laughter. It had faded into a smile by the time Margaret got her camera working. Once more, she had got a historical photograph.

'Margaret Bourke-White became a historic figure while she was still making history,' wrote her biographer Vicki Goldberg. 'Her name, face and photographs were known to millions.' Richard Attenborough in his Oscar-winner *Gandhi* chose Candice Bergman to portray Margaret as Gandhi's 'torturer', a name given to her by the Mahatma himself. Her photographs of India, according to Vicki Goldberg, are her 'most sustained body of work. They offer a kind of stately, classical view of misery, of humanity at its most wretched, yet somehow noble, somehow beautiful.' The subjects are monumental, posed, dramatic, and the philosophy of life is: 'despair over man's inhumanity to man, but a promise that human beings are worthy of compassion and may yet be saved.'

Life magazine commissioned her to cover the exchange of populations that accompanied the partition of India and the birth of two nations. For days she travelled taking photographs of people leaving their homes for an uncertain destiny – 'All roads between India and Pakistan were choked with streams of refugees. In scenes reminiscent of the Biblical times, hordes of displaced people trudged across the newly created borders to an uncertain future.'

She was there to catch the tragedy of the ordinary man caught up in extraordinary events. She was there to photograph Gandhi at his spinning wheel. She was there to photograph Jinnah with his fez. And soon after, both men were to meet their Maker. Difference was that while one had become a Mahatma or saint, the other could barely conceal the 'bitterness of his victory turning stale in his mouth'.

Margaret's many loves were legendary, and in India too, there were many who were enchanted by her. During a train-ride to Shimla, the 'polished-to-the-fingertips' journalist Frank Moraes fell in love with her. He took her by the hand to meet everyone who was anyone in the hurly-burly of Indian politics. Though, for Margaret, the relationship remained a brief dalliance, not one that could penetrate her carefully constructed independence and her single-minded focus on her work.

With all her achievements, fame, sense of excitement, and her unwillingness to entertain regret, Margaret asked much more of life than most people can hope for. But then, her accomplishments were so vast she could be said to have given the world as good as she got, and much of her achievement is still alive in memory and on the printed page.

As early as 1927, she knew she wanted to be famous and she wanted to be wealthy. But fame always came first. She who seemed so self-involved, whose career used up free assistance as fast as film, did not forget a close friend. She had a capacity for loyalty and thoughtfulness that was narrowly directed but infinitely deep.

But an ill-wind was blowing her way. In 1956, at the age of forty-seven, she was diagnosed with Parkinson's. For eighteen years, the disease would become her greatest 'assignment', a project she threw herself in with the rigorous optimism that had stood her in good stead throughout her life. For a while, embarrassed by her body's progressive debilitation, she hid her disease. Then, in 1958, she collaborated with a colleague from *Life*, Alfred Eisenstaedt, on an article on Parkinson's and an experimental surgical procedure that she had undergone. The article, when it appeared in *Life*, became hugely popular and brought her back into the consciousness of millions. It also helped her view her illness as part of her work, something that helped her overcome her fear of it, and ultimately, of death.

Life continued to send her on assignments, but soon, she couldn't manage the work. In 1971, a fall rendered her immobile, and soon, resultant complications ended her life. The camera had slipped from the grasp of the most famous photojournalist of the era, almost at the same time as the golden age of photojournalism was drawing to a close, challenged by television. A year after her death, her beloved *Life* ceased publication in the format that had become popular in Margaret's heyday, and which she had helped popularize to a great extent.

As for summing up her life, Vicki Goldberg says it best. 'Taken all in all, it was a good life – at least the woman who lived it thought so – and she lived it fully to the very last step on the road.'

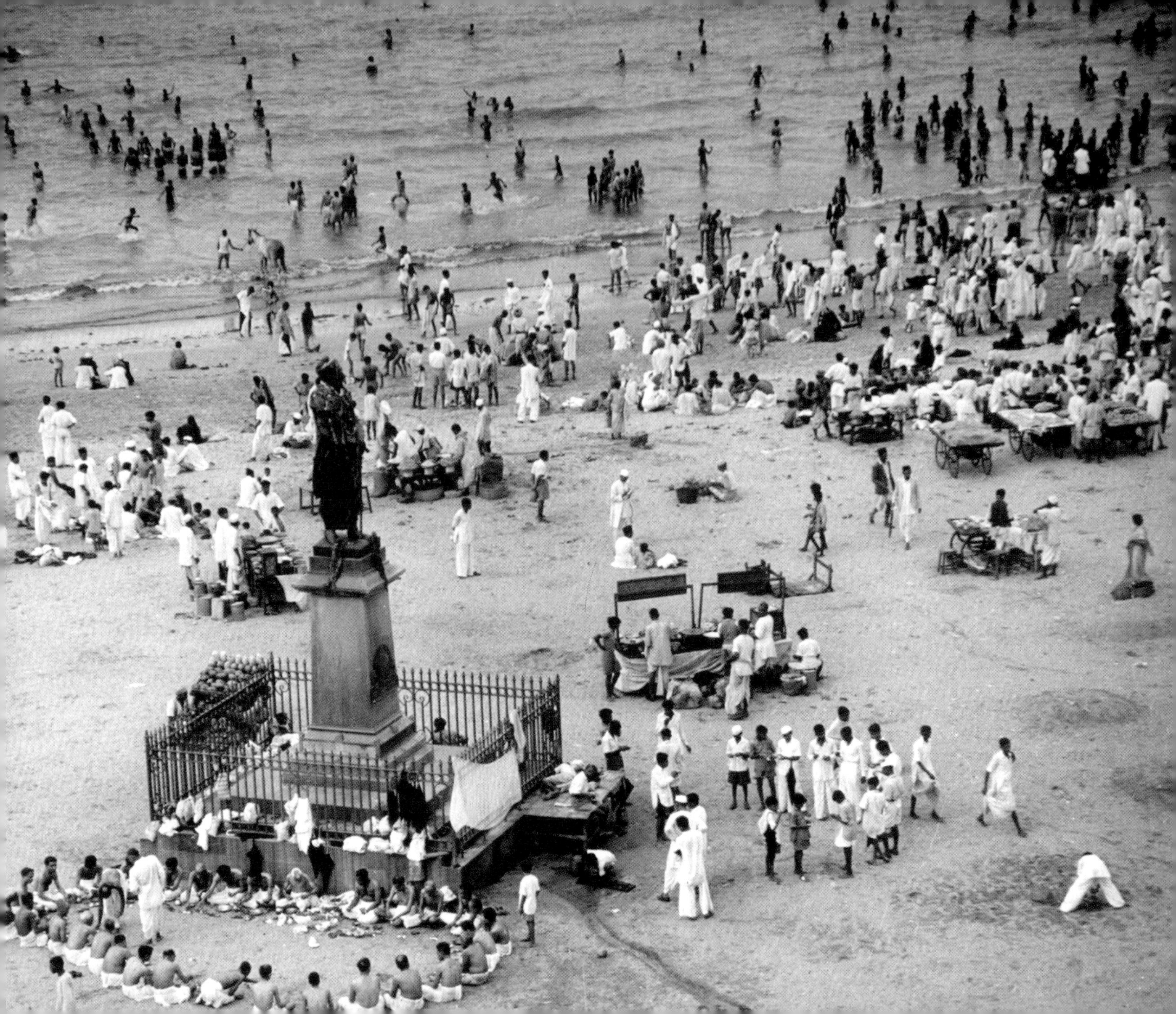

INDIA: A PILLAR OF FIRE

Vicki Goldberg

Life had been eager since the end of the thirties to articulate a role for the United States as a major world power, a role that many had foreseen and that the war would make inevitable. In 1939, Walter Lippmann wrote in *Life*: "What Rome was to the ancient world, what Great Britain has been to the modern world, America is to be to the world of tomorrow." Henry Luce, in a controversial article called "The American Century," made clear in 1941 that he thought American hegemony a kind of holy mission: "The other day," he wrote, "Herbert Hoover said that America was fast becoming the sanctuary of the ideals of civilization. For the moment it may be enough to be the sanctuary of these ideals. But not for long. It now becomes our time to be the powerhouse from which the ideals spread throughout the world and do their mysterious work of lifting the life of mankind from the level of the beasts to what the Psalmist called a little lower than the angels."

From the pulpit of his magazine Luce assured his subscribers that Britain was ready to pass the mantle of leadership to America. "Among serious Englishmen, the chief complaint about America ... has really

Facing Page: For the editors of Life*, the India assignment was a matter of frequent discussions. The country on the threshold of independence needed a 'thorough and interpretative coverage'. Margaret Bourke-White wanted time to stay in India for a long period. She was in the middle of a lecture tour when* Life's *executive editor, Wilson Hicks, telegraphed her that 'the time was at hand'.*

amounted to this – that America has refused to rise to the opportunities of leadership in the world."

In the post-war world America rose to its opportunities. *Life* never let the country forget it. June 14, 1943: "Post-War Plans: Only National Interest Makes Sense – But 'Our' National Interest Is as Wide as the World." November 25, 1946: "World Power: The U.S. Has It and Knows It." September 12, 1949: "A New World Is Shaping Around the U.S., and the British Crisis Is Part of the Change." *Life*, in need of an eyewitness to the fall of the British Empire, sent Margaret Bourke-White to India.

The end of the war spelled the end of the biggest story in the world. *Life* and its photographers had to regear. Margaret, whose themes were always large, needed momentous events to match the levels of challenge she had built into her working life. Wilson Hicks, who understood this, discussed Margaret's career with her and kept a shaping hand on it. Hicks cabled her while she was on a lecture tour that her next story would be India.

She arrived on the subcontinent in March of 1946 and moved quickly to get a picture of Gandhi. She had heard him inveigh publicly and often, through a twentieth-century microphone, against twentieth-century machinery, against the tractor and the textile mill. Surveying the dry land, the hunger, the stupefying poverty of India which she was certain industrialization could relieve, Margaret never quite understood Gandhi's animus toward the machine.

When she made her appointment with him, Gandhi was staying with untouchables in a sprawling slum that smelled of human excrement. As soon as Margaret walked in, his secretary asked if she knew how to spin. The Mahatma's spinning wheel was the symbol of his drive to rid the land of British dominion. Like colonial empires generally, Britain siphoned off the raw materials of its colony to fuel the industrial plant at home. Indian cotton was turned into cloth in British textile mills, then sold back to India for clothing. Gandhi insisted Indians should break the chain of dependency by spinning their own cotton.

Margaret neither knew how to spin nor cared, but the secretary insisted that if she could not spin she could not understand the symbolism of the wheel. He was implacable. At last, because her pictures had to be on the plane that night, Margaret asked for a spinning lesson. When it was determined that she could spin well enough to understand, the secretary advised her that it was Gandhi's day of silence and she must not speak to him. Nor could she use artificial light; he didn't like it. Realizing that the hut would be dark, she pleaded for her lighting equipment and was finally permitted three peanut flashbulbs. She found Gandhi seated cross-legged on the floor in a hand-woven loincloth, reading newspaper clippings through steel-rimmed spectacles perched on his nose. He was seventy-seven, tiny, shrunken, and bald, and he had defied the greatest empire in the history of the world.

He paid no attention to the photographer who had invaded his reading time, and she was grateful, for the bare room was impossibly dark, with sun coming through one high window directly into her camera and her eyes, and she had to maneuver to avoid the halation. As Gandhi began to spin, she used the first of her three bulbs. The flash was delayed. India's heat and moisture frequently sabotaged her machinery. With only two bulbs left, she turned to time exposures, but her tripod soon froze with one leg at its minimum length and the others at the maximum. Carefully checking her flash, Margaret fired the second bulb. It worked exactly as it should – but she had forgotten to pull the slide. At least the third bulb worked.

This sitting, which was every photographer's bad dream come true, resulted in a picture that has been endlessly reproduced. The spinning wheel up close in silhouette spreads its arms over the entire left half of the picture. Slightly behind it sits the Mahatma, wholly involved in studying the papers on his lap. His head is bowed to read, and the light from the window behind him clearly outlines his bald skull with the radiance of a discreet halo. Margaret has composed an icon for a secular saint, humble, meditative, graced by light, and accompanied by his symbolic spinning wheel much as western saints are accompanied by their emblems.

Margaret photographed Gandhi many times afterward. He called her, fondly, she thought, "the torturer." His inconsistencies puzzled her rational mind; it was not until she saw his self-sacrificing bravery in the face of India's convulsive violence that she began to think him akin to the saint she had made him out to be with her camera.

She also photographed Mohammed Ali Jinnah, the Moslem leader, whose features were as sharp as the creases in his western business suits. Jinnah would almost single-handedly bring about the partition of India and the creation of Pakistan. He was the rock against which Nehru, Gandhi, and their Congress party foundered and Mountbatten broke. "We shall have India divided," Jinnah said, "or we shall have India destroyed." Before he died, he fulfilled the first part of his vow and came close to fulfilling the second.

During her first few weeks in India, Margaret met, photographed, interviewed, and charmed scores of officials. Robert Sherrod, a *Life* correspondent on the scene, wrote to a friend: "She knew more about India after three weeks than most reporters learn in three years. She has more energy than anybody else in India, and she works like hell in spite of the deadly heat."

Her cultivated charm had matured to a diplomatic mastery. Sherrod and David B. Richardson, another correspondent, hosted a big party in April. Margaret arranged the invitations, decorations, everything. She invited warring officials who would barely sit down together at conferences: Hindu nationalists, Moslem separatists, Communists, British diplomats, and maharajahs; Nehru, Jinnah, Feroz Khan Noon – the future prime ministers of India and of Pakistan. They all liked Margaret, who dressed to provoke their delight in a backless halter-top dress cleverly run up from a sequined paisley scarf. Sworn enemies became gentlemen accomplices for a few hours, men who were professionally rude to each other reverted to politeness all evening. One British diplomat was heard to exclaim, "Delhi has never seen the likes of this gathering. The catalyst certainly is Bourke-White."

Her diplomacy was subtle, her priorities clear. An Indian photographer named Sunil Janah was recommended as an assistant; she located him at the Communist Party headquarters. He agreed to travel with her because he was scheduled to photograph in the same region, and he thought it humorous that *Life* should pay the expenses of the Communist Party of India. The two of them journeyed to a remote region by river-boat. At the last departure point, their host aboard the boat insulted Janah, who refused to go any further on the trip. "I could see that [Peggy] was angry," he writes, "but she calmly sat down beside me. 'Look, Sunil,' she said, 'you know that I am on your side of the fence, no matter who and what these people are. They and they only can take us where we want to go to do our own work. It is not for our gains and satisfaction or whatever but for being able to tell the world what we may find with our pictures, isn't that what our job is all about? And if our personal feelings get in the way, at any time, don't you think we should get rid of them?'"

He has remembered this all his life. "I remember her not merely as a famous photographer I had worked with but as one of the finest human beings I have ever known, who used her sensitivity, understanding, and her great ability to voice our social conscience through her photography."

Alone, Margaret went north in April to Simla, new site of the freedom conferences and the summer capital of the British Raj, a city of English churches, gardens, and bandstands sitting in the shadow of the Himalayas. She traveled with Gandhi, who insisted on traveling in third-class trains with his followers and his goats; as he had renounced cow's milk, the herd was essential. He needed, in fact, a group of third-class trains. One of his supporters once remarked that Gandhi ought to realize how much it cost to keep him in poverty. Margaret, the only unattached woman on the train, had her own small compartment, between Nehru's and Gandhi's; later she said she was the only American woman to have slept between the two of them.

On the train to Simla, between Nehru and Gandhi and the goats, Frank Moraes, a leading Indian journalist, fell in love with Margaret. Moraes, a good-looking man, his hair black and wavy, cut a romantic figure. A Christian who shared the nationalist views of Gandhi's followers, he drank heavily and smoked regularly among the ranks of ascetic Hindus. He spoke fluently with an upper-class British accent acquired at Oxford and had a slightly Victorian manner of address, a bountiful fund of amusing stories, and a journalist's inexhaustible file of knowledge.

He was married. His son says Moraes adored his wife and that they were "one of the bright young couples of Bombay," giving and going to expensive cocktail parties. The author Ved Mehta, who visited the Moraes household in India, says Frank ran an open house that always attracted interesting people. Mehta found him charming and "very youthful, as if a permanent undergraduate . . . wistful, a little sad." He had extensive free time in which to exercise his numerous social graces, and the ease of a man who likes and is liked by women. Mehta says he was "sexually active, but in a lost way, and lovable, but also in a lost way, like a child." In a warm haze of alcohol, affability, and quick intelligence, Moraes gave the impression of being gentle, sweet, and at the same time cool-headed, an image that he himself mocked.

He and Margaret were soon writing letters every day as she crisscrossed India. His were rapturous, speaking of sexual and emotional bliss. She approached him with her habitual caution and her personal insistence on honesty. Apparently she let him know early on that she insisted on her freedom.

Moraes had seen through the defensive fortifications Margaret had built so carefully. He wrote her that before he'd been interested in her he'd thought she had a streak of hardness.

> As I now know, it isn't hardness but the protective front which a hurt nature offers to an untrustworthy world. Far from being cocksure you're not at all certain of yourself, Darling. All that you've done and achieved you've realized at the cost of hard, sustained work. And you don't want to lose it. The most precious thing to you is Security – a thing you didn't have in your childhood; which you thought you'd achieved when you married Chappie but which was shattered overnight.... You're "hard" only in the sense that you'll fight like a tiger to hold what you have. Because what you have signifies to you what you've made of yourself in the face often of tremendous difficulties and obstacles – and if you lose that, you lose the Big Thing that matters – Faith in yourself – and you feel your world will collapse around you.
>
> ... You've always been understanding but I've a feeling that you're afraid to show tenderness to anybody,

> although lately you've done it to me. . . . It's only people with great reserves of feeling who can really be tender.

Moraes willingly instructed Margaret in Indian politics. She had made it known as soon as she arrived in India that she intended to write a book, and "not a pretty picture book." She probed for information everywhere, pulling her notebook from her purse at formal dinners in a manner so straightforward and ingratiating that people did not hesitate to talk to her. David Richardson, commenting on her bright mind, her infinite capacity for hard work, and the magical, magnetic quality of her striking looks, her poise and animation, says, "I don't think I ever revered any woman journalist the way I did her. ... Up to then, many of us had assumed that if a woman was a journalist she would deal on an emotional level. ... Up to then, women were sort of freaks in journalism abroad."

Moraes, who seemed to know everything, would have helped greatly with her book. She had met his publisher, who was to help her even more: Peter Jayasinghe, a man a dozen years or more her junior, with looks as aristocratic and elegant as Burkes Peerage. Two American women describe him as being the color of coffee with cream, with "velvet black eyes" and delicate hands fingering his luxurious tie, altogether more "handsome, stunning and beautiful than Tyrone Power in *The Rains Came*." He exuded a taste for high living. And he, too, fell in love with Margaret.

He drove her about Delhi in a yellow convertible, chasing along on assignments like a devoted puppy. He helped her so extensively with her research that she offered to share royalties with him, an offer he apparently turned down. Frank Moraes was extremely jealous of Jayasinghe, who dropped hints of his conquest. But Moraes had a much more severe problem with jealousy: his wife's. Beryl Moraes was going mad. Trained as a pathologist, she began to spend her days alone, methodically saying her rosary. A pretty, lively woman, she had become withdrawn and unkempt, her mind seething with suspicions of Margaret.

Dom Moraes, their son, a poet and author, was about eight years old when his mother came into his room one night to tell him about an American woman she'd met at a party the night before. His father, she said, had known this woman for years. He'd been with her in America all during the war when he claimed to be a correspondent in Burma. She demanded that Dom go with her to the woman's hotel and plead with her to leave Frank Moraes alone.

Dom Moraes wrote about the incident in his autobiography.

> We went up to the American woman's room. She opened the door, a tough handsome woman in her

> forties [Margaret was forty-two], smart in slacks. A swell of shame swamped me, but my mother's hand was firm on my arm.
>
> "I want to speak to you," she said in a high trembly voice, "about my husband."
>
> The American woman looked very puzzled. However, she held the door open. "Do come in," she said. "We met yesterday, didn't we? Is this your little boy?"
>
> My mother did not answer, but in the same high, trembly voice launched into an interminable speech about my father's misdeeds, which I tried not to hear. The American woman stared at her in amazement. When my mother paused for breath she said very kindly, "Look, honey, you're not well. Come sit down a moment, and have a cool drink. You wait here, Sonny," she said to me. "There's some picture books in that shelf there. Don't worry, your Mommy's fine."

That afternoon, Beryl Moraes seemed to recover. She told her son on the way home that she'd been "a silly ass." But her madness was not to be stopped by talk, and her jealousy had cause. About this time, Dom Moraes reportedly said he would like Margaret to be his mother because she understood his father and himself and he could depend on her. Frank Moraes was suffering. He cared deeply for his wife and wanted her well. He even asked Margaret to postpone her second trip to India because Beryl was improving. Not surprisingly, Margaret refused. Once she wrote Beryl a letter, which she probably never mailed, saying she did not want to do anything to hurt her or to spoil their friendship. No doubt she meant it.

Certainly she was not the cause of Beryl Moraes's madness. Mrs Moraes would have found another fixation had Margaret not been there. But for a woman who had so little wish to do harm, Margaret had left behind her a wide swath of injured wives. She who did so much to raise the status of women in her profession seldom conformed to feminist ideas of solidarity. (Helen Caldwell Cushman remarks, "I don't say she was above reproach. She was above self-reproach.") Beryl Moraes, in the midst of a nervous breakdown after Margaret went back to America, persistently imagined other people were Bourke-White in disguise. The real Bourke-White could not trouble her much longer; the distance to America was too great for grand passions.

India virtually submerged Margaret beneath its sprawl and clutter. For months she was visually adrift and sent back little of consequence. It took a disaster to focus her talents clearly. Jinnah announced to the press that the Moslem state of Pakistan would be founded on "Direct Action" if necessary. August 16 was to be the day of proof.

That day, the morning dawned white and thick with heat over the bazaars, souks, and fetid alleys of

Calcutta, a city already legendary for its cruelty. At first light, Moslem mobs swarmed up out of the filthy slums. Screaming, burning, rampaging for five days without stop, they clubbed to death thousands of Hindus, leaving the streets clogged with mutilated bodies and the Hooghly River awash with bloody corpses. News of the massacre spread like fire in a high wind. Violence abruptly flared across the country; civil war threatened to explode. The savagery of religious fanaticism in Calcutta changed history in India, unleashing hatreds and reprisals that in time split the country apart.

As soon as she heard the news, Margaret flew to Calcutta. An Associated Press photographer named Max Desfors had been there when the riots erupted; she realized he had come across something extraordinary and badgered him to tell her where. Unwilling to be scooped, he held back the information until he was certain his film had reached his London bureau, then admitted that a driver from the provost marshal's office had found a scene of unparalleled carnage. Instantly Margaret went to the provost marshal, wept when he seemed reluctant, finally got the same driver and found the same place.

The street was short and narrow. Small, single-story houses looked out blindly from locked doors and tiny vertical slits of windows. Lying like garbage across the width of the street and in its open gutters were the bodies of the dead. Some were eviscerated, others in pieces, all hideously swollen by death and exposure to sun. Some had been picked clean down to the bone by vultures, now the street's only live inhabitants, score upon score of them, moving slowly among the corpses. A few had eaten so much they could no longer fly.

David Richardson accompanied Margaret that day. "The sweet stench of death was so strong," he says, "that I clutched a handkerchief to my face while holding out a flashgun ... to fill in the dark shadows among the clustered dead." Margaret was shooting 4 x 5 on a tripod so her pictures would not turn grainy if enlarged. In the grinding heat she put her head under the black focusing cloth and fired one sheet of film after another. The horrors she'd seen in Germany must have steeled her for yet more. "Like Germany's concentration camps," she later wrote, "this was the ultimate result of racial and religious prejudice."

Richardson heard footsteps – "a British colonel, resplendent in fresh tropical khakis and bright decorations, and accompanied, at two paces, by his Indian batman. ... 'I say, old chap,' he asked me, jauntily pointing his swagger stick toward the black-hooded Peggy at her tripod and camera, 'taking a few snaps?'" Margaret's head shot out to glare at the man's retreating back, then she dived again beneath the cloth, where the lurid street hung with preternatural clarity upside down on her ground glass.

When Bourke-White showed Desfors a cable from her New York office that said, "Your vulture pictures simply magnificent," he realized he hadn't yet heard about his own. He cabled London. The return wire read, "Your bodies inedible for British consumption." Bourke-White got a double-page spread in *Life*.

Back in Darien in the fall, Margaret began to write her book. When writing, she gave up all semblance of social life, but she would not deny herself certain pleasures. "Have felt I was living too fast to write it. And I care more about living than writing. I care a great deal about writing but more about living. This is a constant conflict. I dislike conflict and am against it – but this one will never be resolved until the book is written and sealed within two stiff covers." She would not entirely give up men. One longtime lover who had seen her to the plane in London was surprised that she hesitated to let him kiss her in public. He wondered if she was fearful of narrowing her options on the transatlantic flight.

In the States, there was a *Life* artist she cared about for a time, and she resumed the passionate affair she'd had with the Russian expert Maurice Hindus in the early thirties. Peter Jayasinghe flew to America to see her. Totally engrossed in her writing, she did not meet him at the airport and asked him to supper not that night but the next. He never quite forgave the slight and she, writing years later, said it was on her conscience still.

Still, he wanted to marry her. She refused him gently, asking him to stay her good friend. Marriage was out of the question. He was always hurt when her work came first, which was a fatal sign, and once he had committed the cardinal sin: he had given her an order. No one ever gave an order to Margaret Bourke-White, who had won such complete control over her own life, but Jayasinghe one day told her to clean her car. Responding with a rare burst of fury, she threw a wastebasket at him. She knew too much to marry him, but her affection for him was genuine, and they remained friends long after she became ill.

Another good friend, Ed Stanley, who had had an intimate, often interrupted relationship with Margaret since the early thirties, helped her extensively with most of her books. A journalist and a skillful editor, Stanley edited, rewrote, selected pictures, and wrote captions for her. In 1947 he persuaded her to recast her reporting along broader, more balanced lines.

Although Margaret had not overplayed her sympathies with Gandhi and the Congress party but had kept good relations on all sides, Ed Stanley thought she leaned too heavily on left-wing sources. He told her bluntly that she did not know enough to write the serious book she had in mind.

"That made her absolutely furious," he says, "not being accustomed to having her talents challenged. ... I didn't hear from her for weeks and weeks. One day she called up and talked for three hours about going back to India. What should she do? I said one of the things is read one of the British histories of India. ... You need to talk to some other people, not just to Frank Moraes ... no matter how happy you are in his company."

About this time Margaret began to speak often about getting both sides of the story. She also began to plan a second trip to India, telling *Life* she would go on her own if necessary. Her luck held true: *Life* came through with an assignment, and CBS asked her to broadcast news of the upheavals to America. Back in India by the fall of 1947, she studiously set about photographing the length and breadth of the society: jewel-studded maharajahs, peasants reduced by drought to eating leaves, moneylenders in houses aburst with crystal chandeliers that did not work, untouchables, bearded Sikhs immersed in the Pool of Immortality. One day she would photograph the men who worked in the mills of a textile magnate; the next day she would interview the magnate himself. "Really trying to understand what was going on in India," she wrote, "so I could make it clear in my book – this effort had a deep effect on me. I can't overestimate it. It was as though it helped me climb to a higher level of understanding." That was a long-term expedition for Margaret; her sights were always fixed on a higher level.

Halfway to Freedom, the most politically aware of all her books, is a balanced and intelligent, if not scholarly, assessment of a complex situation. She had made Ed Stanley's insistence on objectivity into her credo. Years later, receiving a photography award, she said, "The photographer must know. It is his sacred duty to look on two sides of a question and find the truth." To illustrate, she spoke of her work in India.

In 1947, when *Life* first wired Lee Eitingon, a reporter in India, that Bourke-White was on her way, Eitingon was tempted to quit. She had shared a room with Margaret in Paris one night near the end of the war, and Margaret had asked her to run her bath. She did not quit, and to her surprise found Margaret perfectly reasonable to work with, even quite helpful when Eitingon fell ill.

They traveled for five months in India, one American woman with an extravagant smile, a strong jaw, and a mass of gray hair, and a younger woman who was slim, dark-haired, and instinctively elegant, with finely chiseled features. (Ed Thompson, who later married Eitingon, cabled the two of them that they must be the biggest thing there since the Cherry Sisters. Eitingon cherished the compliment for years; neither she nor Margaret knew that the Cherry Sisters were a turn-of-the-century vaudeville act so prodigally inept that people came to see them on the strength of their bad notices alone.)

Assigned to cover an orgy of destruction that fifty-five thousand armed soldiers had been helpless to quell in northern India, Bourke-White and Eitingon were repeatedly warned that it was too difficult and dangerous for women. The warnings only pushed them farther into the field. Bourke-White's courage had already been on display in India.

When she was a guest at Sunil Janah's house in Calcutta, she never hesitated to go out with her camera into seething streets no Indian would face. Janah was often unnerved by her bravery, saying it might be all right for a white woman to go to Moslem headquarters, but if he went with her he would be butchered without fail. "Over my dead body," she would say, and convince him to come along. She said she would claim he was a black American, impossible on the basis of his looks; improbably, it worked.

Eitingon explains the bravery of women correspondents: "Both of us were whatever the female equivalent of macho is. The smells were so terrible, the officers accompanying us would have handkerchiefs over their faces. We would not. ... That was part of the time and the period. Being women, we had to be tougher. There were very few women doing things like that. One felt more pride in not knuckling under to any feminine weakness." Weakness would have been forgiven of anyone, man or woman, in the Punjab that September, but it probably would have spelled death.

> At the stroke of the midnight hour, while the world sleeps, India will awake to life and freedom. A moment comes, which comes but rarely in history, when we step out from the old to the new, when an age ends, and when the soul of a nation long suppressed finds utterance.
> *Jawaharlal Nehru to the Indian Constituent Assembly, 14 August 1947*

Wholesale slaughter began in the Punjab somewhat before the partition of India. The boundaries of two new nations had split the Punjab in half. Five million Hindus and Sikhs lived in Moslem Pakistan's half, five million Moslems in Hindu India's. On 15 August in Amritsar, home of the Sikhs' most sacred Golden Temple, a roaring mob of Sikhs descended on a Moslem sector, murdered the men without quarter, stripped and raped the women and then marched them, trembling with fear and shame, through the streets to their deaths in the holy precincts.

That afternoon, the long-distance train that rolled into the Amritsar station was ominously vacant, with no one peering from its windows or waiting at its door to descend. Puzzled, the stationmaster looked inside. The compartments were heaped with murdered Hindus, a tangle of human bodies, severed heads, and bloody arms and legs.

Later, Margaret saw a group of Sikhs in all their dignity, their beards rolled and their uncut hair hidden beneath blue turbans, calmly sitting cross-legged the entire length of the platform in this same station. "Each patriarchal figure held a long curved saber across his knees – waiting for the next train." Mobs murdered with profligate abandon for six weeks straight, until the Punjab could count as many deaths in a month and a half as Americans suffered in four years in World War II.

Out on the plains, along the rivers where Darius and Alexander the Great had led their conquering troops, the convoys of refugees began to mass, Hindus headed in one direction, Moslems in the other. They came in high-wheeled carts pulled by bullocks with humped shoulders and crescent horns. They came in little purdah wagons with dark curtains, they came on donkeys, on foot, on improvised litters, on the shoulders of the strong. They walked away from farms and houses with a few possessions in bundles on their heads, then bartered what goods they had for food along the way. Many who survived walked into a strange land without money, a change of clothing, or a hoe to cultivate the alien earth. Ten million people trudged across the face of the Punjab in just over two months, the greatest migration in history. A lone plane on reconnaissance over the wretched procession one day counted a single column of eight hundred thousand refugees.

Margaret and Lee Eitingon followed the exodus in a jeep. A pillar of dust hung over the column by day, a pillar of fire rose from the campfires at night. The monsoon refused to come on time that year. Heat beat down relentlessly; the sky was like a shield of burning steel. Food was scarce and cholera rampant. Those too weak to go on lay down by the wayside to wait for death in a swarm of flies. More than once Margaret saw children pulling at the hands of their dead mothers, tearfully begging to be carried as the convoy marched on without them.

Families mourning a death along the way seemed to compose themselves for Margaret's camera into classic patterns of tragedy. She took memorable pictures of the dogged convoys, photographs like excerpts from some immense frieze symbolic of the grim fate of the dispossessed.

"That frieze," Lee Eitingon says. "We were there for hours. It was the most painful experience of the trip. She found a group she liked. She told them to go back again and again and again. They were too frightened to say no. They were dying." Eitingon protested. Margaret told her to give them some money. "That wouldn't help them. These people just needed to move on. That's why she was such a good photographer. People were dying under her feet.... She thought herself a great humanitarian, but when it came to individual people...."

Yet Margaret herself felt that the Indian experience forced her to think in human terms more than she ever had before, and indeed, whatever the cost to her subjects, she took stark pictures of starving peasants and refugees that convey a sense of humanity *in extremis* with directness, immediacy, and the compositional clarity of the "posed candid" that was her forte. Her photographs of India are her most sustained body of work. They offer a kind of stately, classical view of misery, of humanity at its most wretched, yet somehow noble, somehow beautiful. The rhetoric of the thirties has been toned down, but the subjects are still monumental, still posed, still dramatic, and the philosophy of life is akin to that of *You Have Seen Their Faces*: despair over man's inhumanity to man, but a promise that human beings are worthy of compassion and may yet be saved.

When the monsoon finally broke in September, the rains were the worst in half a century. Walls of water as high as houses thundered down the Punjab without warning, straight across the paths of the struggling convoys. One night at dusk the soldiers accompanying Margaret found a vacant hut near the river Ravi; they set up camp. A British officer who had seen the jeep turn off the road hurried in to warn them of floods. They left instantly; even so, they ended up wading waist-deep in the dark, pushing the jeep through treacherous pools and currents. Others were less fortunate. Margaret photographed a meadow where four thousand Moslems had camped for the night and three thousand had died.

The convoys went on, past skeletal dogs gnawing on swollen bodies in the water, past drowned men buried by the floods, their hands still reaching for the sky. The refugees passed by, too numbed by loss, too concentrated on survival to cast a sidelong glance. Margaret photographed it all.

She was ready to return to America in January of '48, when Gandhi announced a fast and she canceled her reservations. He swore to fast to death unless violence was quenched in Delhi and the warring factions vowed peace for India. The fast is a peculiarly Indian weapon that Gandhi used brilliantly. In a land where hunger is endemic, Gandhi asserted his claim on men who were blood enemies of each other but not of him. In his fragile state he forced them to consider their differences in an atmosphere of urgency.

Gandhi's philosophy of nonviolence was at stake in this fast, a philosophy that had defeated the British Empire but seemed to have no hold over his own people. He was seventy-eight. Within two days his life hung in the balance. Only at the last instant did every faction meet his terms. The little man with the dream that changed history had once more mobilized a community and a nation. He broke his fast.

Margaret made reservations again and arranged an interview with Gandhi, now nearly recovered, on the day before she left. Until that day, she had never reconciled herself to the inconsistencies of his thought. She spoke to him about the atom bomb, which had dealt the second great blow to her faith in rational idealism, already shaken to the core by the Nazis.

She asked Gandhi how he would meet the bomb.

> "I will go out and face the pilot," he responded, "so he will see I have not the face of evil against him. I know the pilot will not see our faces from his great height, but that longing in our hearts that he should not come to harm would reach up to him, and his eyes would be opened. Of those thousands who were done to death in Hiroshima, if they had died with that prayerful action – died openly with that prayer in their hearts – then the war would not have ended as disgracefully as it has. It is a question now whether the victors are really victors or victims ... of our own lust ... and omission."

She was moved by the force of his spirit. What seems to have impressed her most was that, directly confronting the terror at the heart of the modern world, he still believed in the power of the human heart and the ultimate triumph of good. Margaret spoke of Gandhi afterward with reverence and some awe. He seems to have reconfirmed for her the faith she had inherited and the optimistic world-view she had lived by.

She was surprised to hear herself wishing Gandhi good luck as she left the interview. At seventeen minutes past five that afternoon, as he was walking to the prayer ground to conduct a public meeting, a member of the RSS, a militant right-wing Hindu sect, stepped out of the ranks of devotees waiting for the Mahatma and fired three bullets into his chest. Gandhi spoke the name of God and died.

Margaret raced back to Birla House, where Gandhi had been staying. His body lay on a straw mattress next to his spinning wheel. The room was filled with mourners – people who had been close to him and important Indian officials. No photographers. Margaret, who knew the people around him so well, was permitted into the room without her equipment.

At six-thirty, or so it was reported to the American embassy by several distraught Indians and subsequently to the American secretary of state, Margaret suddenly pulled out a concealed camera and set off her flash. The soft mourning chants of the Gita abruptly changed to loud indignation. Someone seized the camera and threatened to smash it. Instead, the film was removed and destroyed, the photographer was unceremoniously escorted out of the building and told to leave the grounds immediately. She did not. Surreptitiously she reloaded the camera, concealed it again, and tried, unsuccessfully, to regain entrance to the building.

Her scoop having been shredded by angry people who had trusted her, Margaret turned to Gandhi's public funeral. The body rested on a weapons carrier decked with flowers; its machine-age power stilled, it was pulled by two hundred and fifty sailors over a five-mile route to the cremation grounds. The throngs were so dense they seemed to go on forever, Moslems and Hindus, Brahmans and untouchables, the religions and castes that Gandhi had hoped to unite in life truly united for that moment by his death.

Margaret could scarcely find a place to stand. A vantage point for photographs was harder still. When the flames of the funeral pyre rose in the air, she scrambled atop the hood of a truck to photograph the fire before the light died. As she tried to hold the camera still for a long exposure, the two men in the truck began to shove her back down into the churning crowd. Margaret clung to the truck, snapping as fast as she could, begging for a foothold, and still they pushed her off. Suddenly the crowd started to yell at the drivers to let the woman stay. A Moslem woman shouted out with authority: "She has the agility of a snake, hair like flax, a face like the sun, and eyes like the eagle. You should learn from her zeal!"

Even Margaret's zeal could not produce first-rate photographs where speed was so essential and her control so limited. But Gandhi had given her hope that the promise that appeared moribund after Germany and dead after Hiroshima might yet be fulfilled. She wrote that in the night beside his funeral pyre, she had liked to believe "that a tiny flame was kindling in each of those million hearts. ... His supreme sacrifice in the cause of tolerance and unity could mean the turning point for India. He had given his life to light the way." A woman with a face like the sun and eyes like the eagle does not easily relinquish her dream of humankind.

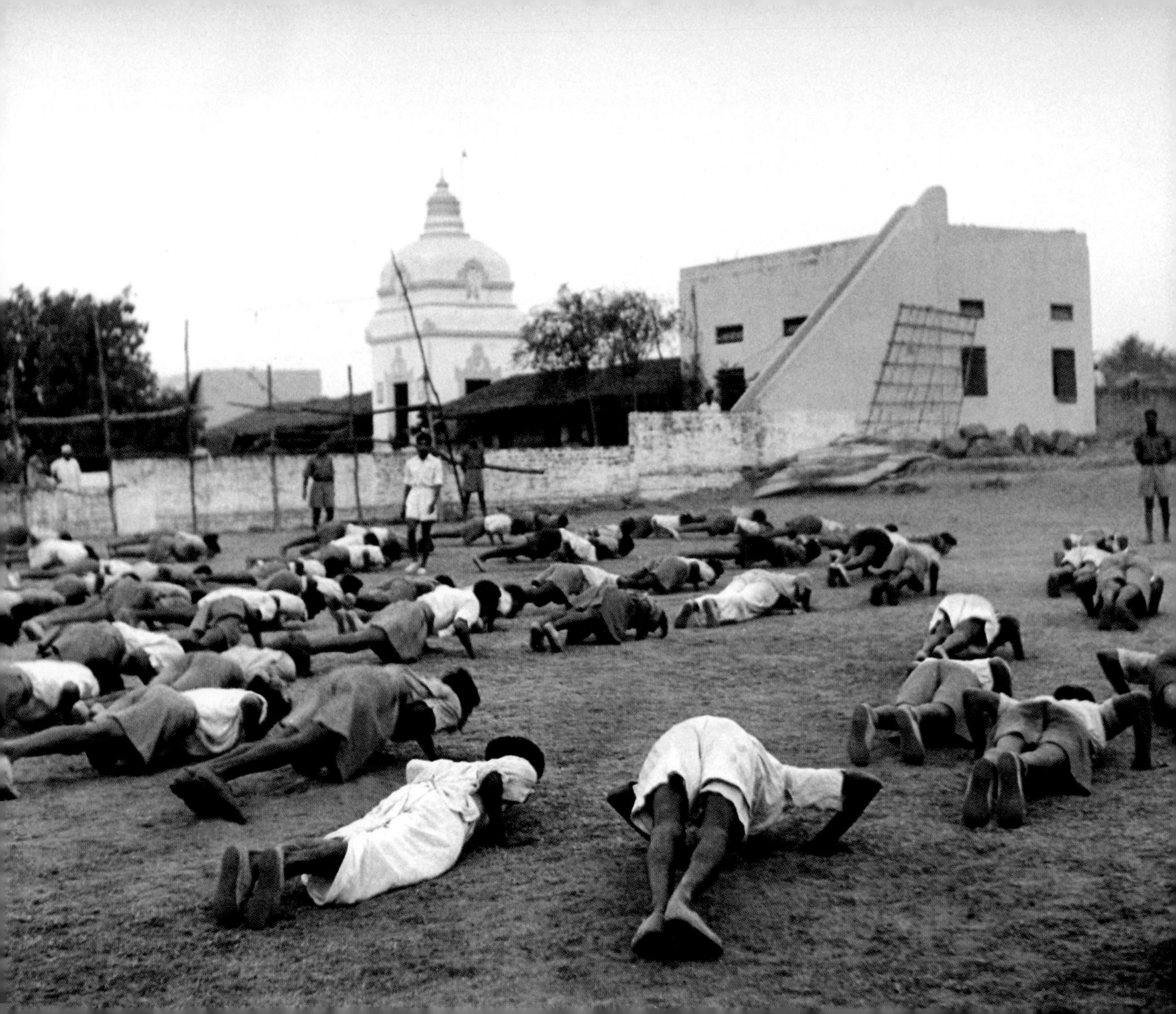

On the threshold of new life, Mahatma Gandhi was the only hope for the people of India. Thousands of young men and women were drawn to him and worked with him as volunteers. About this quality of Gandhi, Pyarelal told Margaret Bourke-White:

'They were drawn…by the "radiance" about him, by the "granitelike strength combined with terrific calm," by "something of activity in the voice." Pyarelal chose his words carefully, trying to describe this precise quality of voice… "he spoke like someone in authority, a man with whom the frontiers of responsibility are unlimited… There is something of the prophet in him."'

Left: Gandhian volunteers exercising early morning near the Valmiki Temple.

Right: A vendor carrying a box of figures in the likeness of Gandhi.

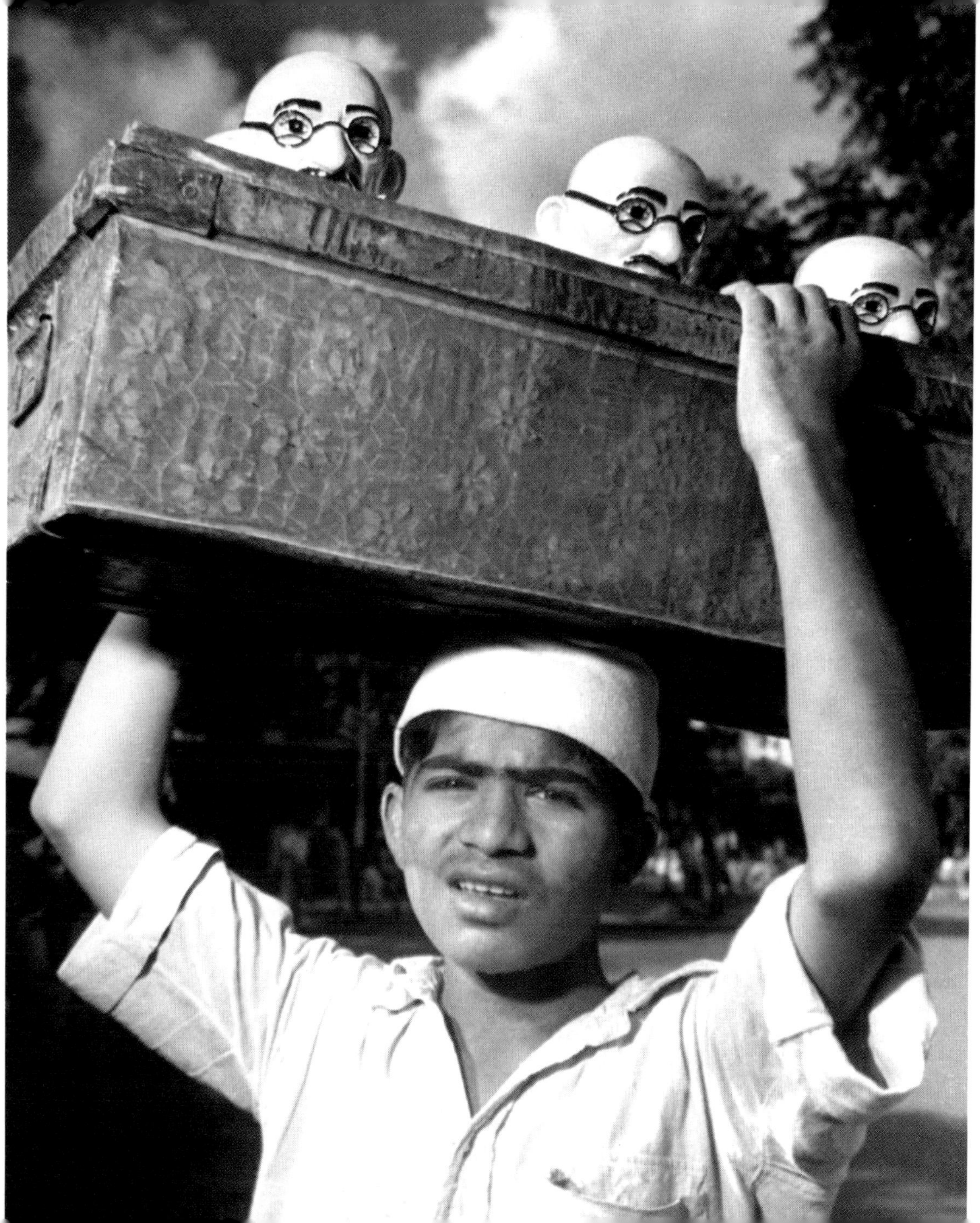

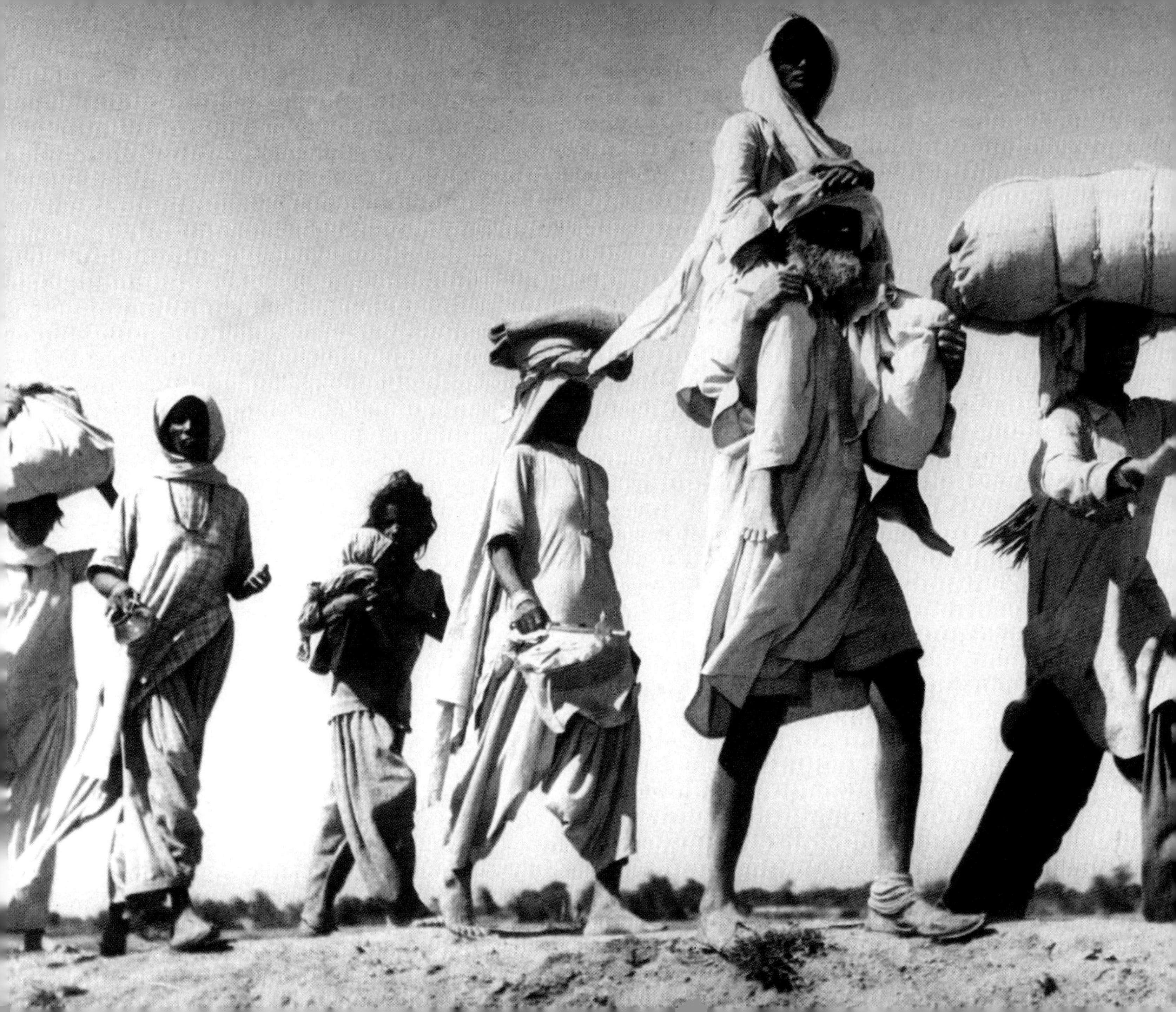

Margaret Bourke-White considered herself fortunate to have witnessed and documented the historic 'birth of two nations' – a birth accompanied by strife and suffering. During the months following the division, she travelled extensively through the entire northern region, covering the 'Migration' story with Lee Eitingon, a Life *reporter.*

'The division of India into two separate nations – based on religious differences – blew fanaticism to such heat that great caravans of desperate, terror-stricken refugees began to crawl along the inadequate roads, millions of them, Hindus and Sikhs to India, Muslims to Pakistan. They had almost no defences against the hazards that beset them – famine, cholera, gangsters and exhaustion… This inhumanity was described as an "exchange of population".'

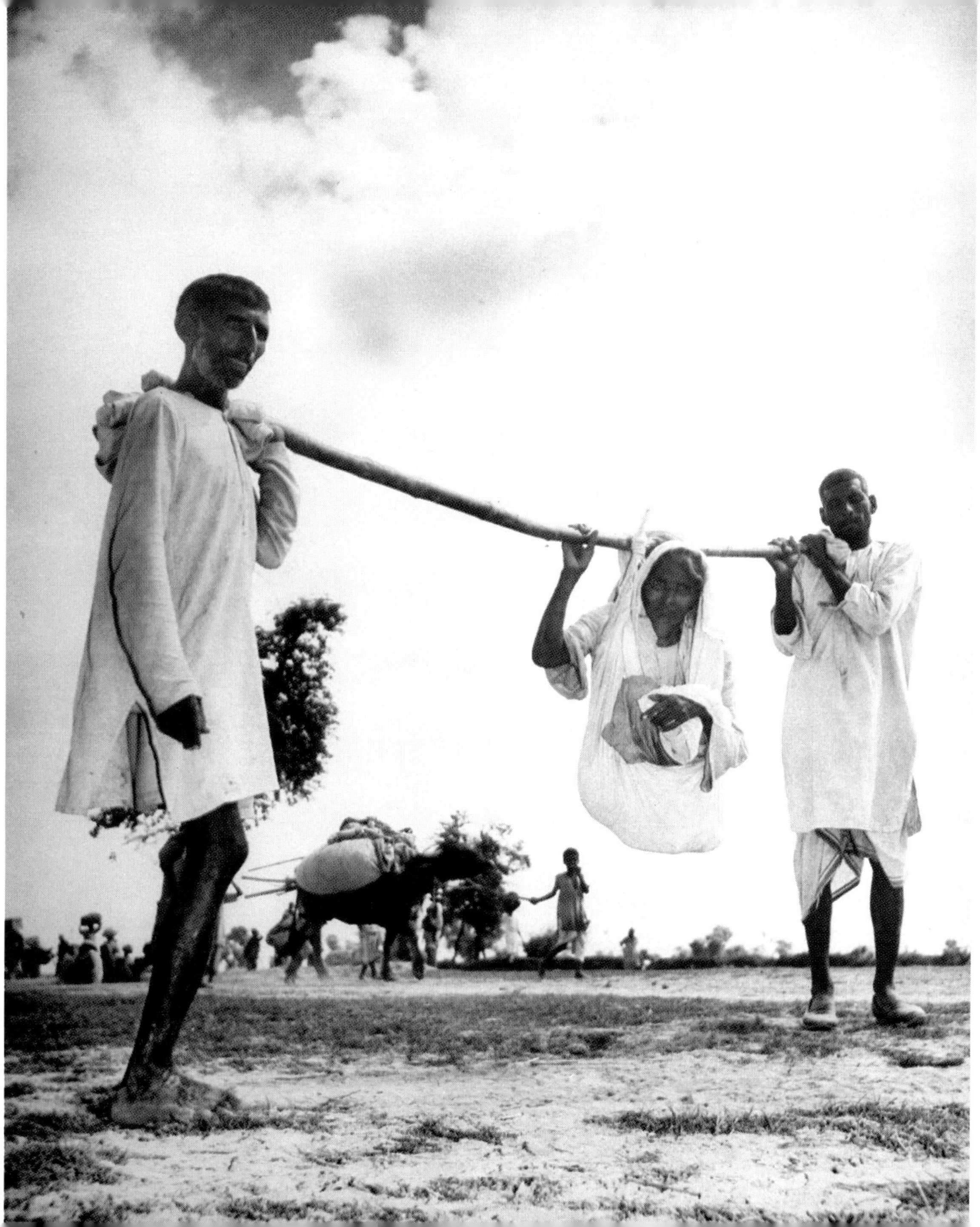

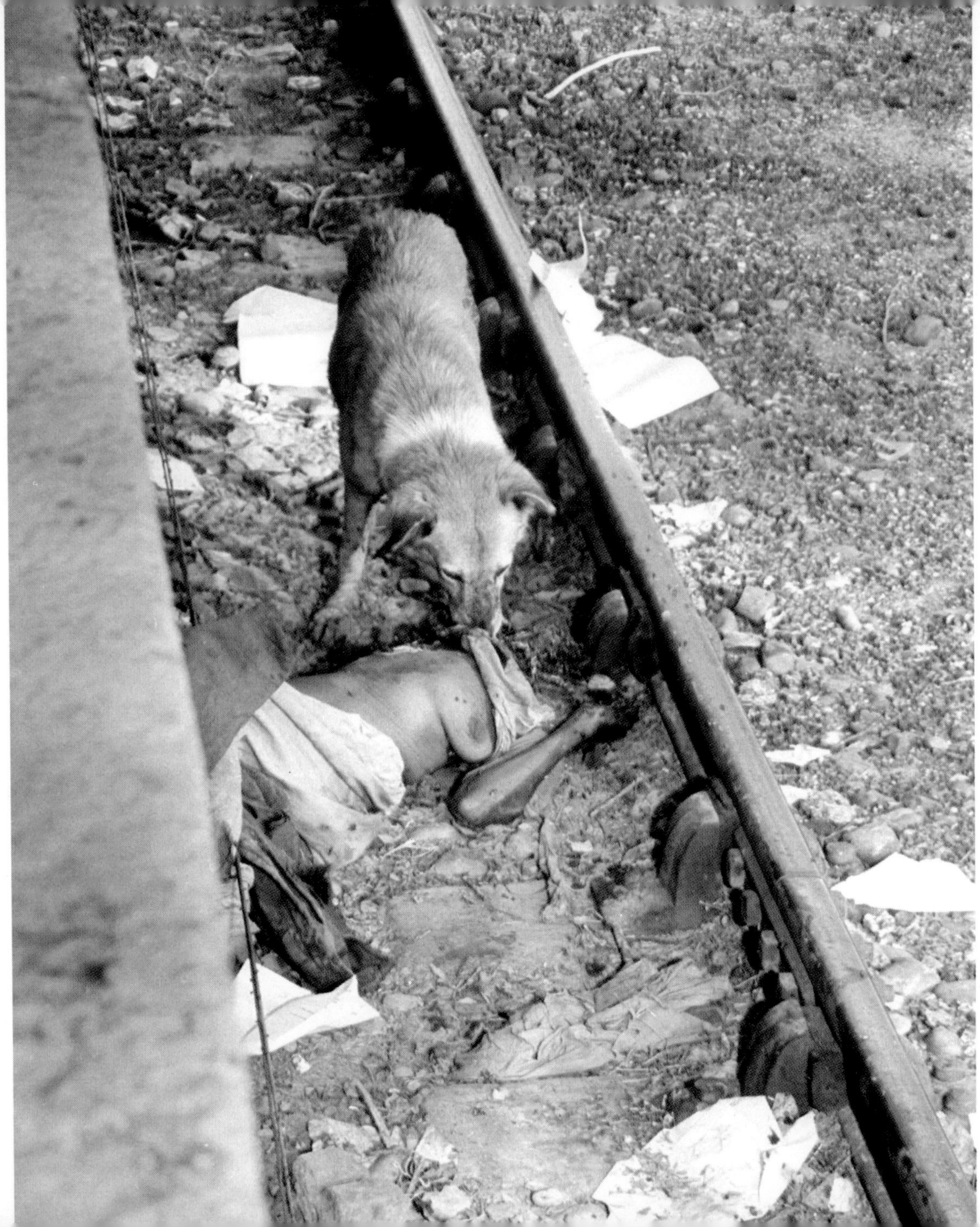

'Hoping against hope' people were moving to safer cities across the new border. Travel by train was unsafe as it was easy to stop it on the track to attack and loot. In these two photographs, the railway station at Amritsar, the last big junction trains had to pass through before crossing into the new Pakistan territory, wears a dreaded and frightful look after a train leaving for Lahore was attacked by a mob.

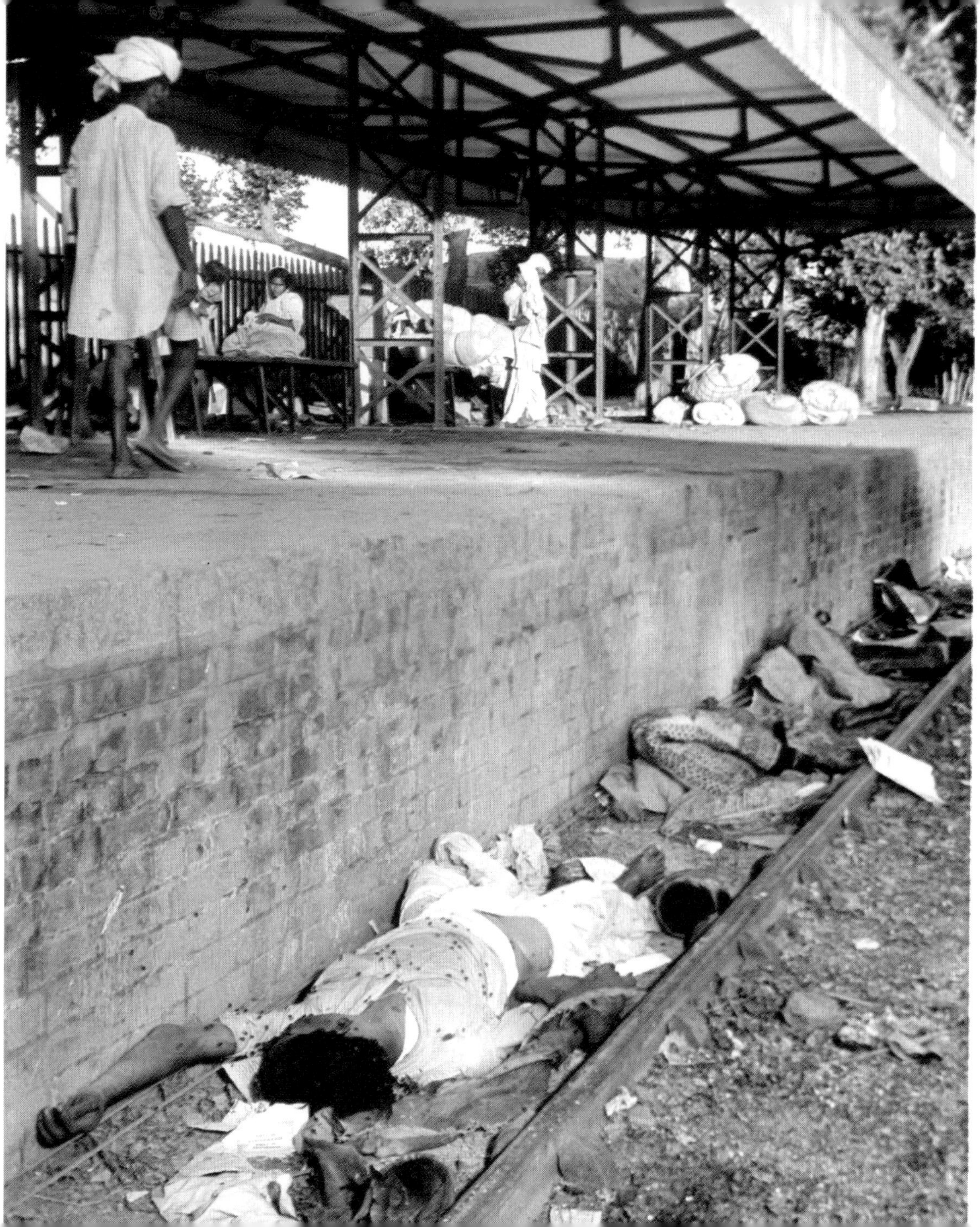

'I remember visiting the frightfully littered railroad station after an attack which had cost the lives of a thousand Muslim refugees, and seeing a row of dignified-looking Sikhs, venerable in their long beards and wearing the bright blue turbans of the militant Akali sect, sitting cross-legged all along the platform. Each patriarchal figure held a long curved saber across his knees – waiting quietly for the next train.'

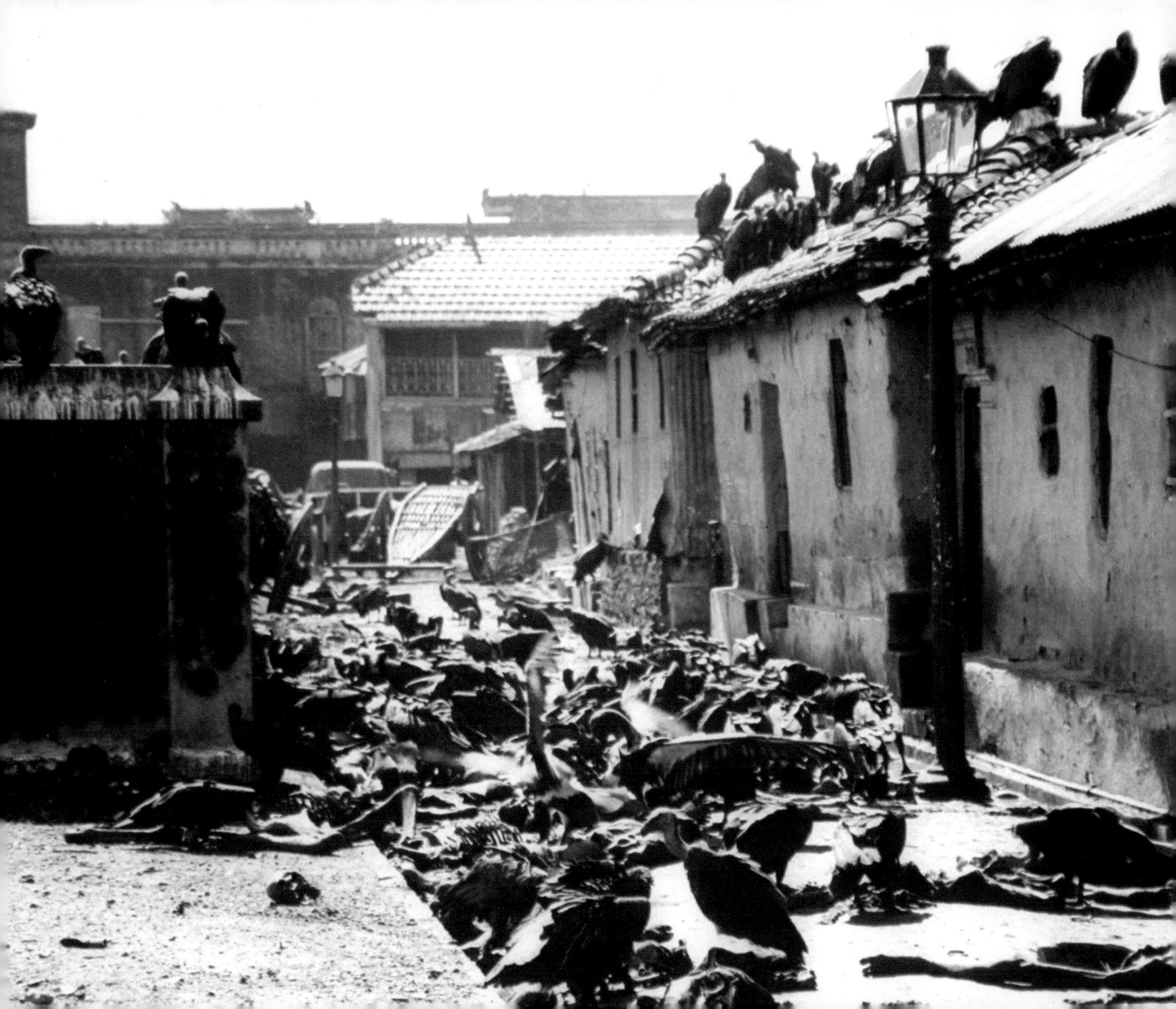

The problems were multiplying with vast populations on the move. Floods, starvation and epidemics like cholera were killing people in millions. Margaret Bourke-White with Lee Eitingon travelled with the convoys for weeks photographing the 'heartbreaking subjects' where bloated bodies lay unclaimed after the floods ... the best they could get was a mass burial.

'There were heartbreaking subjects to photograph.... There were scenes straight out of the Old Testament.... I have always thought that if I could turn back the pages of history and photograph one man, my choice would be Moses. While I traveled with the migration, my respect for Moses grew, for I glimpsed the colossal problem he had to solve. But these people had no Moses.'

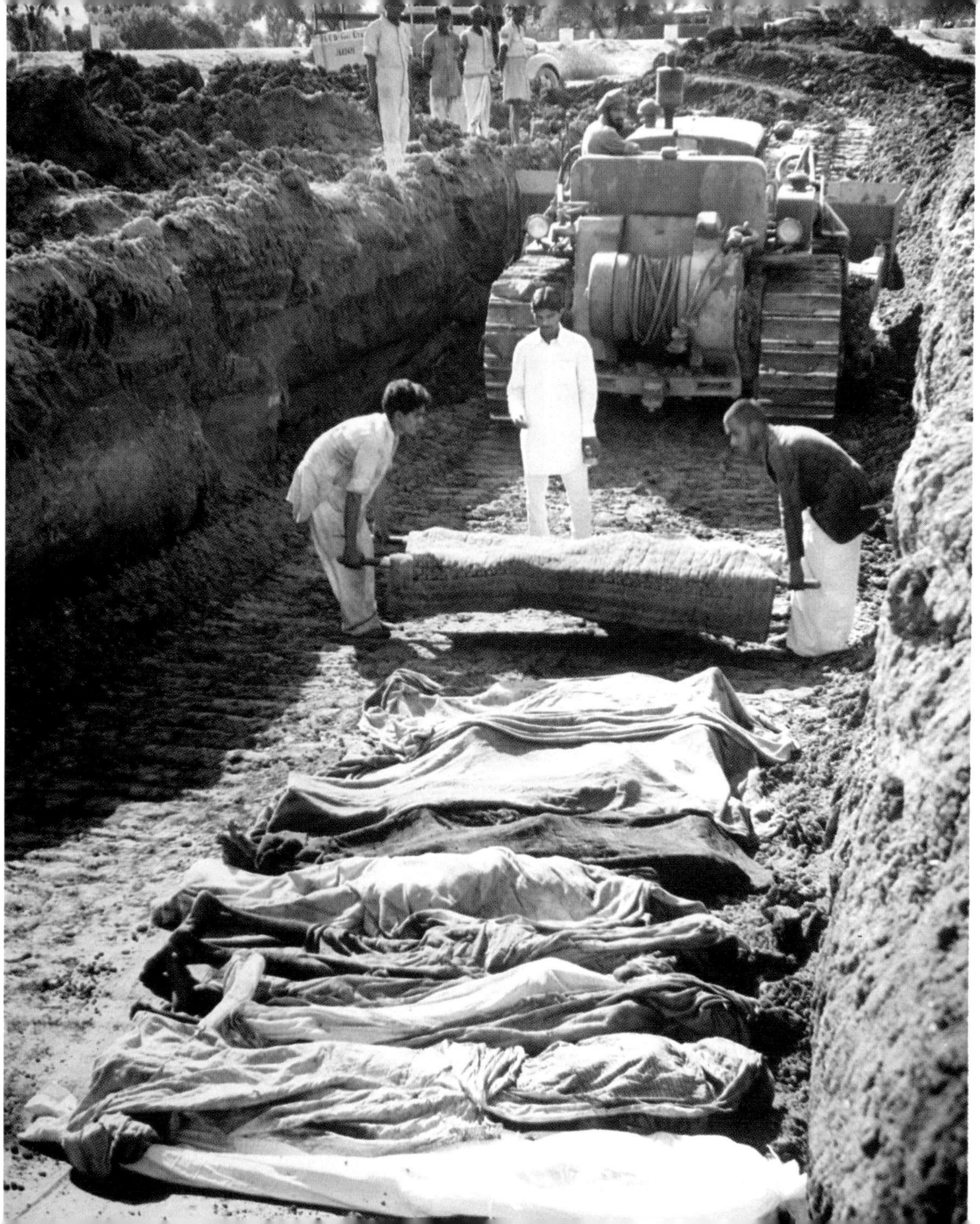

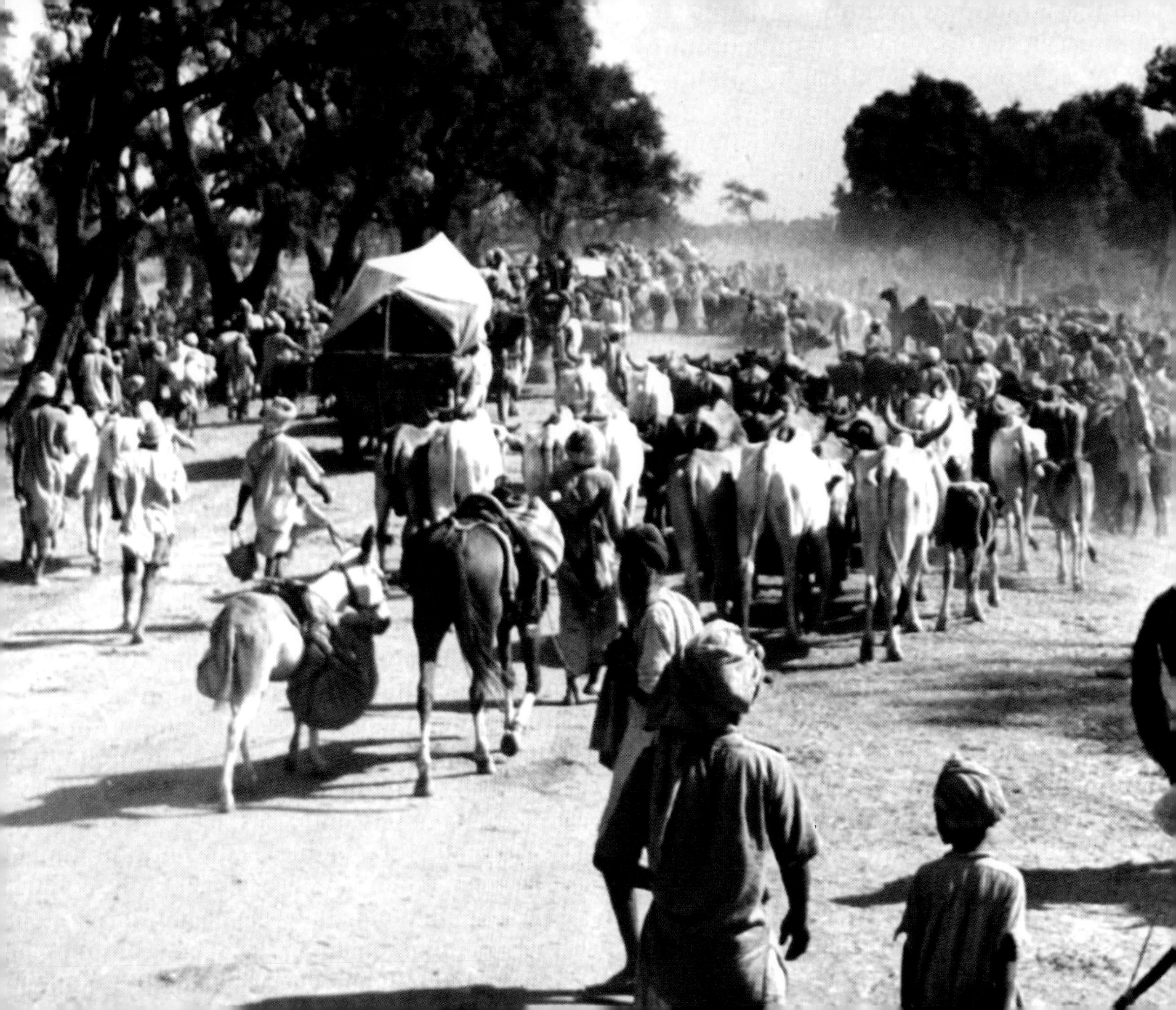

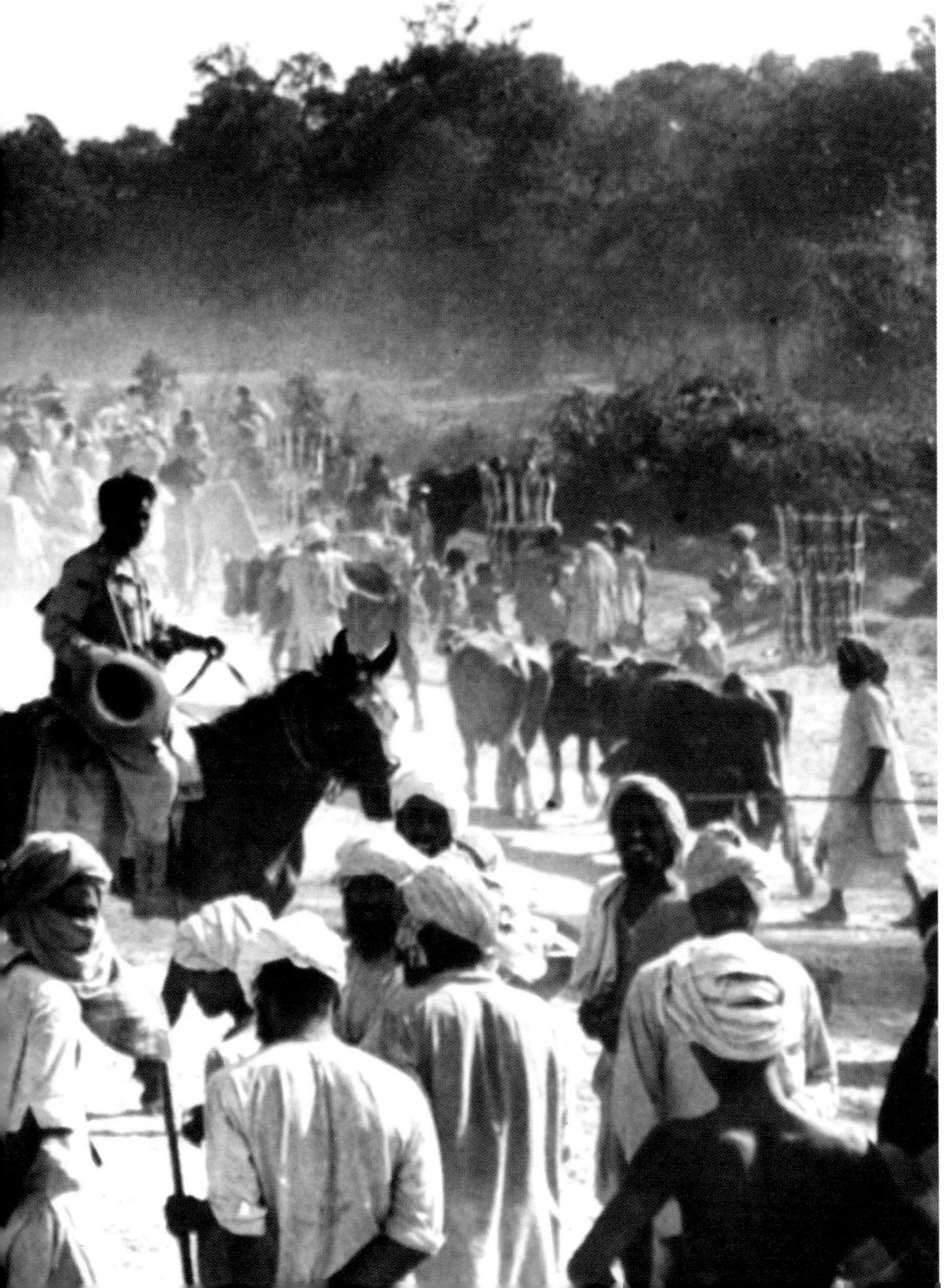

'They flowed in a two-way stream across the border. Into the Indian Union came the Hindus and Sikhs; the Muslims poured into their new Pakistan, which they looked on as their Promised Land. All were led by fear, by highly questionable leadership, by ever dwindling hope. What had been merely arbitrarily drawn areas on a map began emptying and refilling with human beings – neatly separated into so-called "opposite" religious communities – as children's crayons fill in an outline map in geography class. But this was no child's play. This was a massive exercise in human misery.'

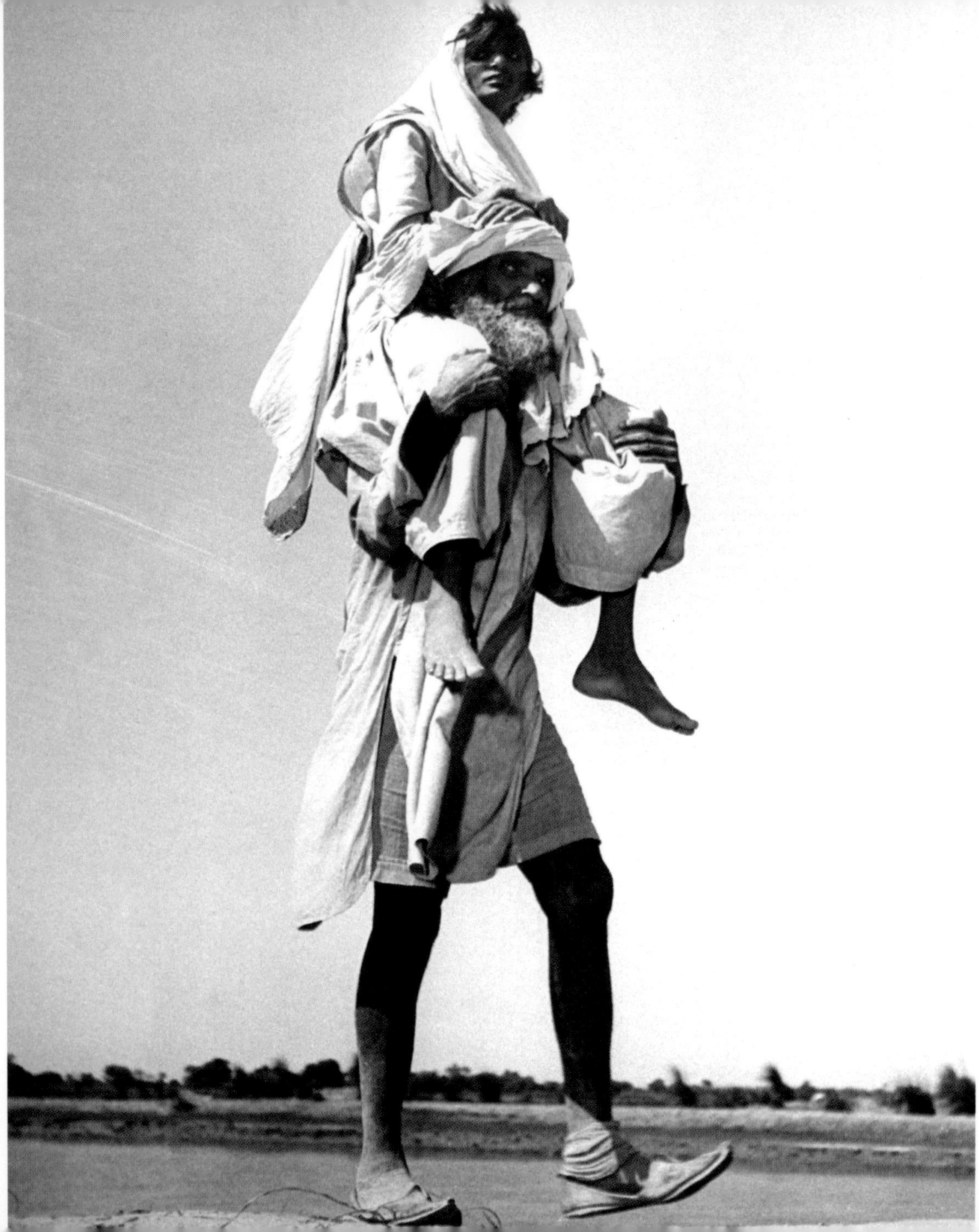

Everybody – men, women and children, felt the burden of the Promised Land. The peace that was promised to come with a separate nation was elusive. The multitude of people Margaret Bourke-White spoke to for her stories for Life *had one common emotion – helplessness. Hindus, Muslims or Sikhs, they all were 'victims of the same fate'.*

'For the bewildered Sikhs out on the roads, disaster had fallen so suddenly that they couldn't guess at the cause. "Our leaders didn't tell us we would have to leave our land," they told me, as they plodded away from the land which they had carved out of the wilderness and over which they had sweated so much. Over and over I heard Sikh peasants say, "We thought it was an understood thing that we would get the whole of the Punjab. We heard we were going to have our own Sikhistan." … And, one of them, whom I shall always remember for the great dignity of his bearing in spite of the dust which caked his turban and patriarchal beard, added a moving thought: "For the Mussulmans too the future is dark. They are helpless just like us. They have been rendered homeless just as we have been. They are victims of the same fate.'"

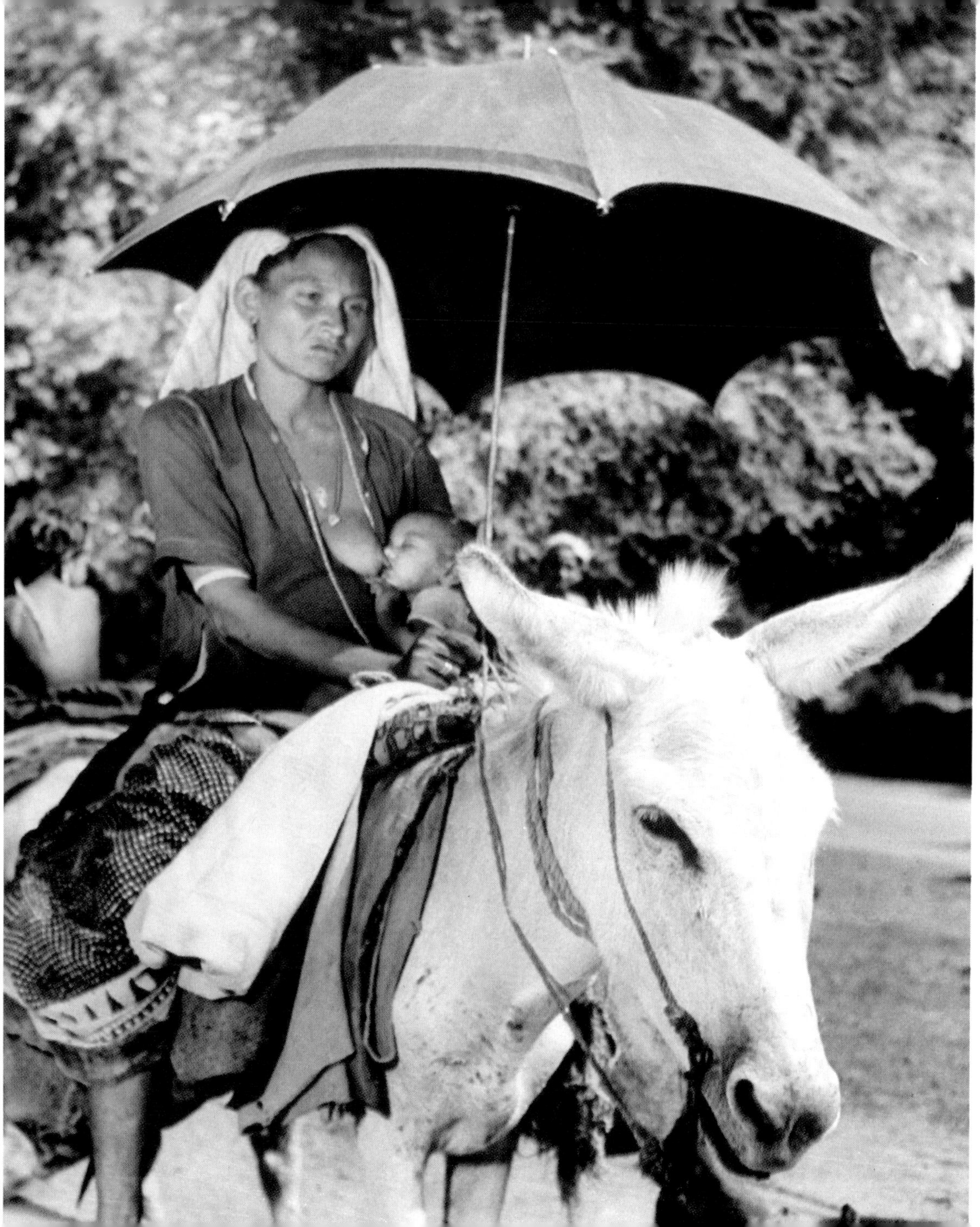

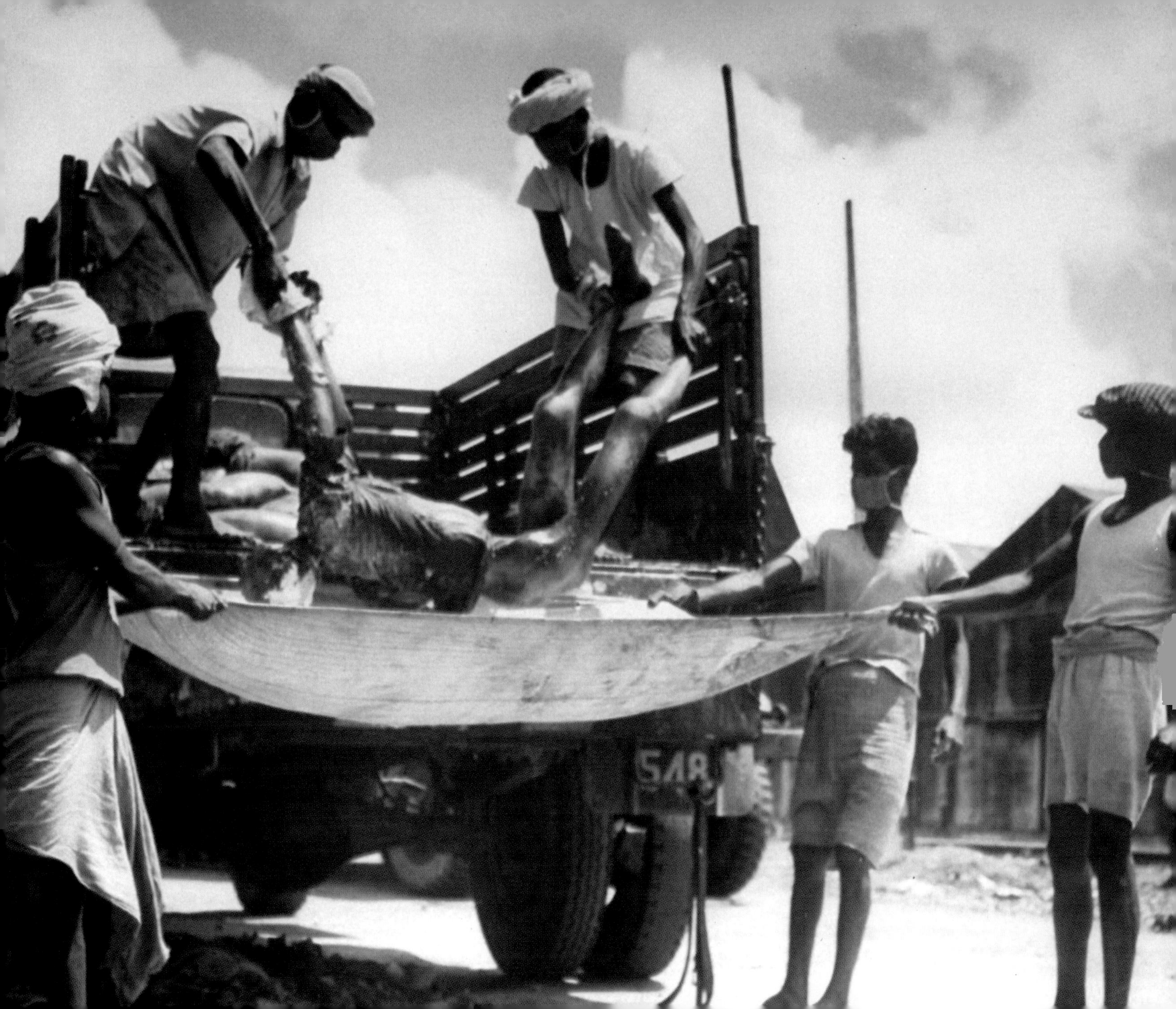

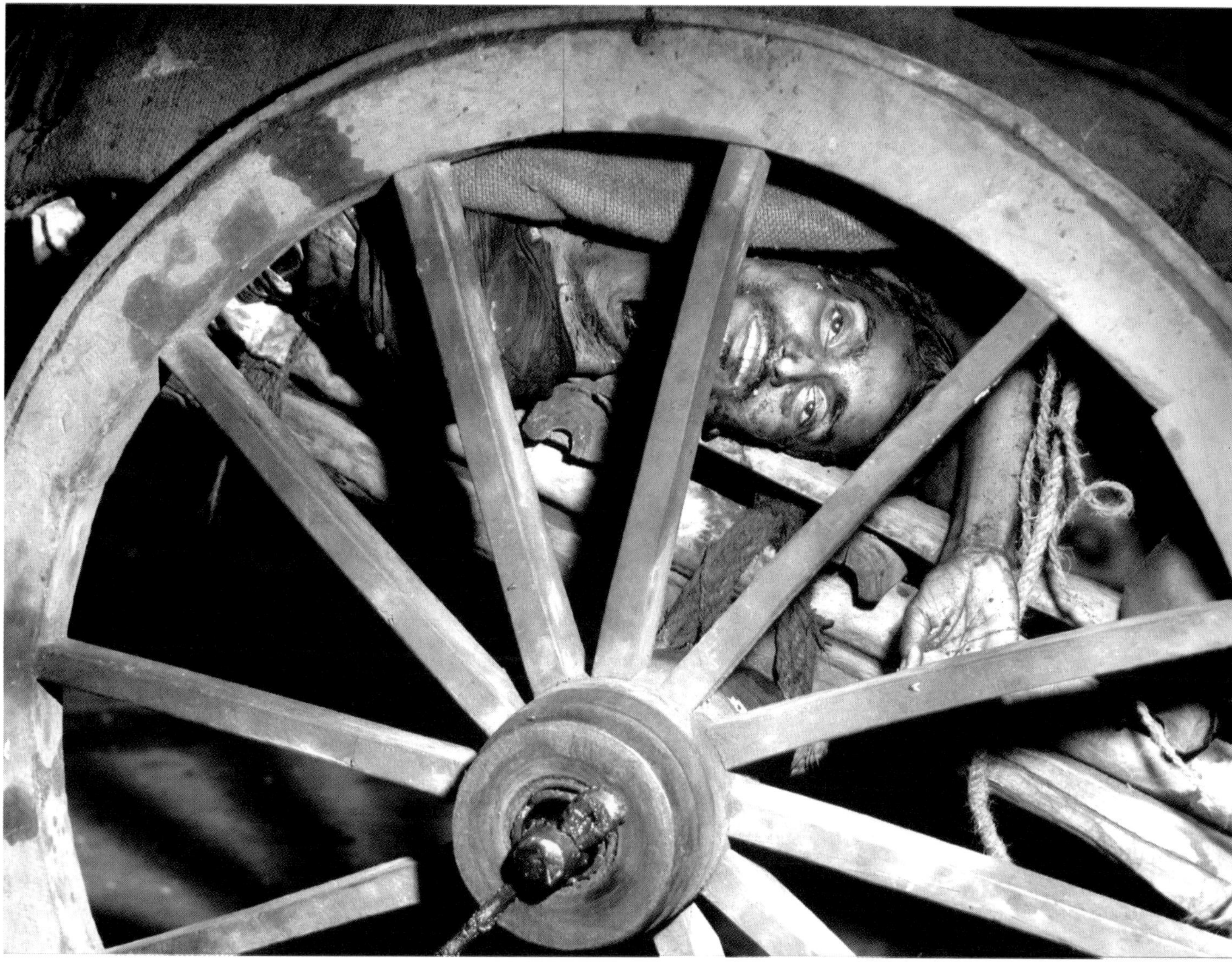

Communal violence killed an estimated one million Hindus, Muslims and Sikhs on both sides of the border. Margaret Bourke-White was an eyewitness to this bloodshed and mayhem for weeks.

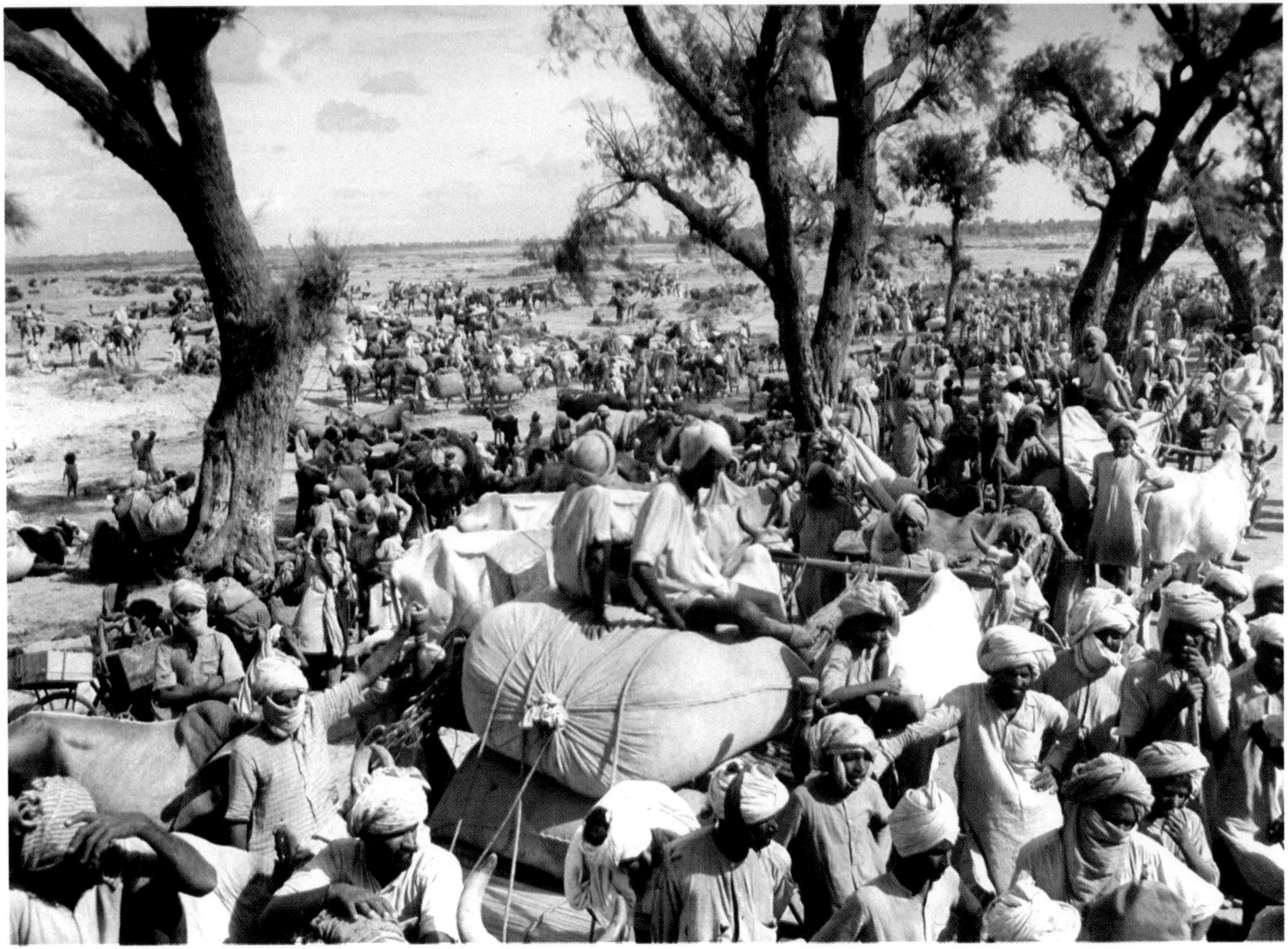

'… long after the last of my negatives had been dispatched by air to *Life* . . . those millions of peasants were still trudging blindly forward on their tragic journey. The total of Sikhs and Hindus leaving Pakistan had reached four million, but with six million Muslims coming in [Pakistan], this infant Land of the Pure seemed in danger of being swept away by the very numbers of the pure pouring into it.'

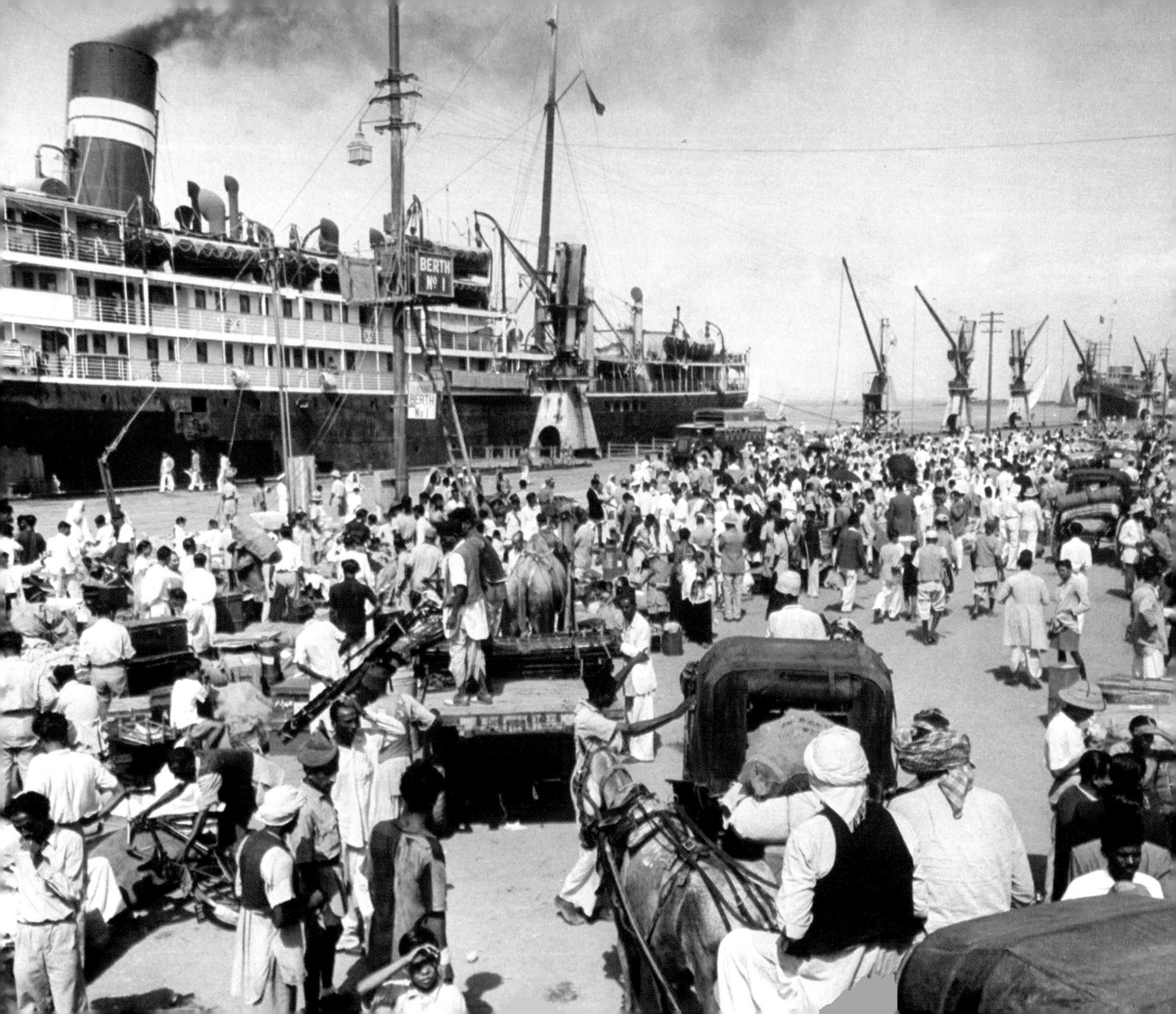
BERTH
Nº 1
BERTH
Nº 1

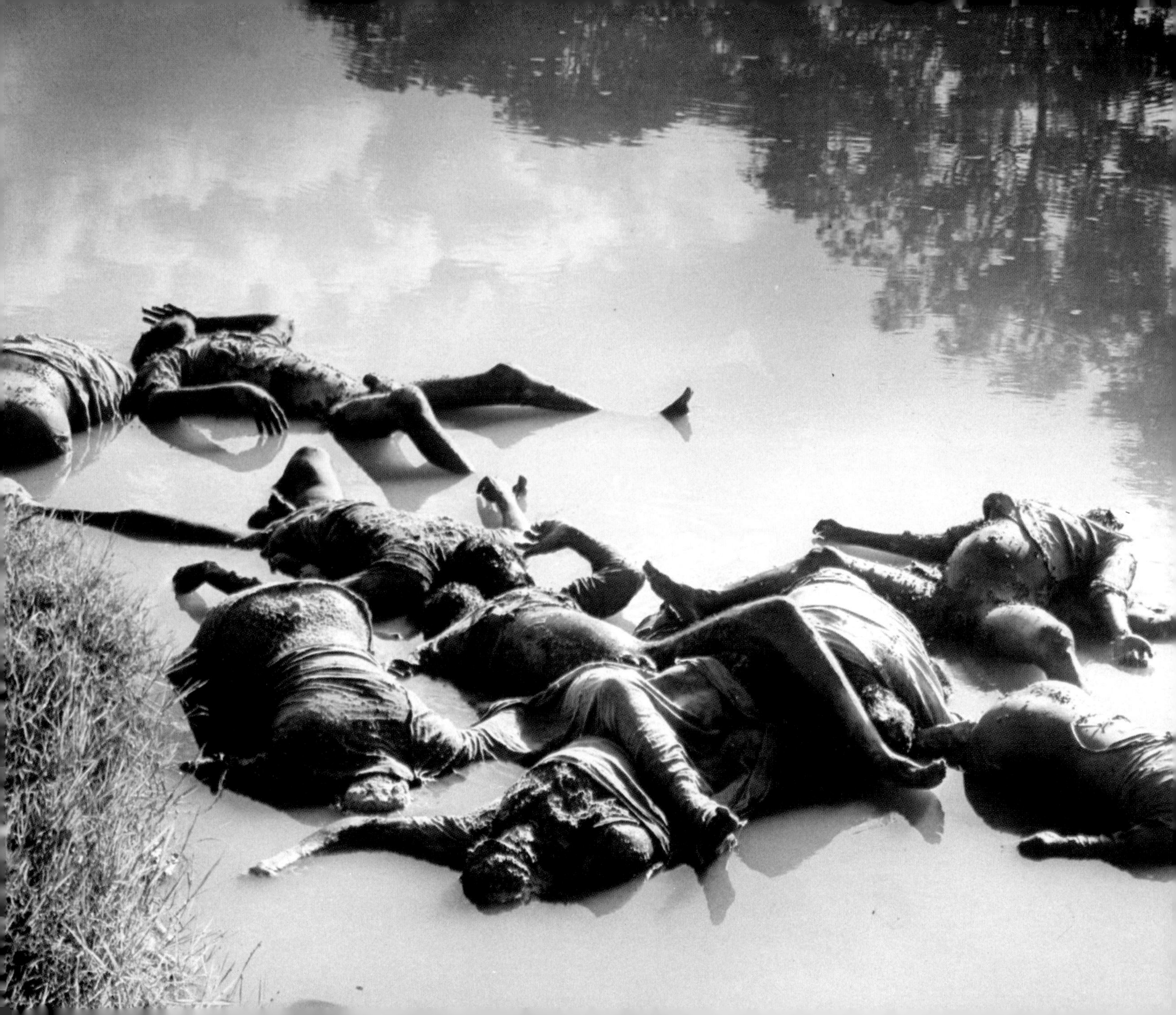

THE DELUGE

About 14.5 million people crossed the border to what they hoped was the relative safety of religious majority – a safety of the promised land with no defence against famine, cholera, gangsters, rioting, killing or any natural disaster like floods that deluged the land of five rivers.

'As though the travail of a people divided by pen strokes was not enough, North India, in this year of all years, suffered the worst floods since 1900. In the Punjab, which means Land of Five Rivers, all five began overflowing their banks, tearing away the earth barriers in the network of canals, spilling into the fields, and trapping entire encampments of refugees. I was almost caught myself in the rising of the River Ravi. …

'Thousands of peasants less lucky than I were trapped – they had no jeep, no one to warn them. The River Beas claimed the most victims. When the water began receding sufficiently for me to get to it, I photographed one meadow between the river and a railroad ramp where four thousand Muslims had gone in to camp for the night. Only one thousand had come out alive. That meadow was like a battlefield: carts overturned wildly, household goods and farm tools pressed into a mash of mud and wreckage. Several nights later I chanced on an encampment of the survivors of the Beas disaster just as they were settling down for the night. I talked with one man who was digging a grave by the side of the road. His name was Rasik; he came from Jullundur, where he and his brothers had owned a ten-acre orange grove. The grave was for his eight-year-old son, who had died just that afternoon. Rasik had been carrying the child's body until he had a chance to bury it properly and recite prayers over the grave, as any father would wish to do. …

'The convoy had pitched camp with much more cheer than usual on the night of the disaster, … because the border of Pakistan was less than fifty miles away. At midnight he was awakened by the shouts of his neighbors. Rasik found the water was rising swiftly, and he and his family climbed to the top of their bullock cart. The water rose to the wheelhubs, to their knees, to the top of the cart, to their chests. For two days and nights the family stayed on the cart, standing in water, without food, watching many of their friends being swept away…. When the water went down, they trudged on their way, but the little son never seemed able to retain his strength and died.'

Excerpted from *Halfway to Freedom* by Margaret Bourke-White

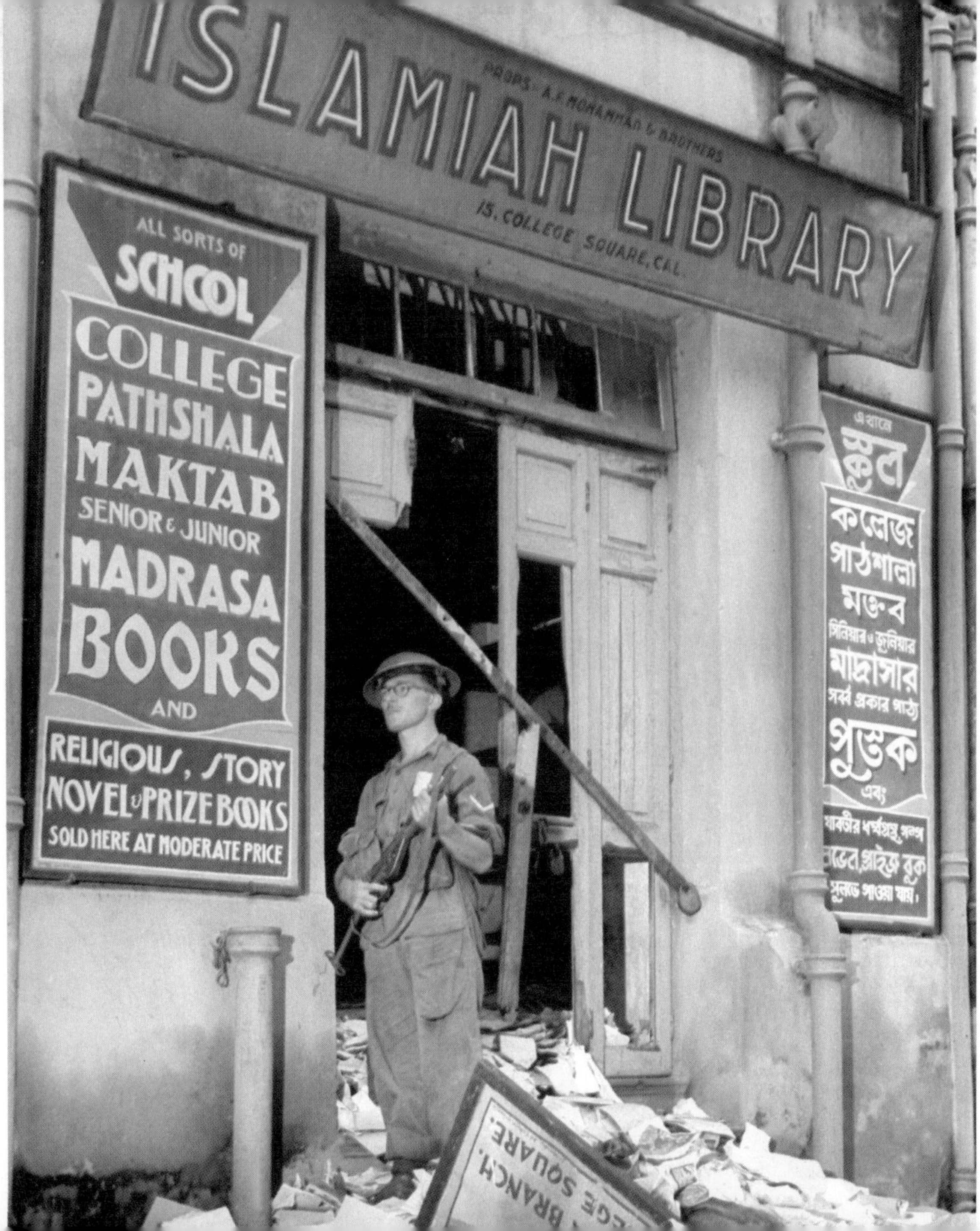

'India suffered the biggest Moslem-Hindu riot in its history' reported Time *on 26 August 1946 about the 'great Calcutta Killing'.*

Left: A British infantryman standing guard outside a vandalized bookshop in Calcutta.

Right: July 1946, Mohammed Ali Jinnah, leader of the Muslim League with Liaquat Ali Khan at a press conference at his Malabar Hill home in Bombay. At the press meet he 'intimated – rather boldly – the coming of Direct Action Day'. The terrible riots that raged Calcutta for five days starting 16 August 1946 could only be controlled after the Army was called in on 21 August. Also known as the 'great Calcutta killing', within seventy-two hours more than 4,000 people lost their lives and 100,000 residents were left homeless. Margaret Bourke-White attended this press meet in Bombay and rushed to Calcutta.

'His [Mr Jinnah] statement to the press was in the form of a monologue, delivered in an icy voice, which was a forecast of fiery events to come. "We are preparing to launch a struggle. We have chalked out a plan." … He had decided to boycott the Constituent Assembly. He was rejecting in its entirety the British plan for transfer of power to an interim government, which would combine both the League and the Congress. He lashed out against the "Hindu-dominated Congress" in his flat, chilled monotone. It seemed clear, now the bondage to the British was drawing to an end, that he was free to concentrate all his fire against the opposite party.'

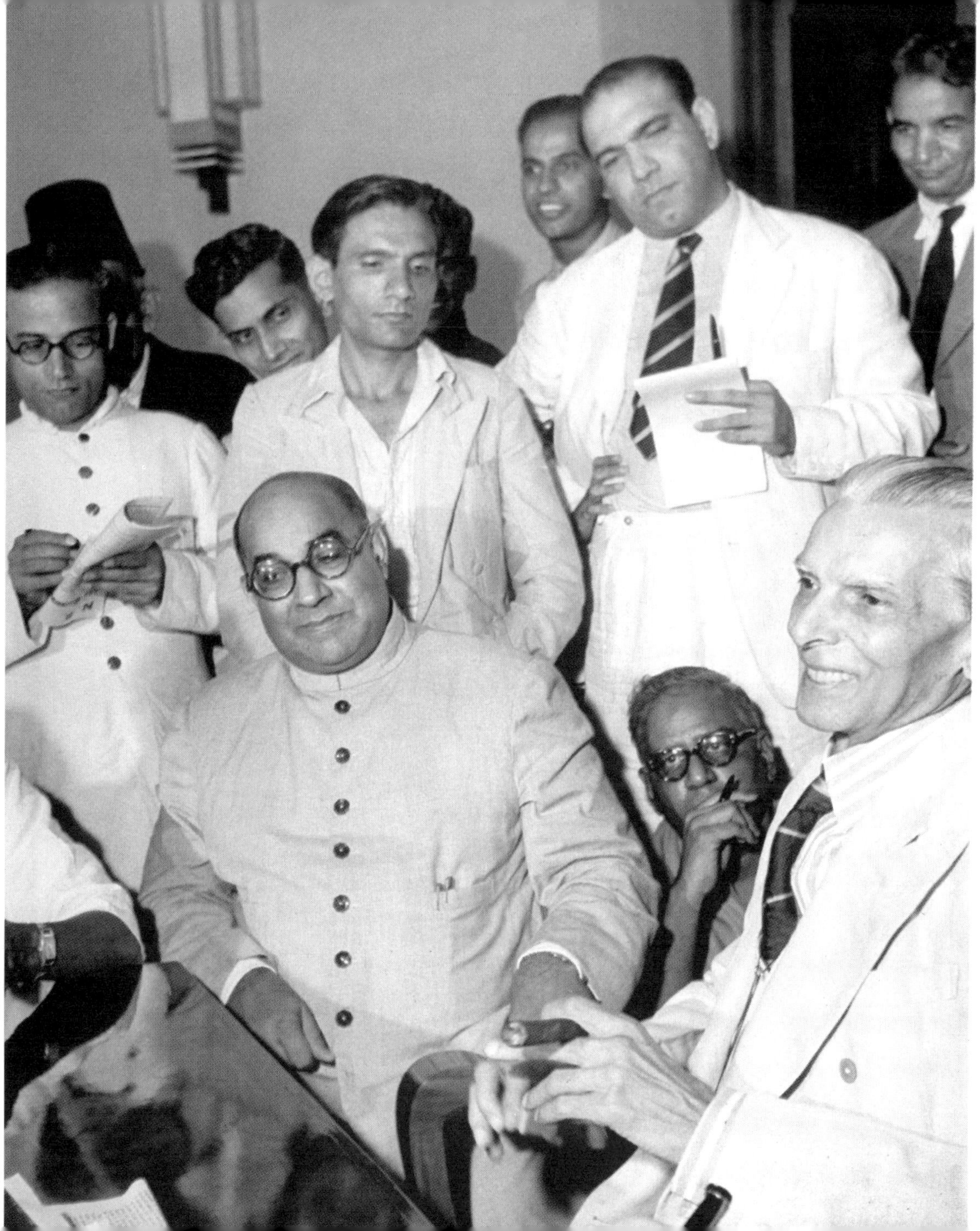

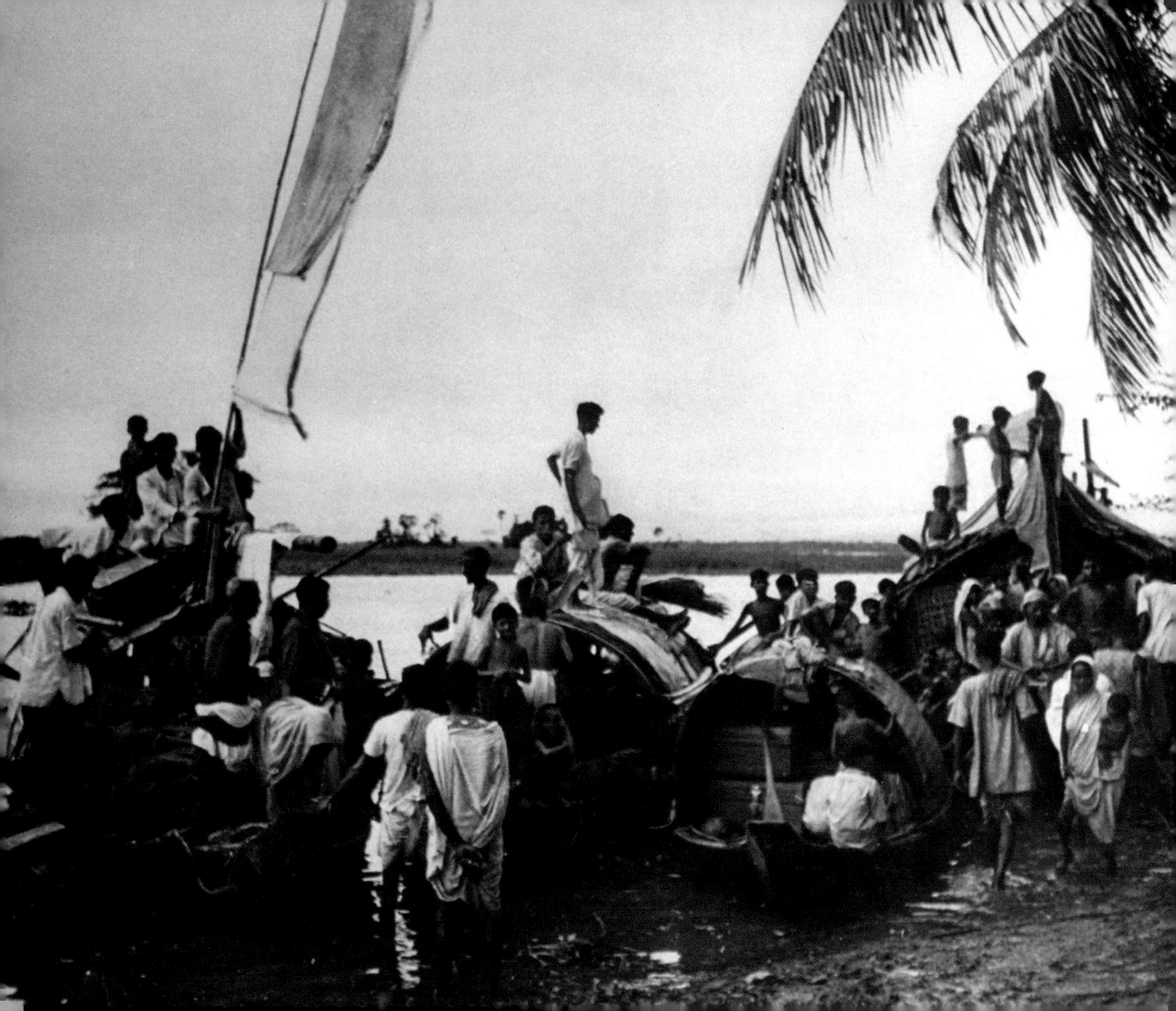

DIRECT ACTION DAY

In response to the Congress Party's rejection of the plan to divide the nation into a Hindu-majority India and Muslim-majority Pakistan, the *Muslim League leader Mohammed Ali Jinnah intimated the coming of Direct Action Day. The action on 16 August 1946 though direct, wasn't peaceful. Before the disastrous day was over, blood soaked the 'melting asphalt of sweltering Calcutta's streets'.*

'Most of what I learned about that day came from a little teashop keeper in Calcutta, where the explosion began. As soon as I heard of the incredible events taking place, I had flown from Bombay to Calcutta. … Hunting for a survivor who had been an eyewitness to the first stroke of direct action, I found Nanda Lal.

'Nanda Lal's little "East Bengal Cabin" at 36 Harrison Road, was located in one of those potential trouble spots where a by-lane of Muslim shops crossed the Hindu-dominated thoroughfare.… It was the sight of the first tram that confirmed Nanda Lal's fears ... Normally it was so crowded with commuters that they bulged from the platform and clung to the doorsteps and back of the car. Today there was hardly a passenger on board.…

'The streets and by-lanes were throbbing with cries of "Jai Hind. Victory to a united India" from the Hindus, and "Pakistan zindabad. Long Live Pakistan" from the Muslims…

'On the fourth day Nanda Lal noted that the weapons in the street fighting had grown heavier. Soda water bottles had given way to iron staves, and unfortunately the neighbourhood had a plentiful supply of rails from the fence surrounding the near-by Shraddhananda Park. Finally, as the skirmish of the iron pikes reached its fiercest, a convoy of three military tanks rolled through and machine-gunned the mobs, and along with them the police made their belated appearance.… 'When peace returned to Calcutta on the fifth day, the streets were a rubble of broken bricks and bottles, bloated remains of cows, and charred wrecks of automobiles and victories rising above the strewn figures of the dead. …

'Thousands began fleeing Calcutta. For days the bridge over the Hooghly, … was a one way current of men, women, children and domestic animals, heading toward Howrah railroad station … Calcutta was only the beginning of a chain reaction of riot, counter-riot, and reprisal which stormed through India for an entire year.'

Excerpted from *Halfway to Freedom* by Margaret Bourke-White

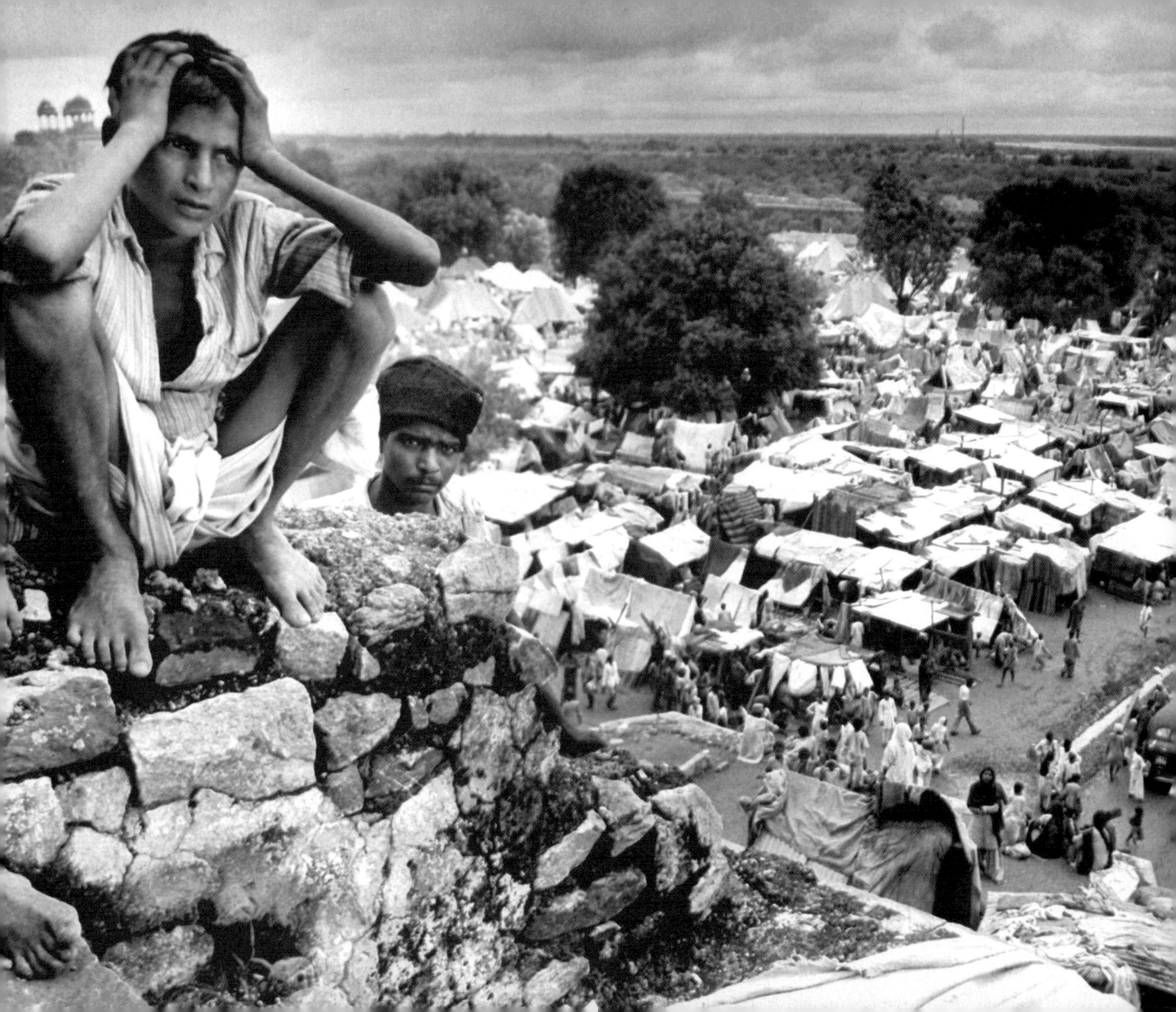

THE GREAT MIGRATION

The birth of 'twin nations' in 1947 on the lines of different religious identities led millions to leave their homeland of generations and move to a future unknown and unpromising. About 11.2 million or 78 per cent of the population transfer took place in the west, with Punjab accounting for most of it. Almost 5.3 million Muslims moved from India to West Punjab in Pakistan, while 3.4 million Hindus and Sikhs moved from Pakistan to East Punjab in India.

'When I went to the Punjab area, in the North of India, in the fall of 1947 to begin photographing the newborn sovereign states, massive exchange of populations was under way. The roads connecting the Union of India with Pakistan looked as our Pulaski Skyway or Sunset Boulevard looks during the rush hour. But instead of the two-way stream of the motorcars there were endless convoys of bullock carts, women on donkey back, men on foot carrying on their shoulders the very young or the very old.

'... Babies were born along the way. People died along the way. Some died of cholera, some from the attacks of hostile religious communities. But many of them simply dropped out of line from sheer weariness and sat by the roadside to wait patiently for death. ...

'Indeed, there was a Biblical atmosphere about this mammoth two-way exodus that I turned to the Old Testament to compare its size with the migration of the Israelites … the exodus of the children of Israel was dwarfed by the great migration of Muslims, Sikhs, and Hindus which took place upon the partition of India. At the time that I was photographing … there were five million people on the move, with several more million due to follow as soon as room could be found for them. This, for these wretched millions, was the first bitter fruit of independence.'

Excerpted from *Halfway to Freedom* by Margaret Bourke-White

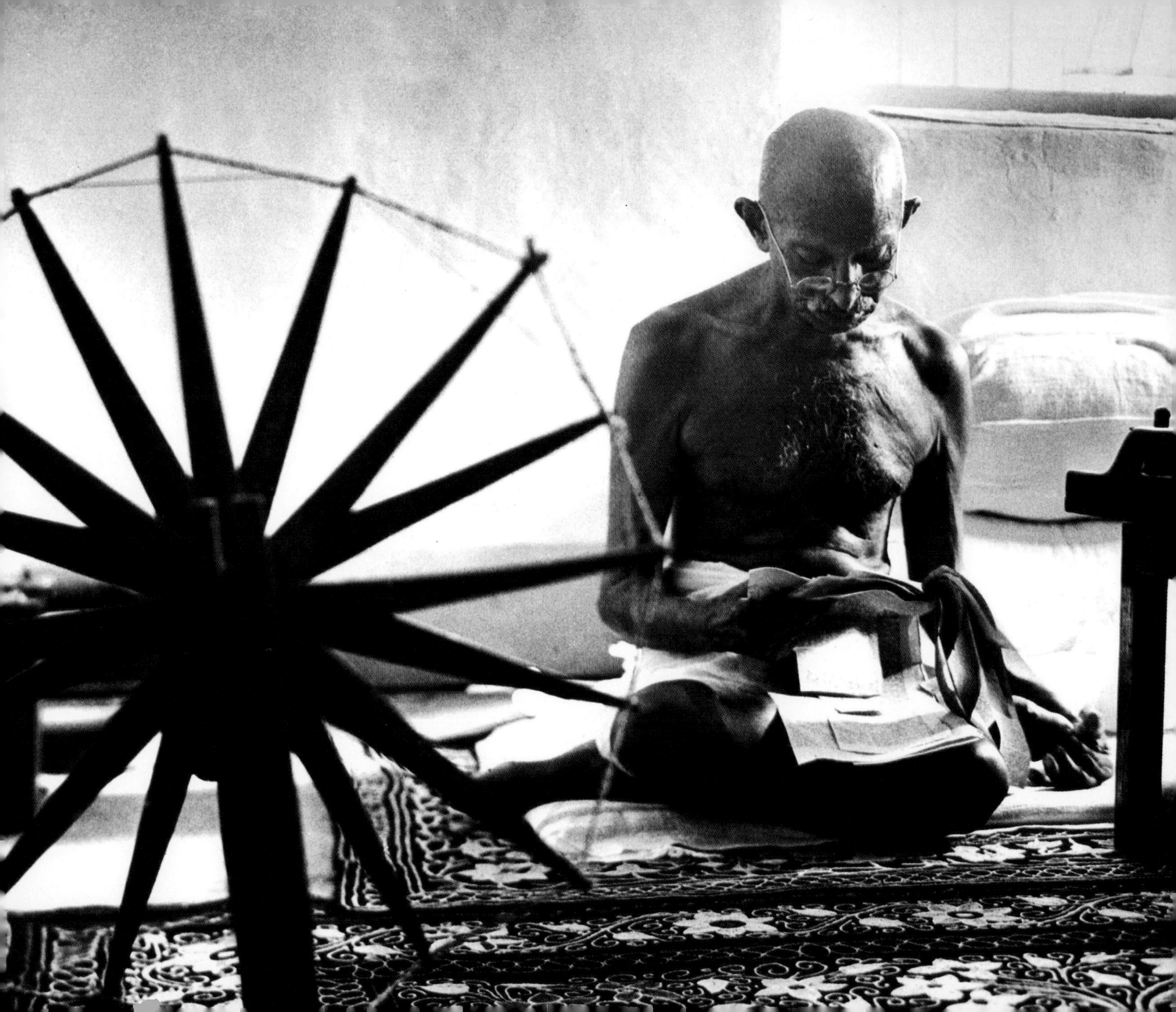

MEETING THE MAHATMA

While Gandhi fondly called her 'the torturer', Margaret Bourke-White felt that Gandhi looked like a 'great white mushroom on legs, under the huge wet turkish towel on his head' constanty dripping. It was their admiration and respect for each other that led them question the beliefs they believed in. Margaret Bourke-White always found it hard to accept his antiquated ideas on the machine age. For he believed in the greatness of the 'labour of man', and that the poverty and backwardness could be overcome 'by working with … hands and brains'. This famous photograph (facing page) was taken during the period for a scheduled feature on India's political leaders for the *Life* magazine. In her book *Halfway to Freedom*, she writes:

'I shall always remember the day we met. … Having thought of Mahatma Gandhi as a symbol of simplicity, I was a bit surprised to find that I had to go through several secretaries to get permission to photograph him. When I reached the last and chief secretary, an earnest man in horn-rimmed spectacles, and dressed entirely in snow-white homespun, I explained my mission. This was the beginning of my acquaintance with Pyarelal.

"Do you know how to spin?" asked Pyarelal.

"Oh I didn't come to spin. I came to take pictures of the Mahatma spinning."

"And you are not familiar with the workings of the charkha?"

"I'm afraid not. Just with the workings of the camera."

"How can you photograph Mahatmaji spinning until first you understand the spinning wheel, a most delicate, intricate, and marvelous instrument?… It illustrates a major tenet of Gandhiji's: when individually considered, man is insignificant – even like a drop of water. But in the mass he becomes mighty and powerful like the ocean. When the millions of drops combine, they make a sea which bears on its bosom the whole fleet; even so it is with the masses when they have learned to combine…"

"You will make me drop photography and take up spinning," I said politely, wondering when we could get back to the subject of my appointment.

'I was caught like a fly in the twisted threads of the charkha. The more I cried out that I had a deadline to meet, the more I struggled… I was being crucified on the charkha.

'I do not remember exactly how I persuaded Gandhi's secretary that I must have my spinning lesson today – this very day. And that the appointment with the Mahatma must follow. My methods were non-violent – but just barely.

'Translated into the many instructions a photographer must meet, the rule set up by Gandhi's secretary was a good one: if you want to photograph a man spinning, give some thought to why he spins. Understanding, for a photographer, is as important as the equipment he uses. I have always believed what goes on, unseen, in back of the lens is just as important as what goes on in front of it. In the case of Gandhi, the spinning wheel was laden with meaning. For millions of Indians, it was the symbol of the fight for freedom. Gandhi was a shrewd judge of economic pressures as well as spiritual ones. If millions of Indians could be persuaded to make the cloth they used themselves, instead of buying manufactured textiles from the British colonial power, the boycott would be severely felt in England's textile industry. The charkha was the key to victory. Non-violence was Gandhi's creed, and the spinning wheel was the perfect weapon.

'During the limping course of my lesson it helped me very little to have Pyarelal remark that progress in spinning was directly related to the level of the I.Q. As I kept making awkward mistakes and breaking the thread, I began to appreciate as never before the machine age with all its ball bearings and steel parts and maybe an occasional nail to take over from the human hand. But finally I was told I might pick up my equipment and go into Gandhi's hut.

"You understand. He will pay no attention to you."

'I understood. It was his day of silence. And I was overjoyed. If he paid no attention to me he wouldn't stop me.

'I found the inside of the hut even darker than I had anticipated. A single beam of daylight shone from a little high window directly into my lens and into my eyes as well. I could scarcely see to compose the picture, but when my eyes became accustomed to the murky shadows, there sat the Mahatma, cross-legged, a spidery figure with long, wiry legs, a bald head and spectacles.

Could this be the man who was leading his people to freedom – the little old man in a loincloth who had kindled the imagination of the world? I was filled with an emotion as close to awe as a photographer can come.

'My shutters and synchronizers, which normally work quite well, suddenly develop idiosyncrasies and refuse to function properly when confronted with some difficult and important personality. It happened with King Farouk of Egypt, with Prime Minister Churchill, with the Emperor of Ethiopia, and with the Pope. Probably the change from a cold to a warm climate did not help my equipment any. I tried loosening up the equipment by taking some slow time shots before using up my flashbulbs. The shutter began catching on the automatic release device, gaping wide open and refusing to close. When I coaxed that into action, the blade-arrester gadget thrust itself in the way. The film adapters kept slipping in crooked and sticking. The paper pulls on the film pack tore in half when the films were only partly drawn. As I turned to my tripod, two legs stuck at their shortest position while a third became wedged at its maximum length.

'Then Gandhi laid aside his clippings and started to spin. I decided to risk the first flashbulb. It was quite plain from the span of time between bulb flash and shutter click that the camera hadn't synchronized. The second shot sounded perfect and I was overjoyed, only to observe in the next second that I had forgotten to pull the slide. I drew a long breath before taking the third, checked everything, watched Gandhi carefully, and when he touched the fine cotton thread with his brown hand, gathered it up skillfully and beautifully, I caught him on the upstroke, and the camera sounded perfect. I threw my arms around the equipment and rushed out of the hut, feeling that I wasn't so sold on the machine age after all. Not until I held the finished photograph in my hands did my faith return completely.'

Excerpted from *Halfway to Freedom*
by Margaret Bourke-White

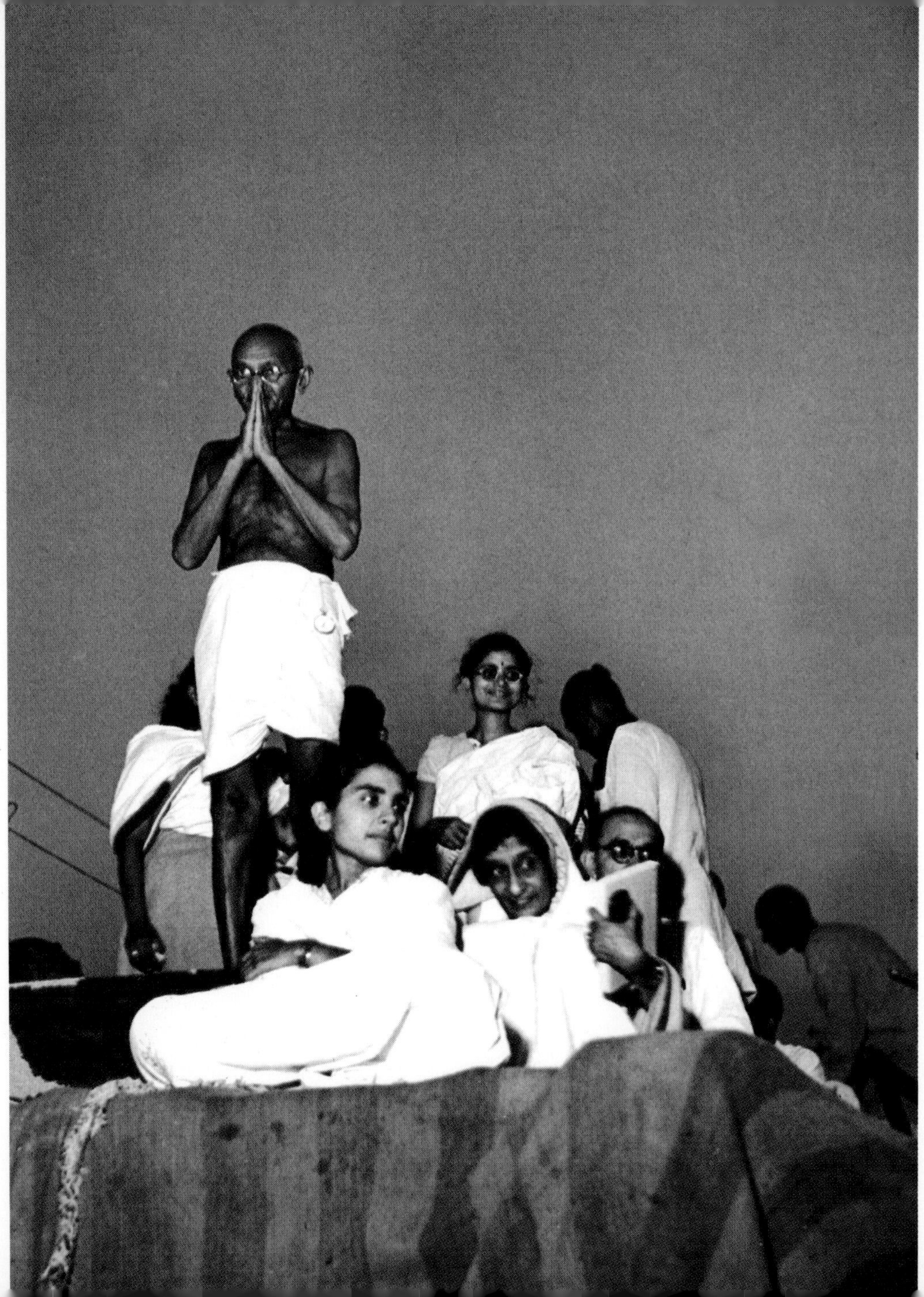

Left: At a prayer meeting: Mahatma Gandhi with Kanu and his wife Abha (standing), and Dr Sushila, Rajkumari Amrit Kaur and Pyarelal (sitting).

Right: Mahatma Gandhi with Kanu (singing a bhajan), Abha (seated in front) and Anis Ahmad, a Muslim League leader.

'The crowds often ran into the thousands, and the listeners into the millions, as his prayer talks were broadcast each day. The loudspeaker, though labeled "Chicago", was manufactured in Bombay. These evening prayers gave Gandhi a great pulpit from which to comment on any subject, large or small. What Gandhi said one evening would be on the tongue of every Indian by morning, and in times of crisis his words were followed closely.'

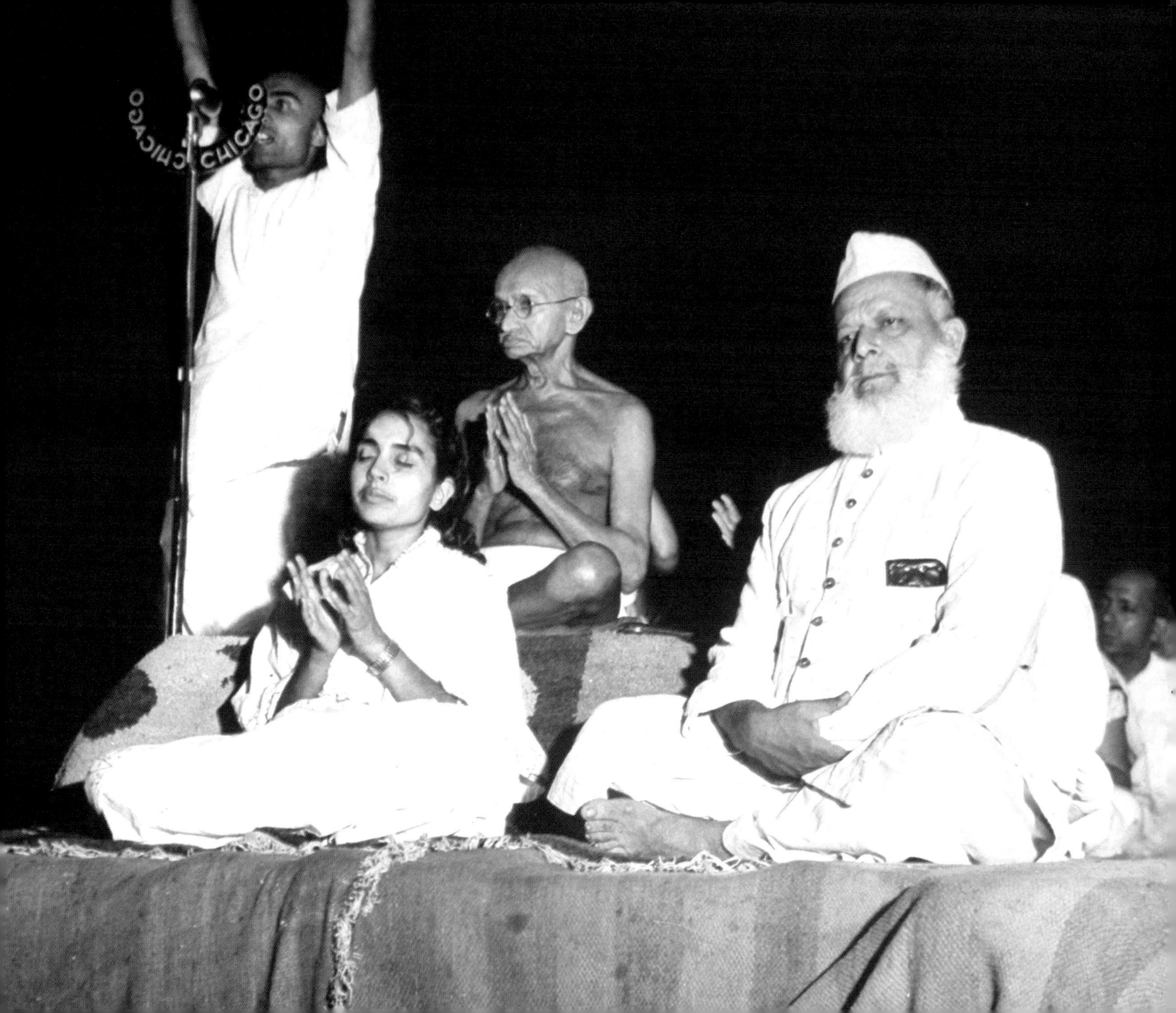
CHICAGO
CHICAGO

A frequenter to Gandhi's ashram, Margaret Bourke-White used to reach the ashram early morning to photograph the Mahatma during his morning walks. Pyarelal told her once, "Gandhiji has often said that if he had to make a choice between missing a meal and missing a walk, he would miss the first."

'There was one morning when Gandhi walked in the volleyball court beside the Bhangi Colony, and I had planted myself at one side opposite an opening between two tall trees. … Flanking Gandhi in a soldierly rank were the key members of his ashram. Gandhi was leaning as usual on the shoulders of two women; this morning he had his grand-niece-in-law Abha on the left and his attractive little granddaughter Sita on the right … During his last turn around the court the first golden ray stole through the gap in the trees. As he streaked past me Gandhi chuckled, "Now all your efforts will be in vain," and the column of figures swept on and away. But he was wrong. I had kept two cameras with lenses of different focal lengths focused on the crucial spot, and as he strode through the sunbeam I got two splendid negatives, one showing the entire rank with Gandhi and his followers , and the other a close-up of the Mahatma leaning on the shoulders of the two girls.'

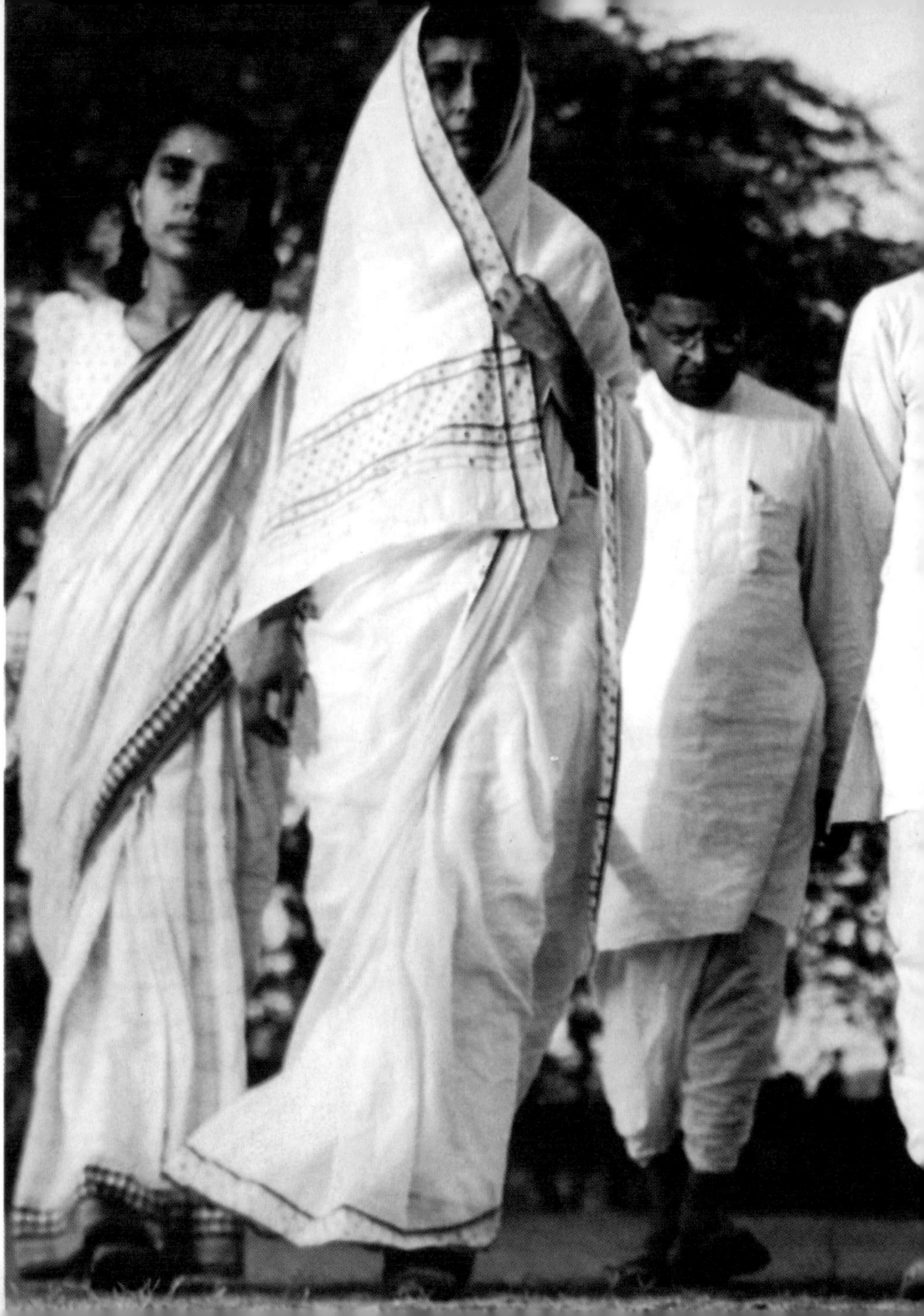

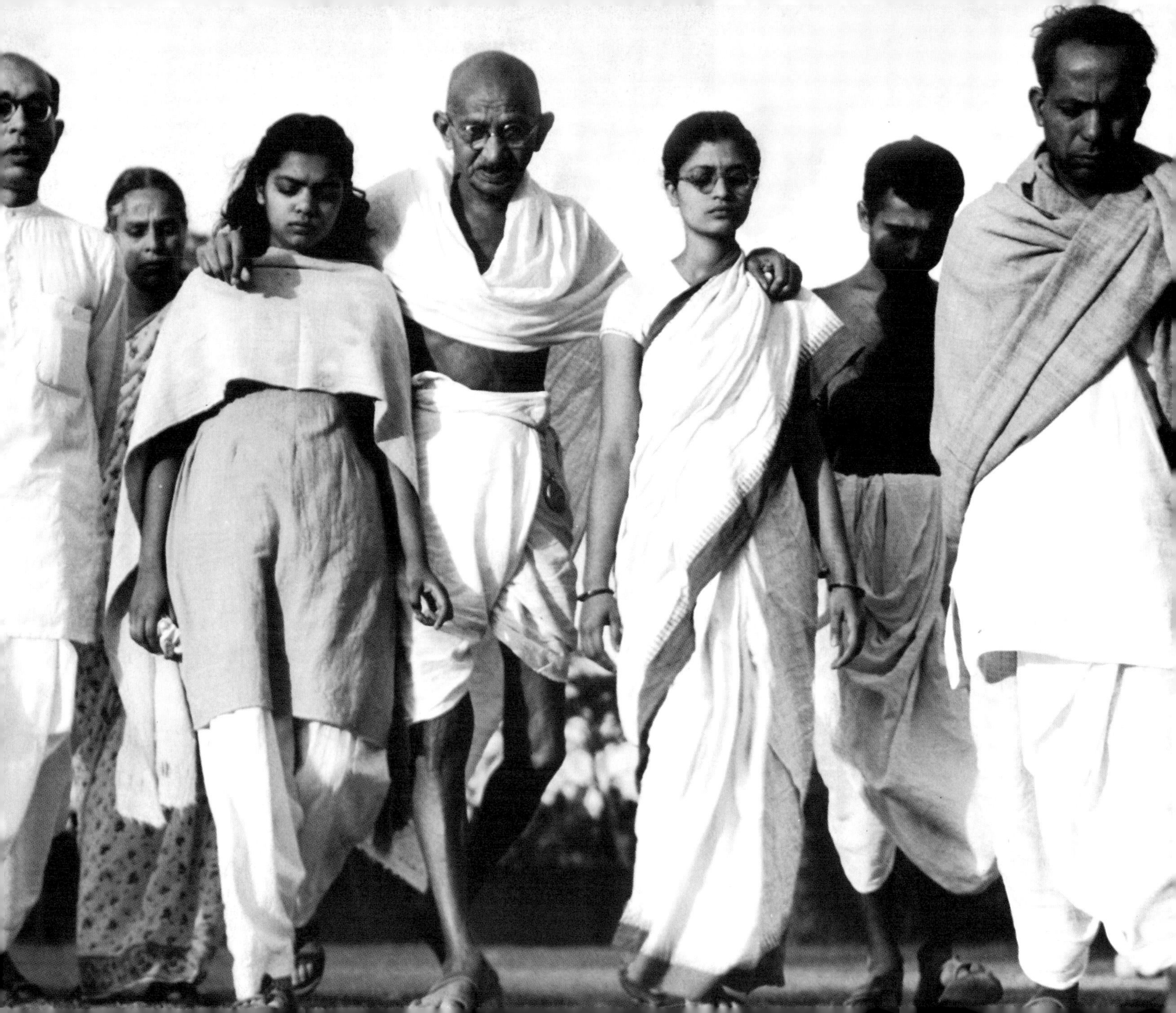

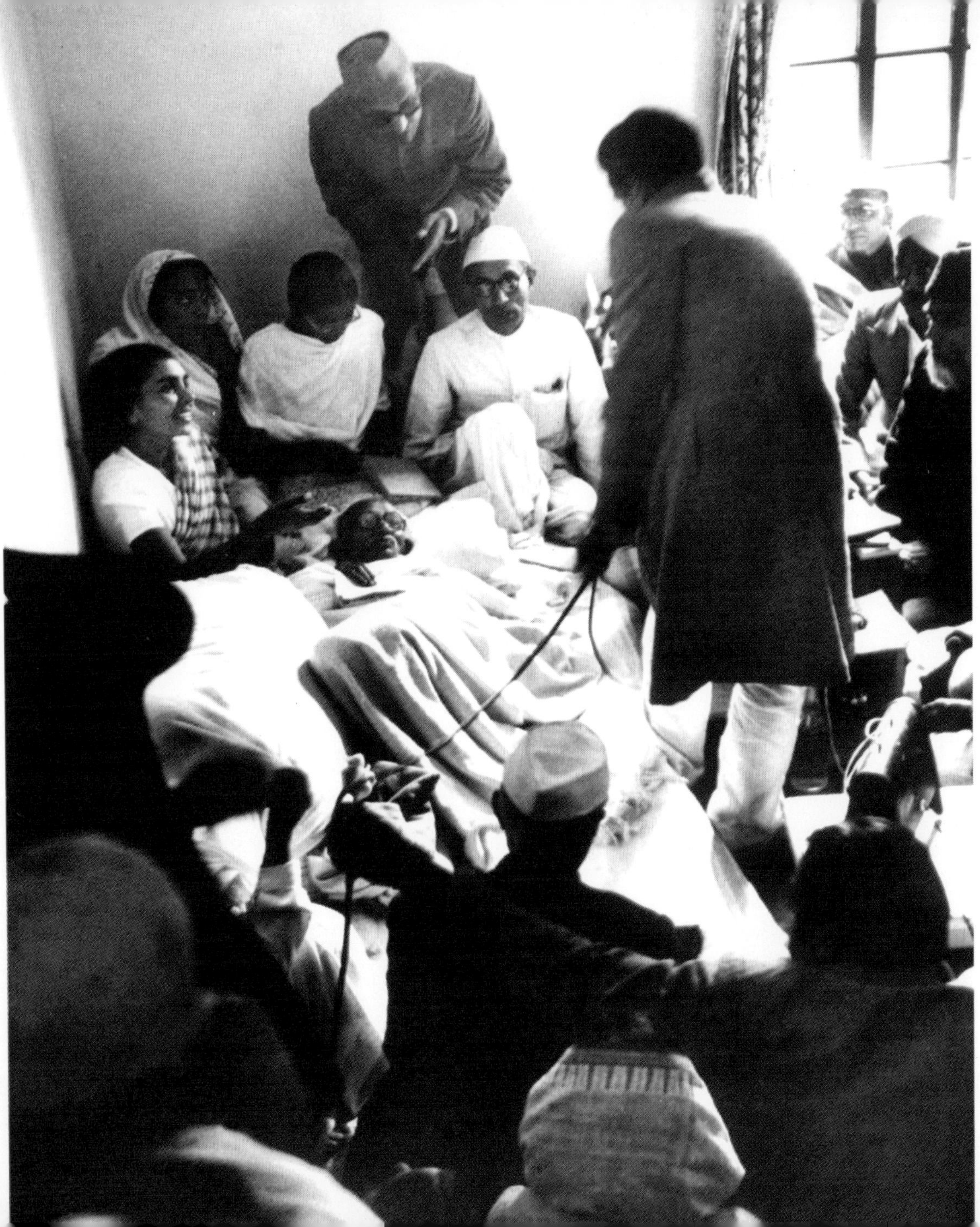

On 12 January 1948, Mahatma Gandhi decided to go on a fast in the hope of 'bringing peace to the hearts of the people of all religions in India' ... This was the sixteenth fast of Gandhi's life. It was more of a 'bombshell than the previous fifteen had been'. While the others had been directed against the British Raj, this was for the unity of his own people, his own children.

'It was plain that Gandhi was launching the hardest battle of his life: the battle to conquer inner hatreds. For thirty years he had fought an outside power and with his weapon of non-violence had been spectacularly successful in leading his people along the road to freedom. Now he was faced with a still more difficult job: the task of winning tolerance and unity within men's hearts. As he talked on in his quiet voice I had the feeling that he possessed a real power to call on these people's inner strength, for, I thought, he is closer to the soul of India than any other men.'

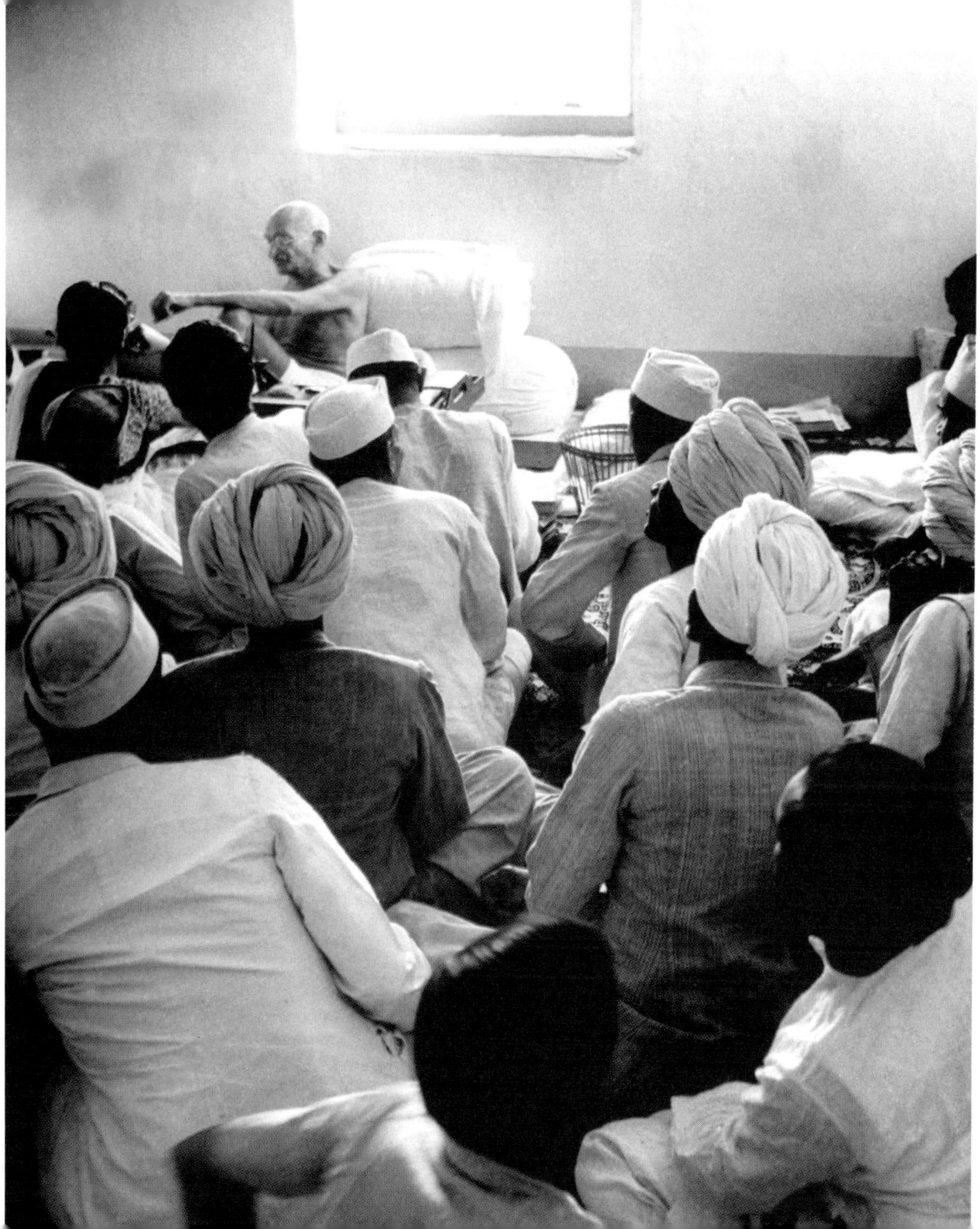

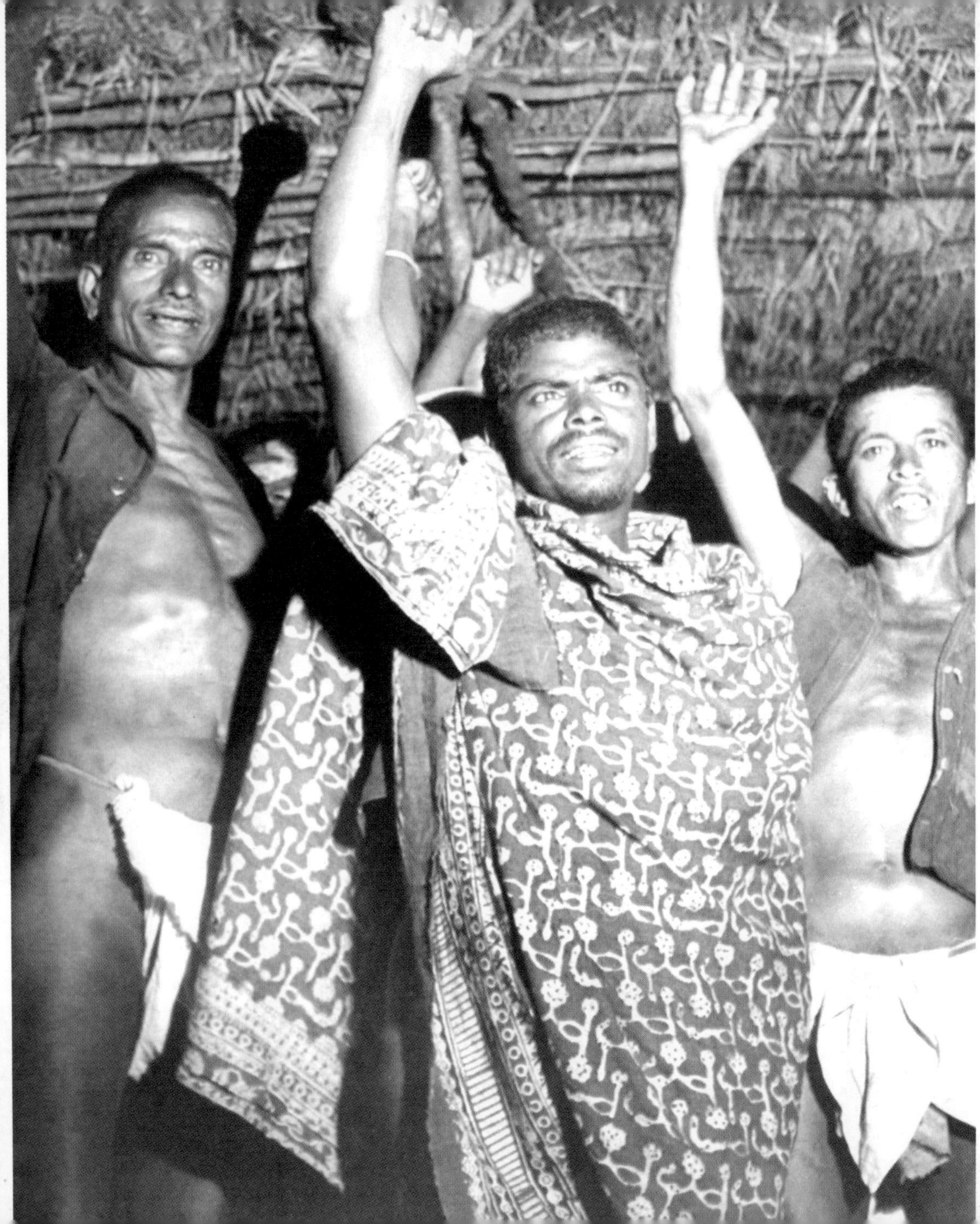

'With anxiety over the spread of Communism in Asia so prominent in the minds of Western leaders, it is pertinent to ask how far the government can compromise with the feudal princes over the land question, and with industrialists over collective bargaining, without strengthening the Socialists and the Communists. Though both groups are relatively young and still weak, they are powerful in the growing labor unions and in the various movements in the princely states. In outbreaks such as the Telengana uprisings and peasant seizure of the farmlands in eastern Hyderabad, there are unmistakable signs that the Communistic voice is reaching the potentially rebellious poor peasantry and threatening Congress party control of rural India. Government suppression of the party is an even better indication of its increased potency.'

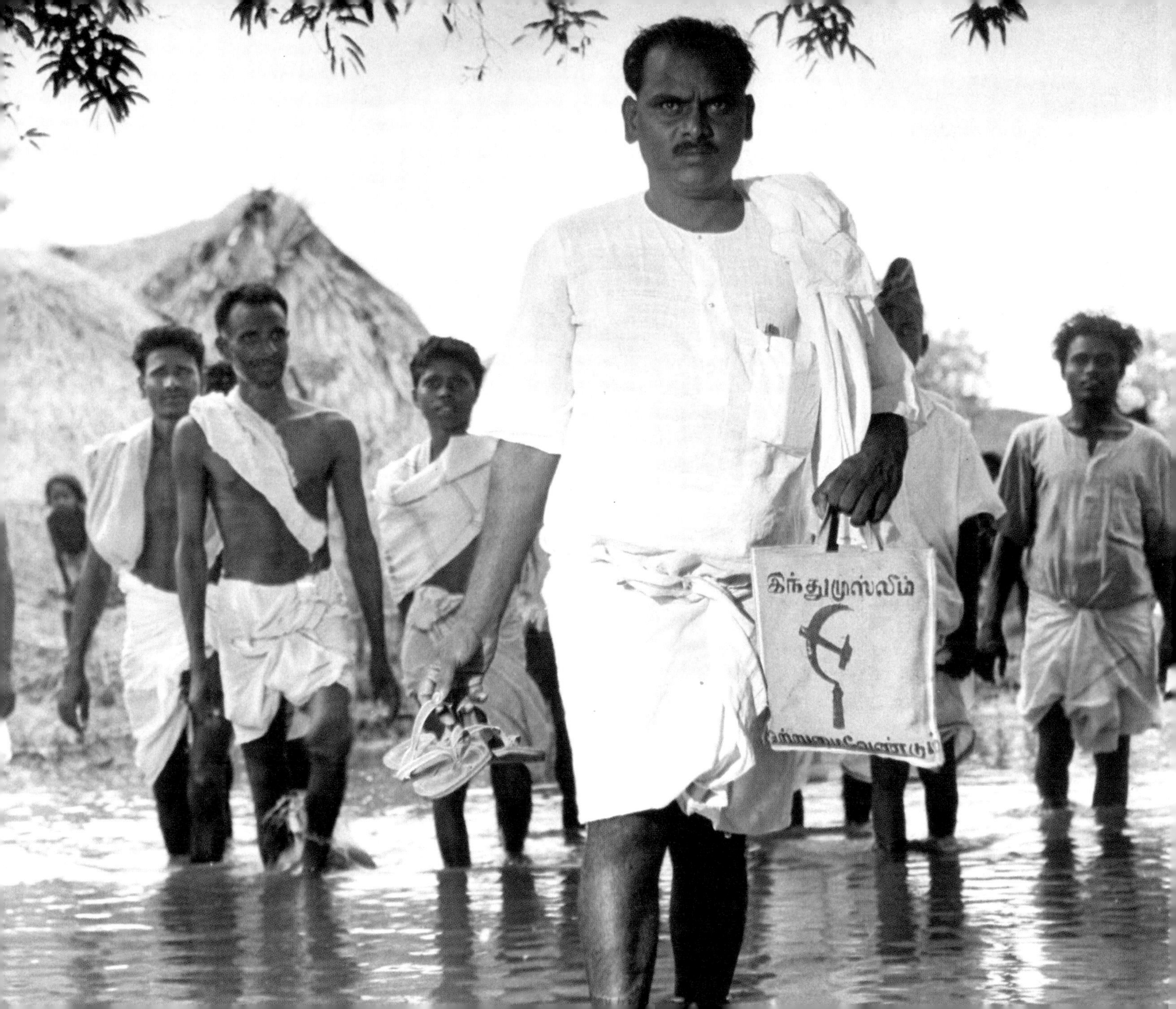
இந்துமுஸ்லிம்

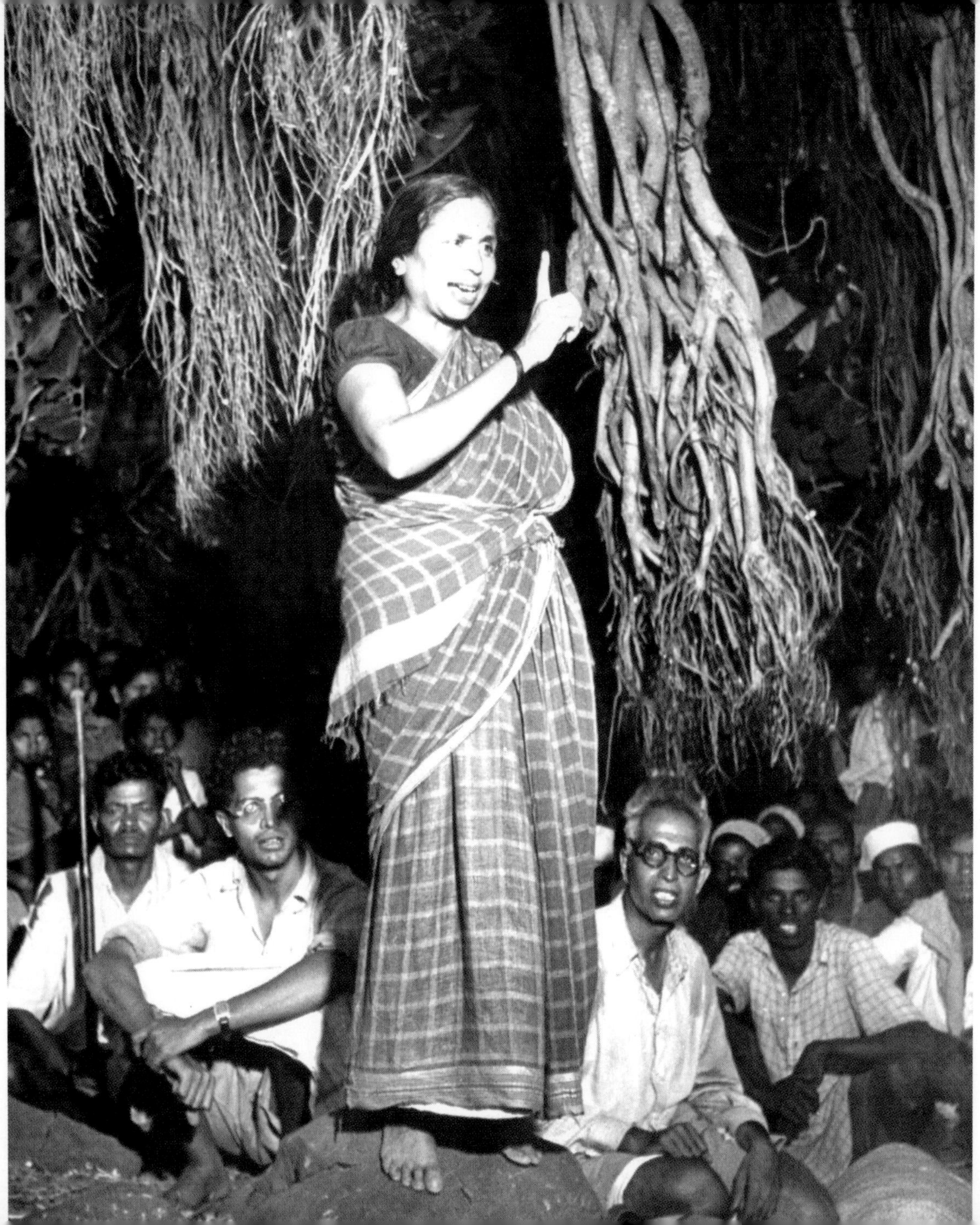

At one of the Trichy Tannery Workers Union meetings that Margaret Bourke-White attended she spoke to the workers about freedom and education for every child. Communist leaders Gadivari (left) and SV Perulekar (right) addressing the meeting.

'It was an unusual union meeting which I photographed that night, with its large proportion of children. They began arriving at twilight, as they were released from their work in the pits, and they took their place quietly on the ground under the banyan tree. Long after darkness fell, the leather workers came streaming in, until the ground far beyond the banyan tree was filled with hundreds of untouchables, most of them children … the lamplight fell on the first few row of faces, lighting up childish eyes grave and wise beyond their years, and illuminating the red banner which listed the union's demand.'

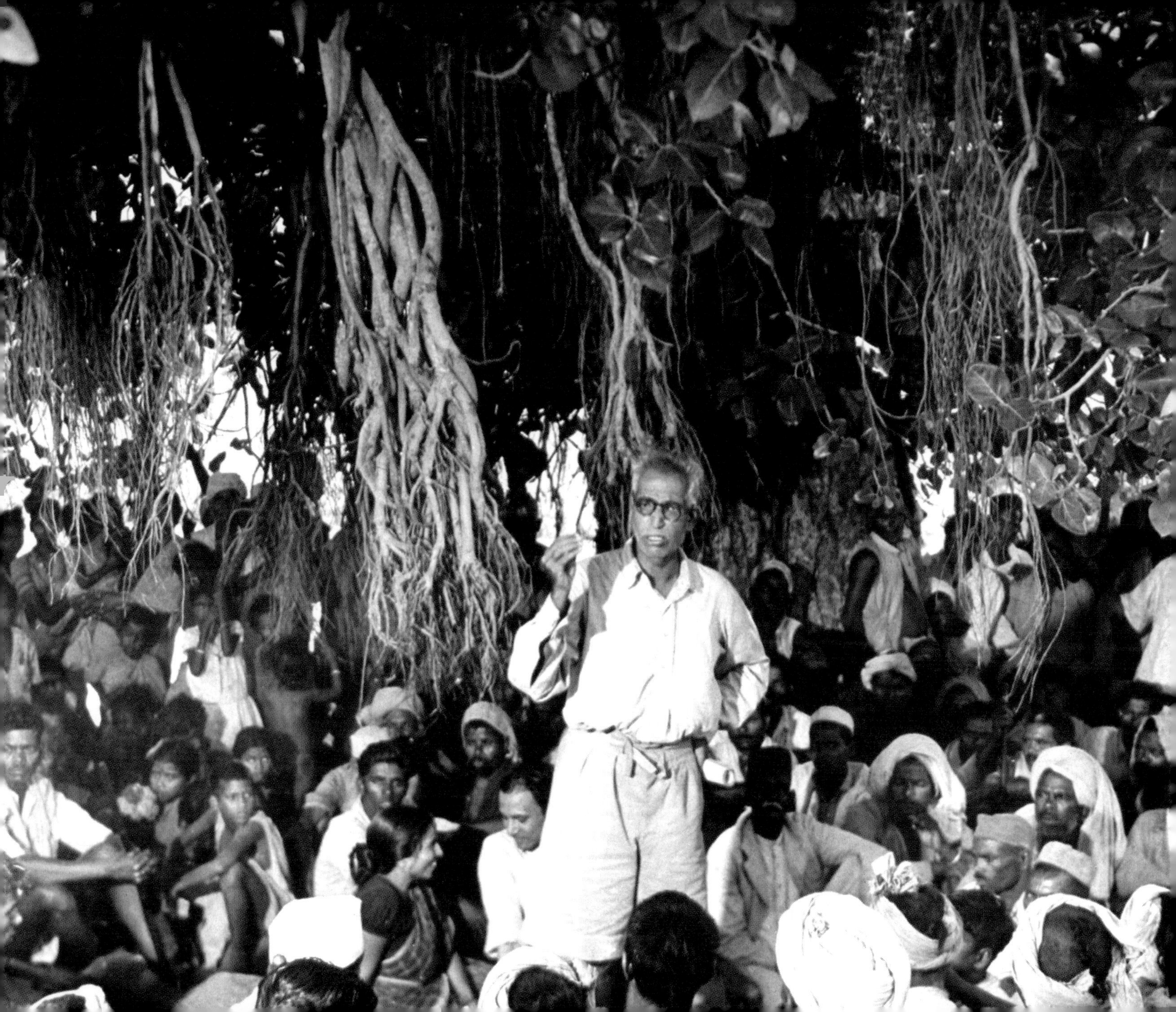

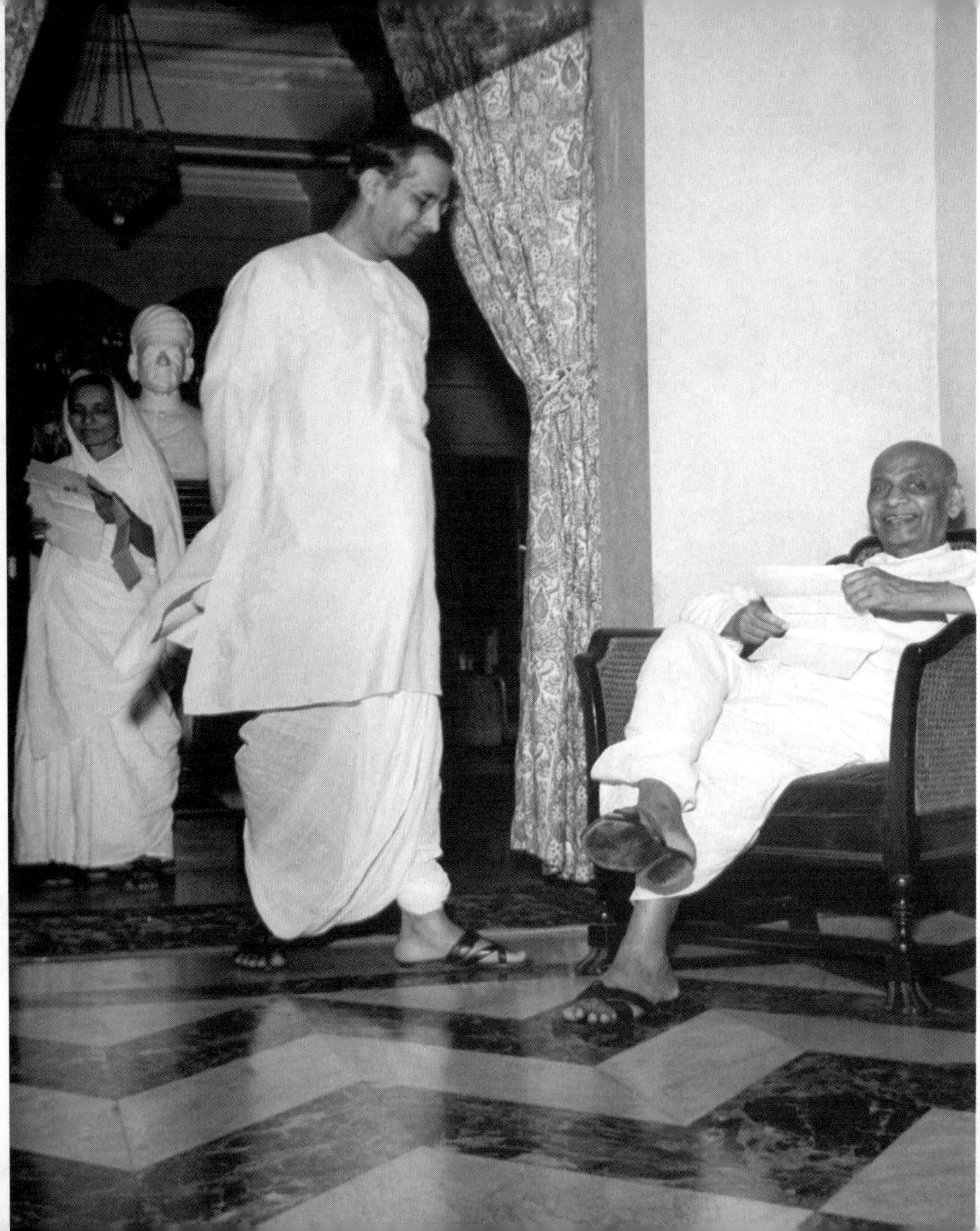

Birla House on Albuquerque Road, now Tees January Marg, in New Delhi where Mahatma Gandhi usually stayed when he was in the city, was the meeting place for the top brass of Indian politics.

Left: Industrialist Ghanshyam Das Birla with Sardar Vallabhbhai Patel.

Right: Mahatma Gandhi leaving Birla House.

'To the man in the street, Seth Birla was the personification of big business, and Patel was its spokesperson. In the popular mind Patel was associated with rightist and Nehru with Leftist trends; Patel with the industrialists and the maharajas, and Nehru with the rights of the common man.'

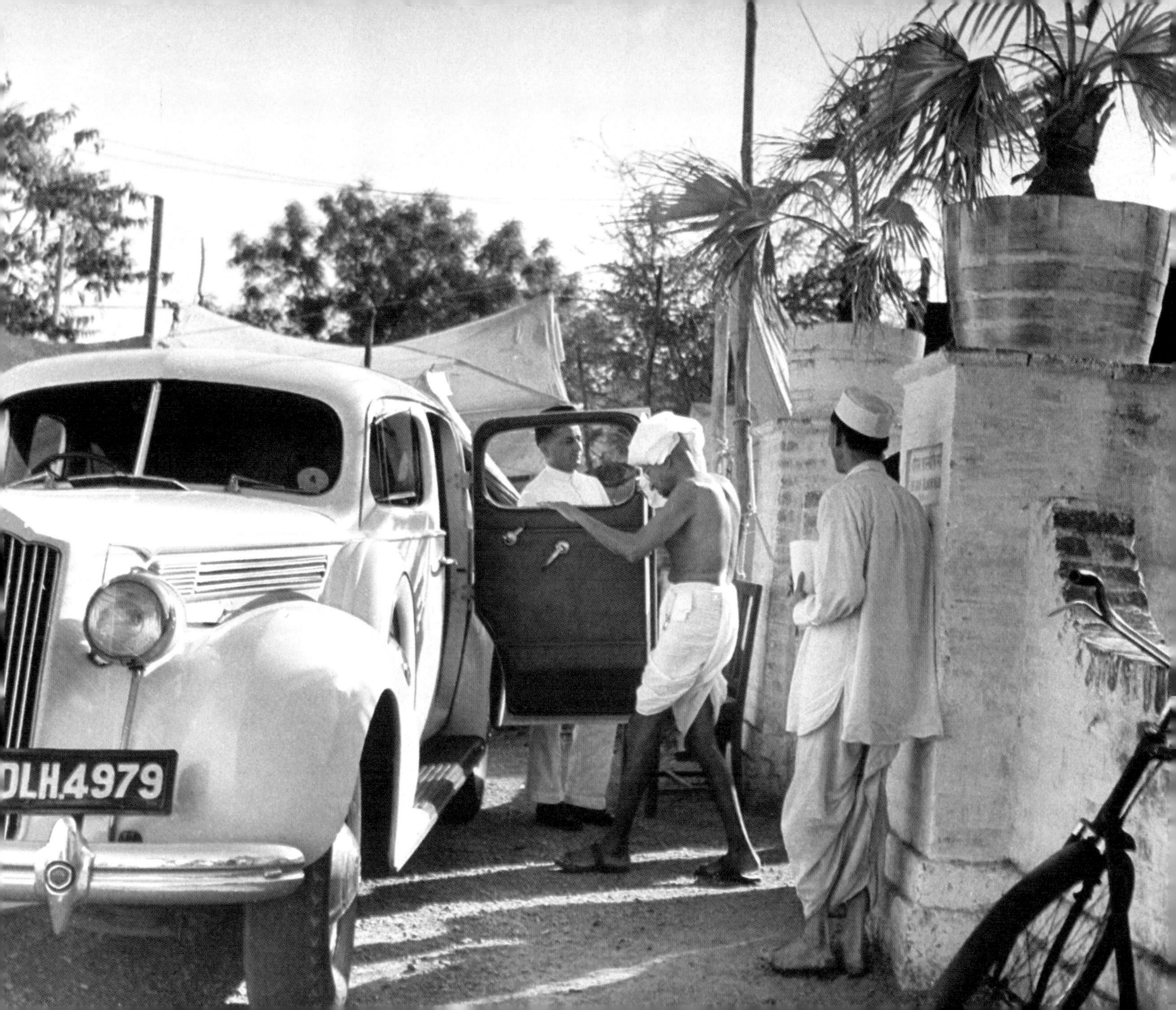
DLH.4979

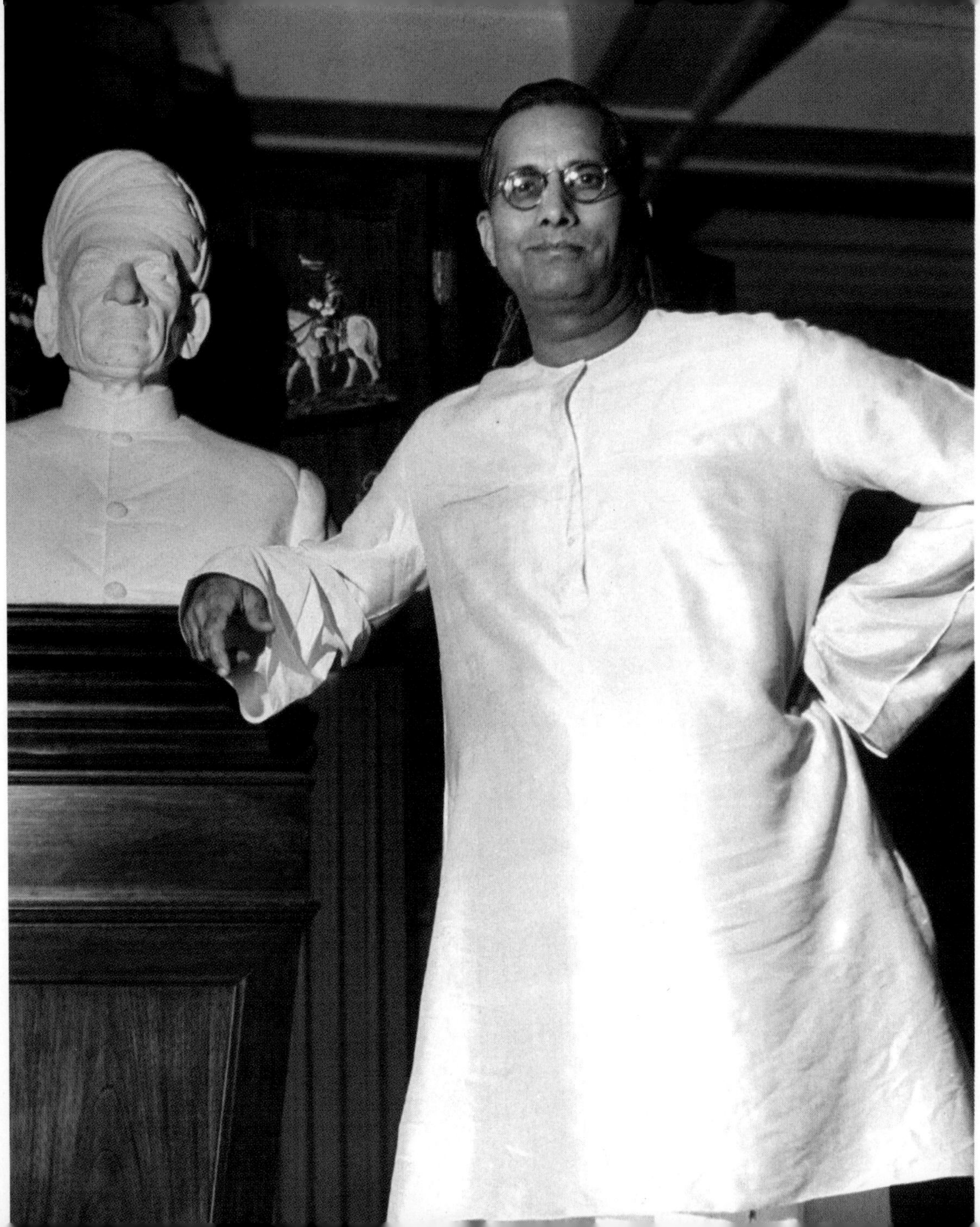

Left: Ghanshyam Das Birla posing next to the bust of his grandfather, Shiv Narain Birla, founder of the Birla Firm.

Right: Managing Editor of Hindustan Times, Devadas Gandhi, Mahatma Gandhi's youngest son, chatting with a colleague.

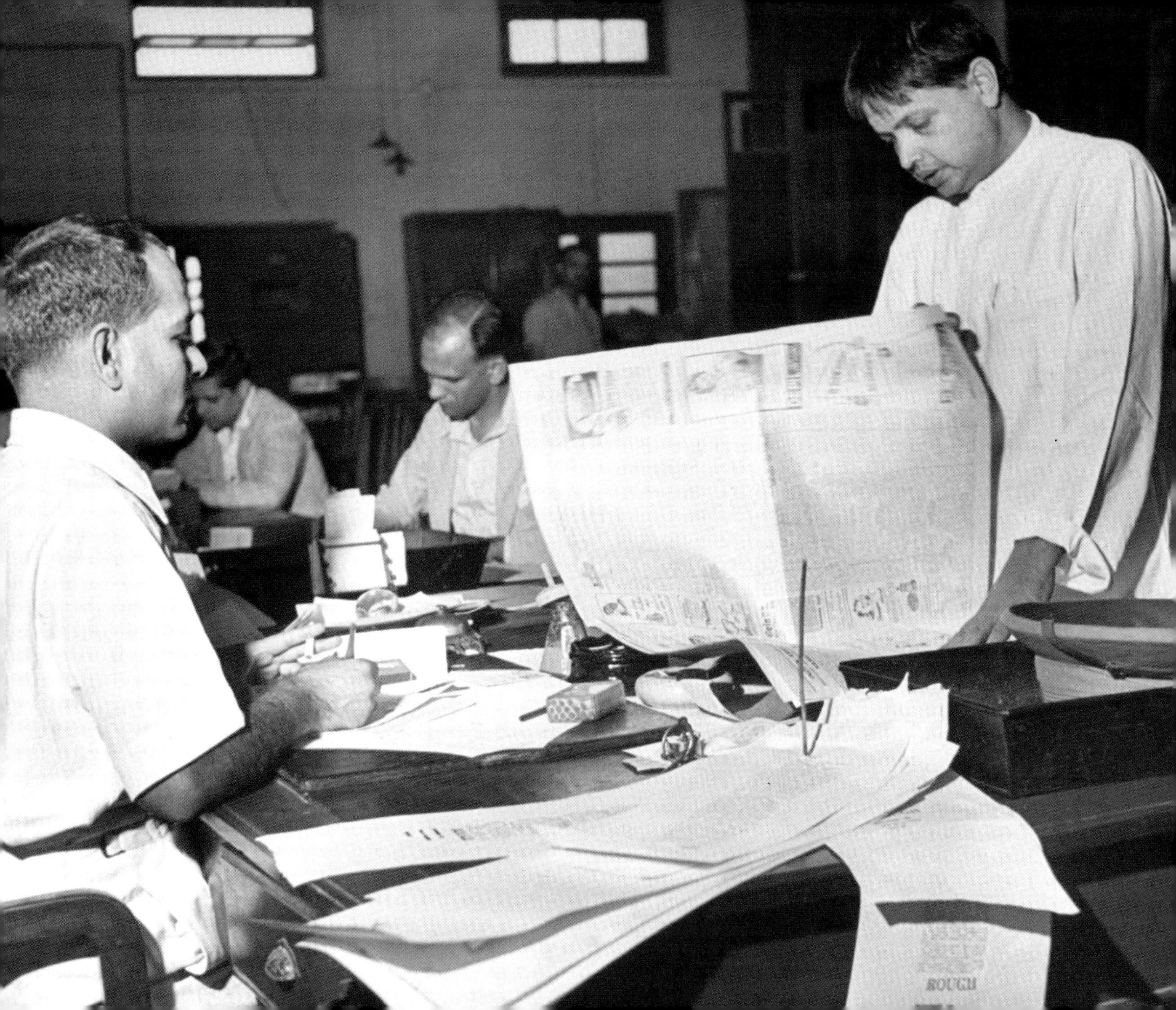
ROUGH

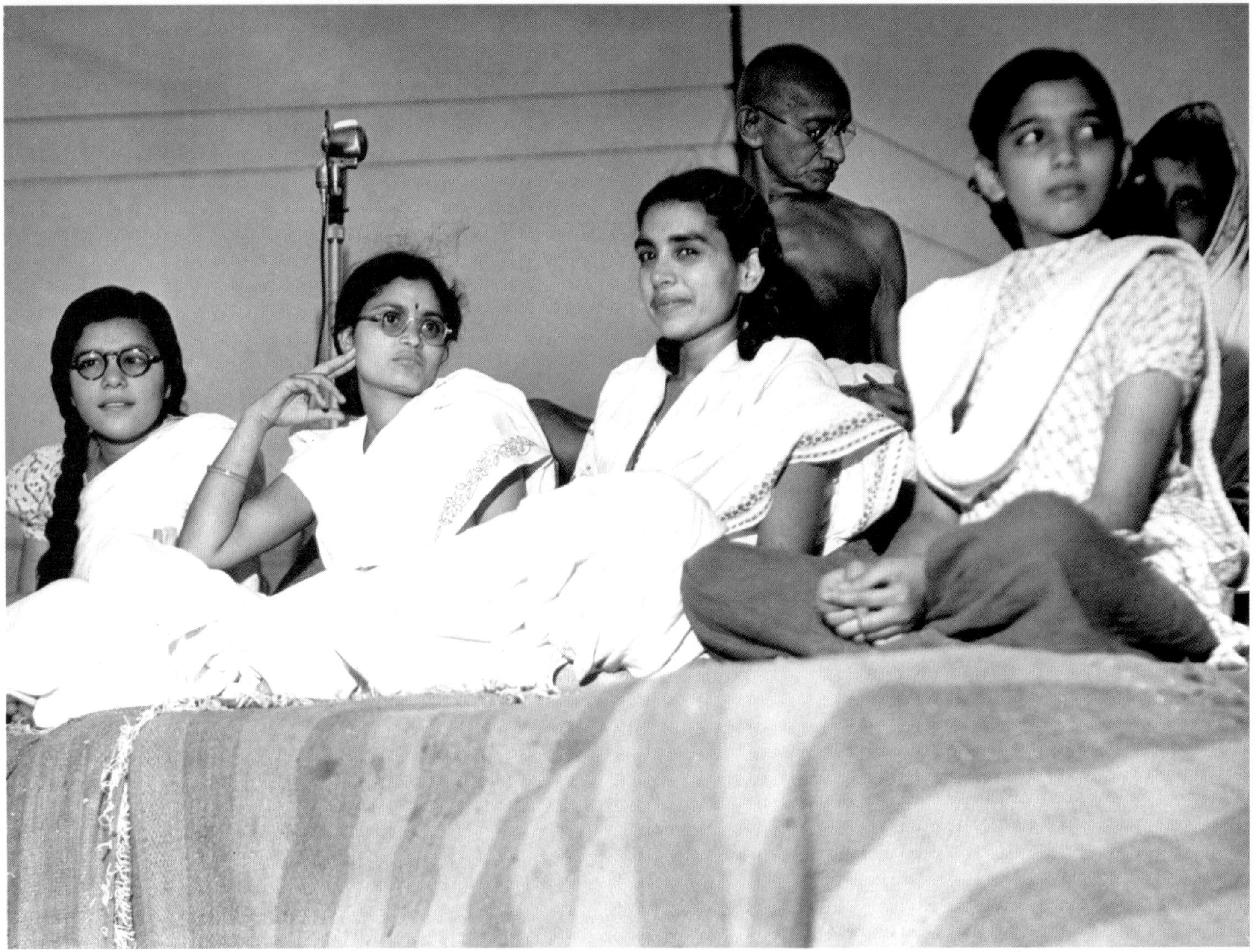

Mahatma Gandhi at a twilight prayer meeting with (from L to R) his granddaughter Mohun, nephew's wife Abha, Dr Sushila, granddaughter Tara, and Rajkumari Amrit Kaur.

Facing page: Dr Rajagopalachari with his grandchildren (L to R) Gopu, Mohun, Ramchandra and Tara – children of Devadas Gandhi.

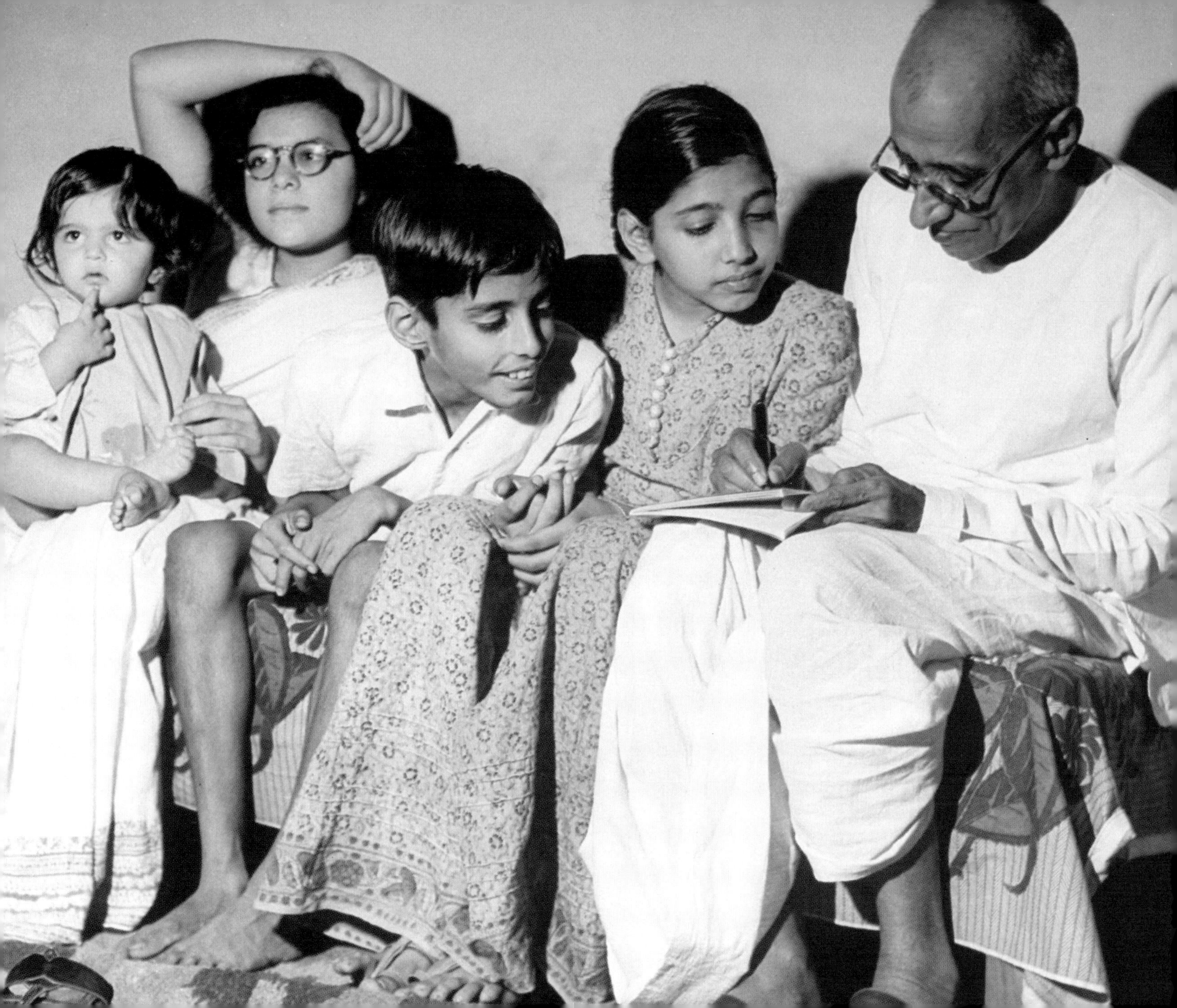

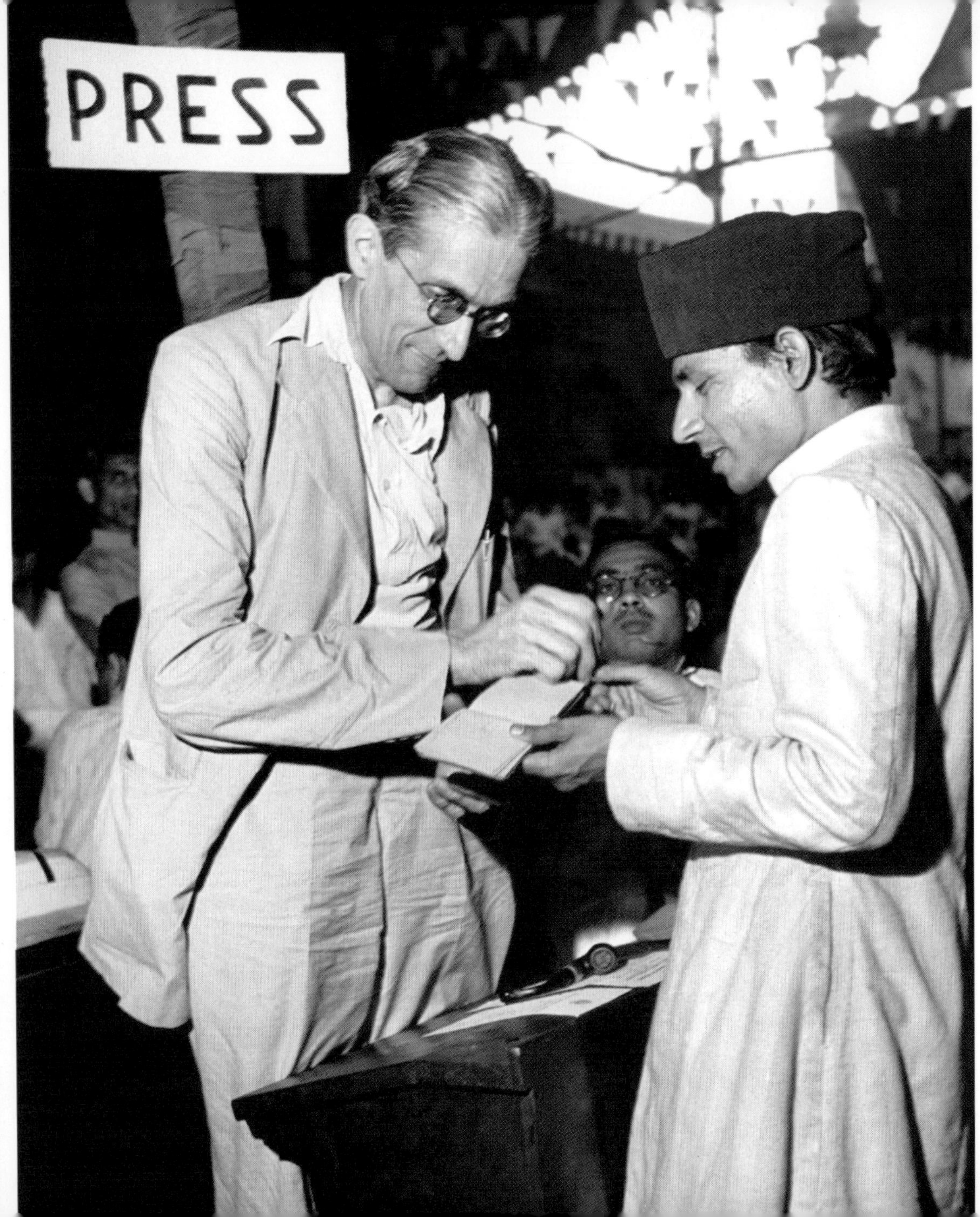

Left: A leading journalist and theoretician in the Communist Party of the Great Britian, Rajani Palme Dutt (L), was in India in 1946, covering the Cabinet Mission for the London Daily Worker.

Right: Chaman Lal, a journalist, talking on telephone in the Press Tent at Gandhi Colony compound.

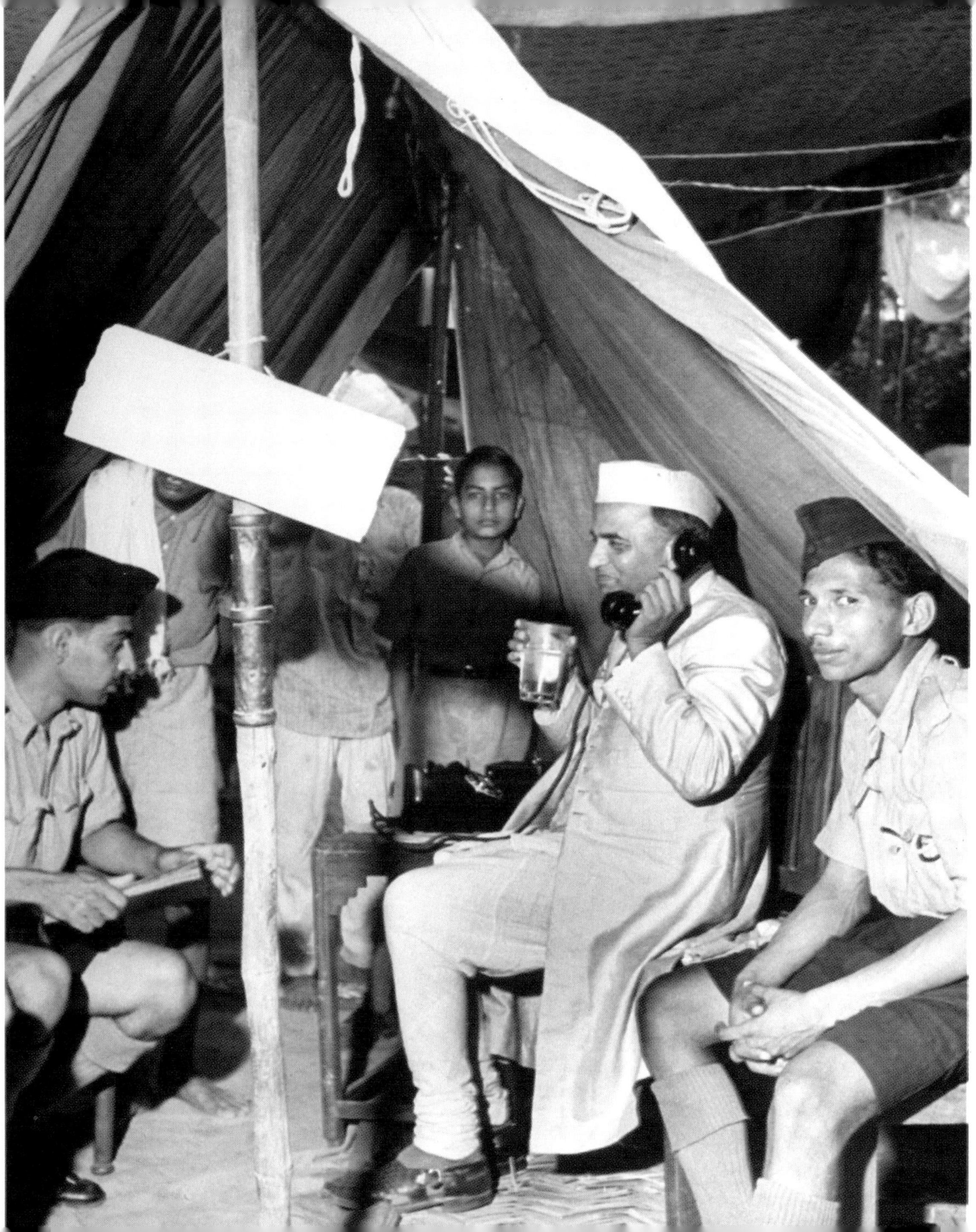

'The members of the working press in Delhi had formed the habit of visiting the Bhangi Colony every day to observe the mounting preparations for Gandhi's arrival, which had been going on for several days. The residents of half the Bhangi Colony had been moved out – I never discovered where, perhaps to that part of the colony which had been left in its virgin squalor.'

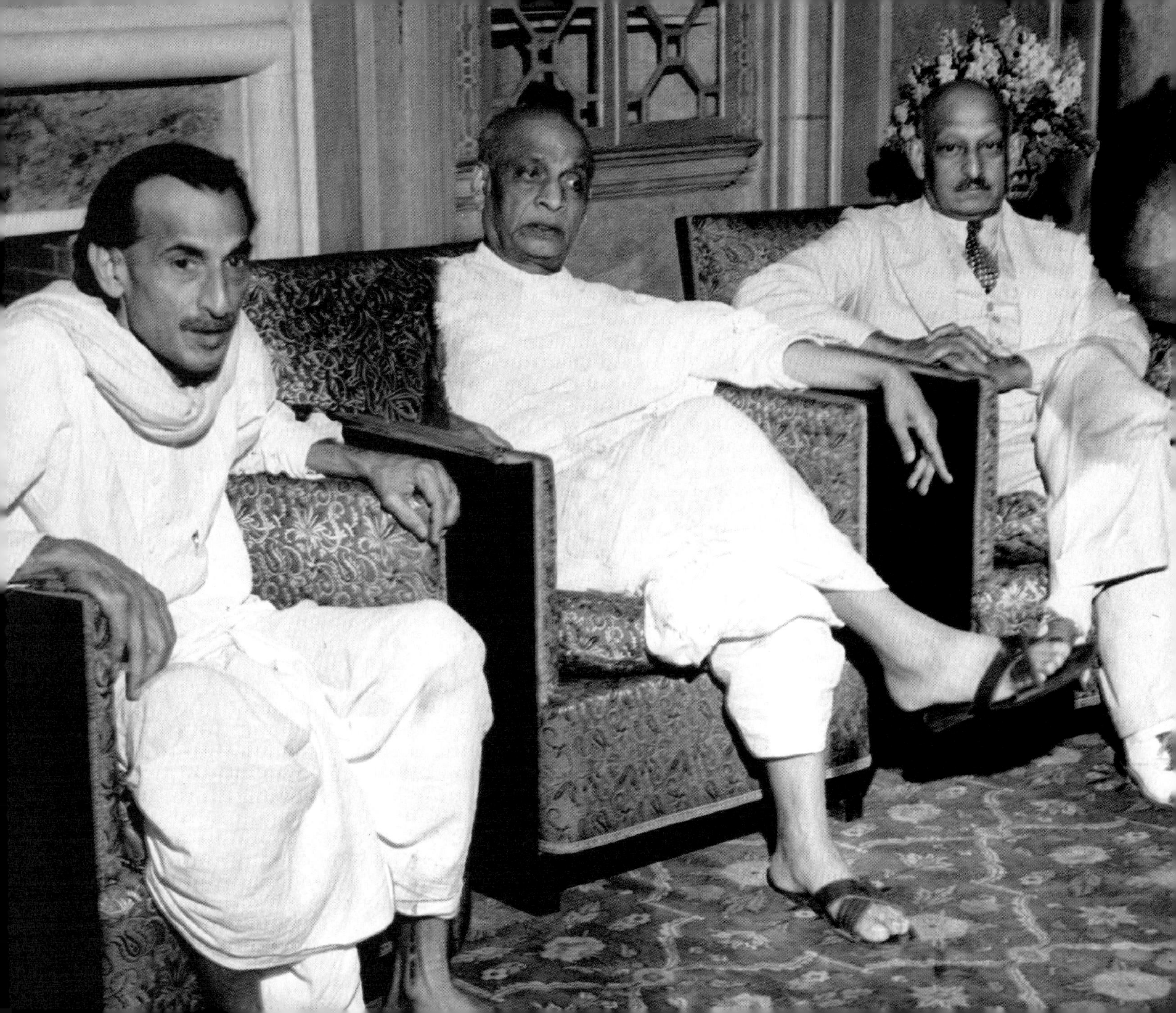

Left: (L to R) Acharya J.B. Kriplani, Sardar Vallabhbhai Patel and Sir Vala Nath Sen at G.D. Birla's house.

Right: (L to R) Satyanarayan Sinha, member of legislative assembly; Gopinath Bardoloi, chief minister of Assam with Rohini Kumar Chaudhri, member of legislative assembly, waiting at the Gandhi Colony compound to meet the Mahatma.

'In March of 1946, all Indian leaders were flocking to Delhi to meet with the British Cabinet Mission, to lay the ground plan of the coming freedom. The British ministers were Sir Stafford Cripps, Lord Pethick-Lawrence, India's Secretary of State, and Mr A.V. Alexander, First Lord of the Admirality.'

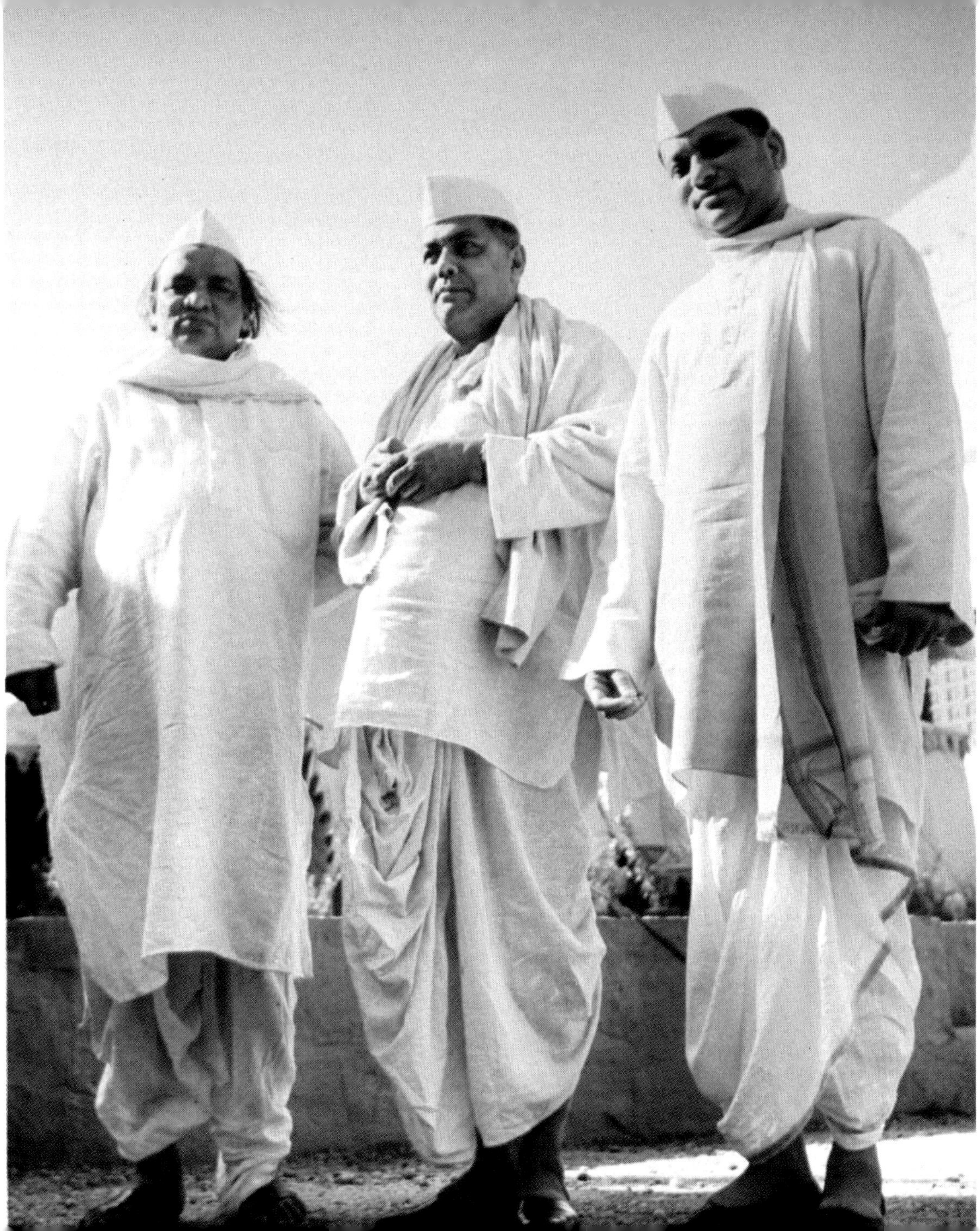

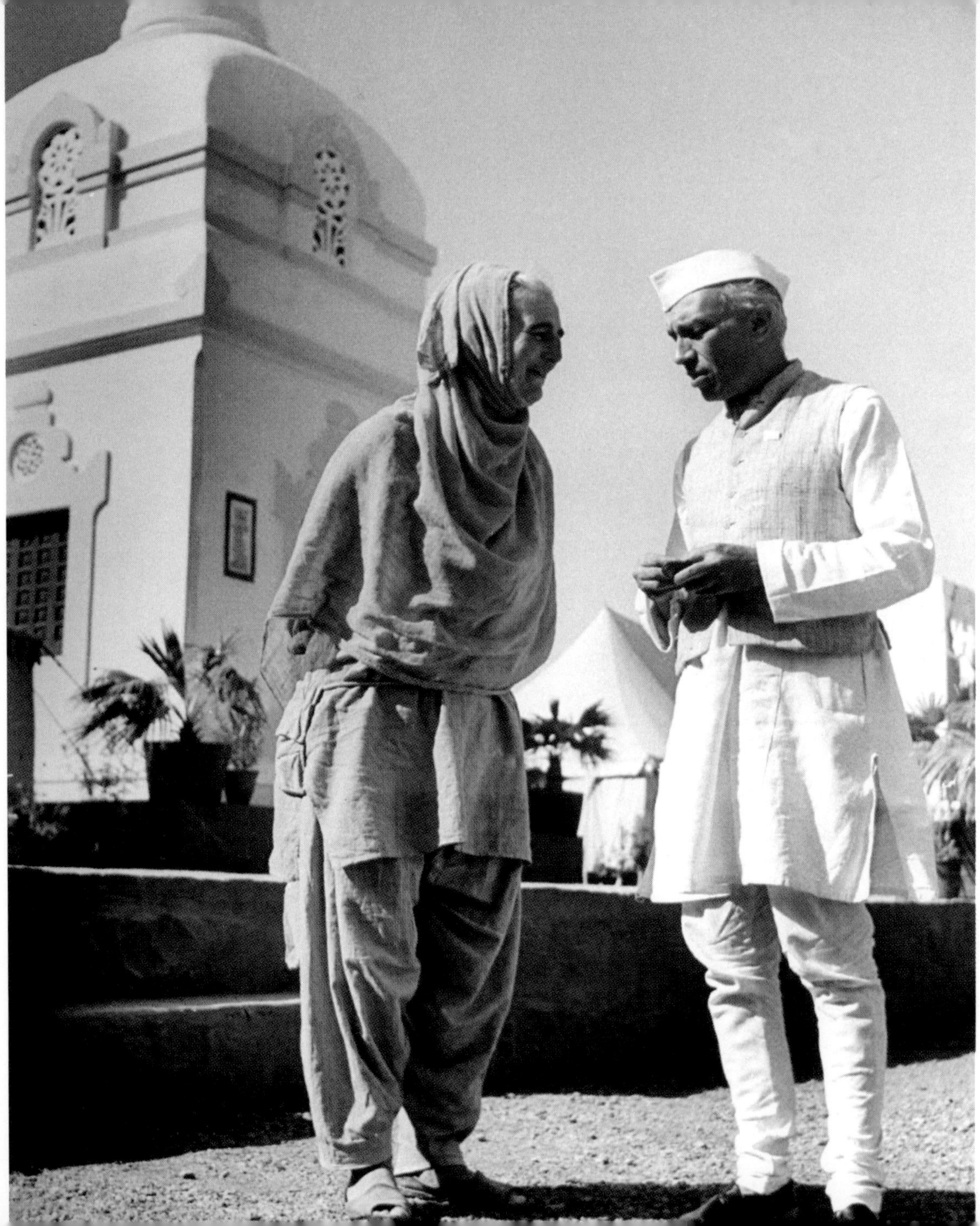

Pandit Jawaharlal Nehru with Mira Behn (Madeleine Slade) standing in front of the Valmiki Temple.

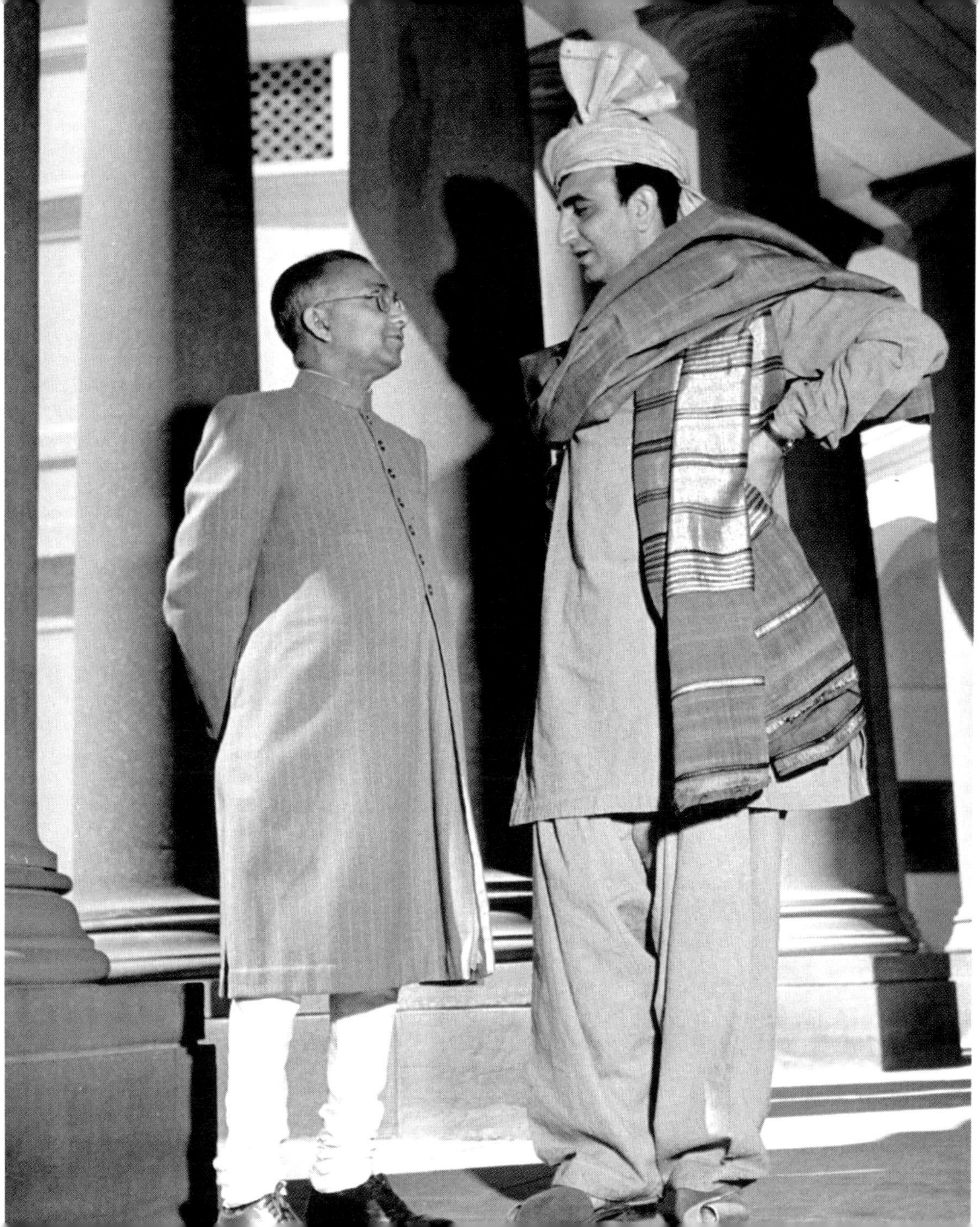

Abdul Ghani Khan (R), son of 'Frontier Gandhi' Khan Abdul Ghaffar Khan chatting with Shiva Rao, a leading journalist, at the Council House in Delhi, 1946. Ghani Khan was a poet, artist, historian and politician. Often known as one of the foremost poets in the Pastun language, Ghani Khan was imprisoned by the Pakistani government in 1948 despite having left active politics.

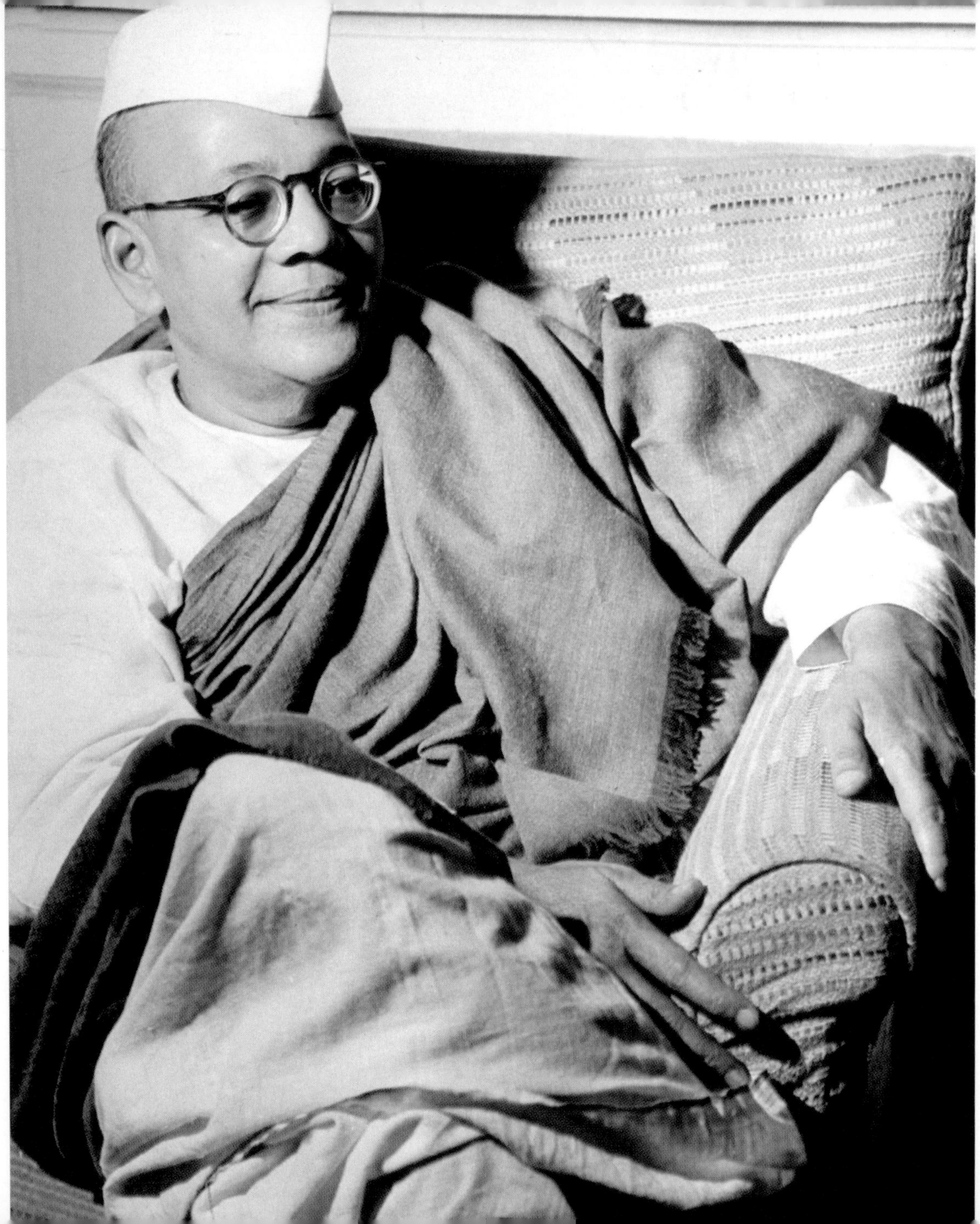

Netaji Subhash Chandra Bose relaxing at home.

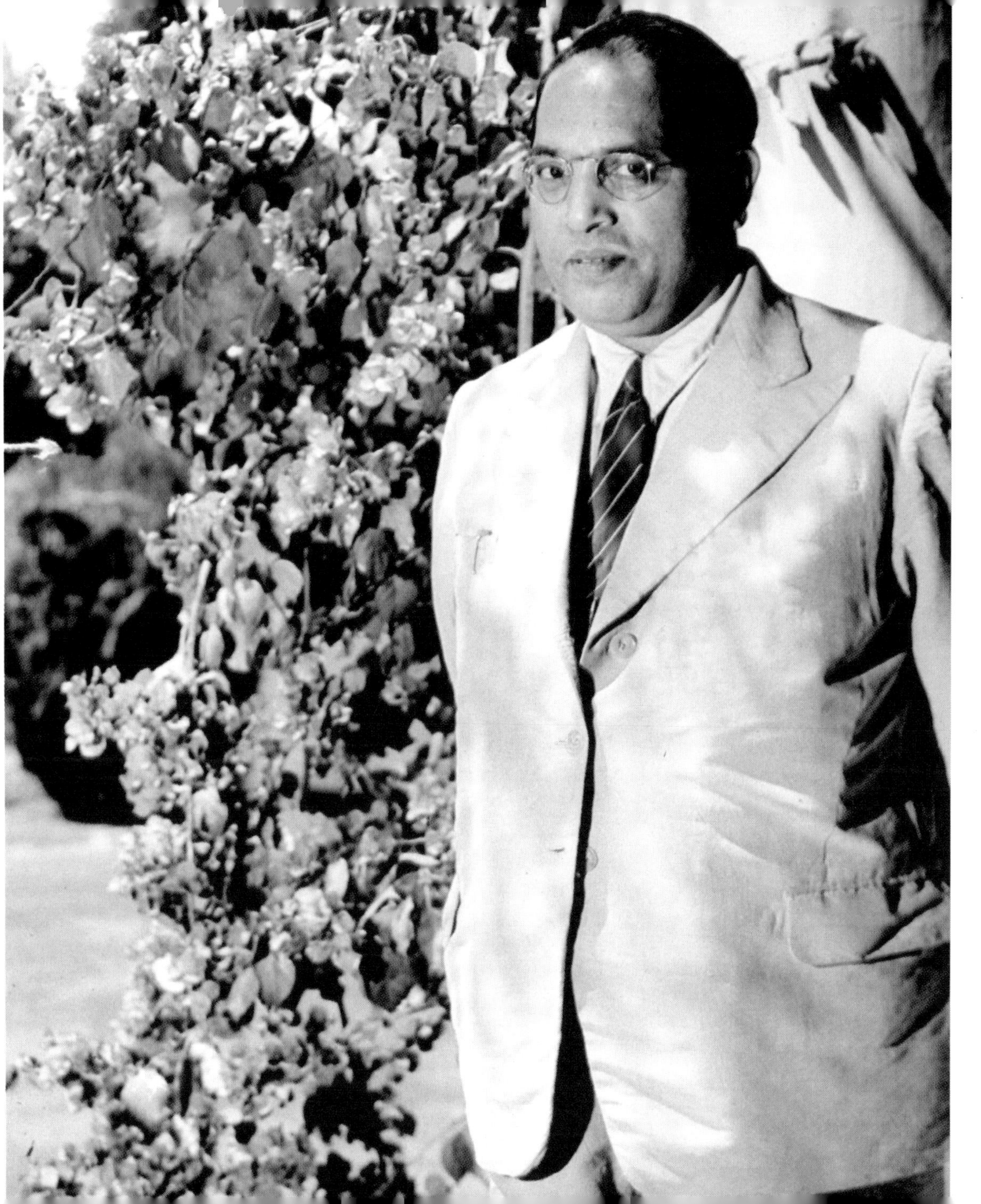

Dr Bhimrao Ambedkar.

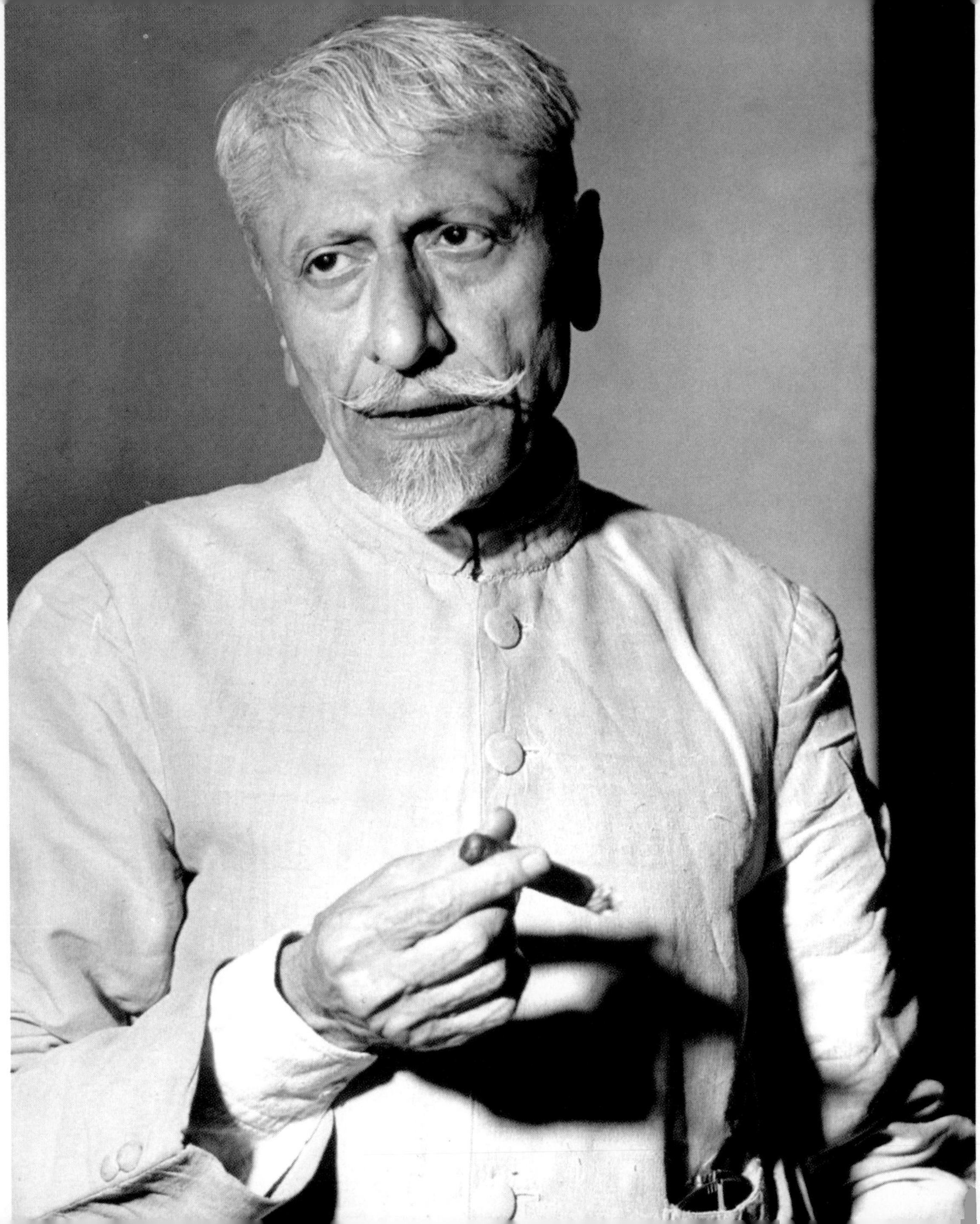

Left: Maulana Abul Kalam Azad

Right: Pandit Jawaharlal Nehru. 'If Gandhi's great mantle falls on any one man, Nehru is that man,' writes Margaret Bourke-White. According to her Nehru was one leader who was influenced by the West and formed a great balance between the Western and Asian worlds.

'With India entering the world stage, Indians were saying, "Panditji is the greatest man in Asia." Nehru's stand that the Western world should "stop treating Asia like a poor relation" won the hearts of his people. They realized with pride that their Prime Minister commanded the overwhelming respect of both the Eastern and Western worlds. His European education and many years abroad, combined with an intimate knowledge of his own country, fitted him for a unique international role. His closest friends had their affectionate jokes about what Nehru himself called his "queer mixture of East and West". Maulana Azad, the great Urdu scholar, once said, "When Jawaharlal talks in his sleep he speaks in English."'

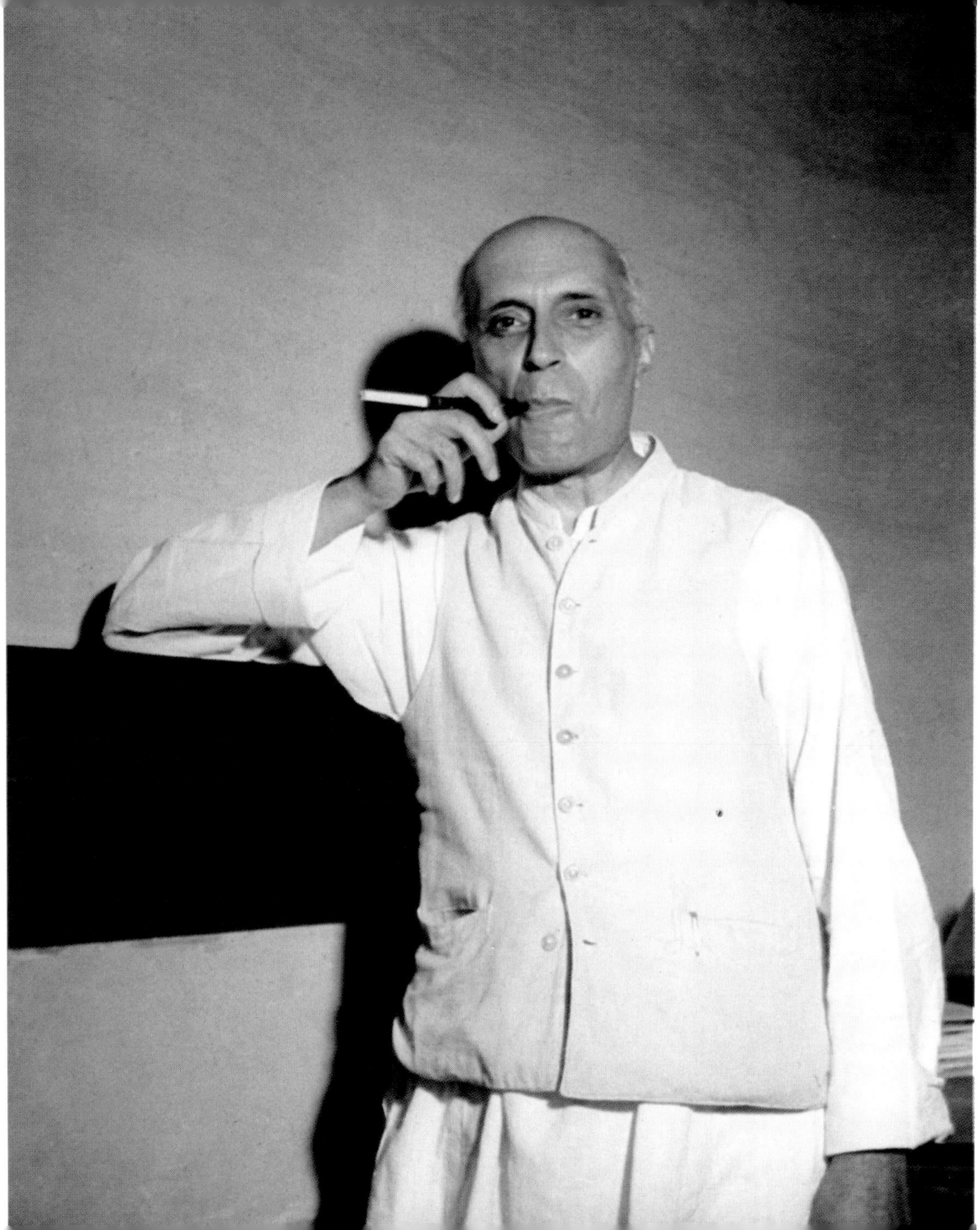

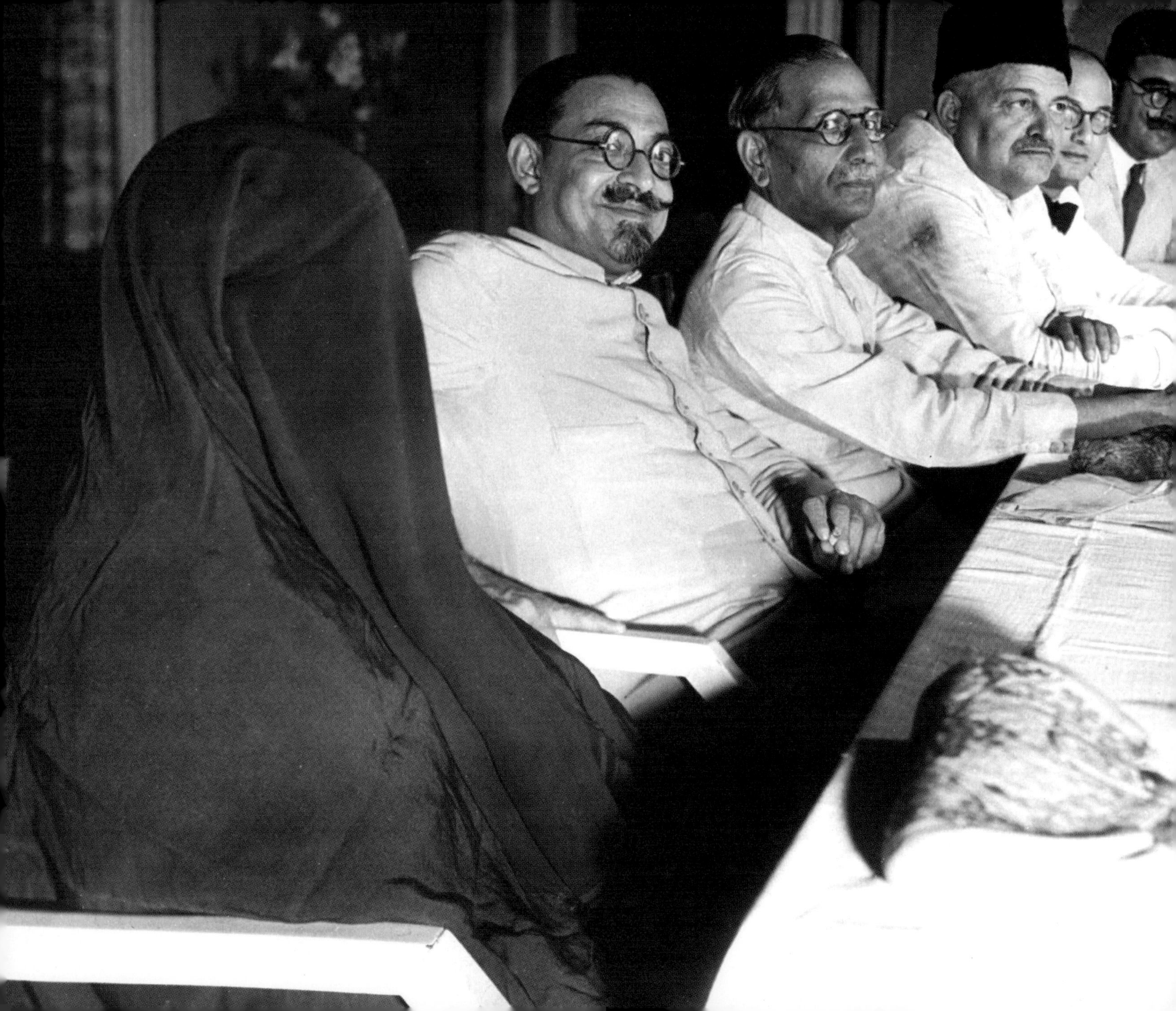

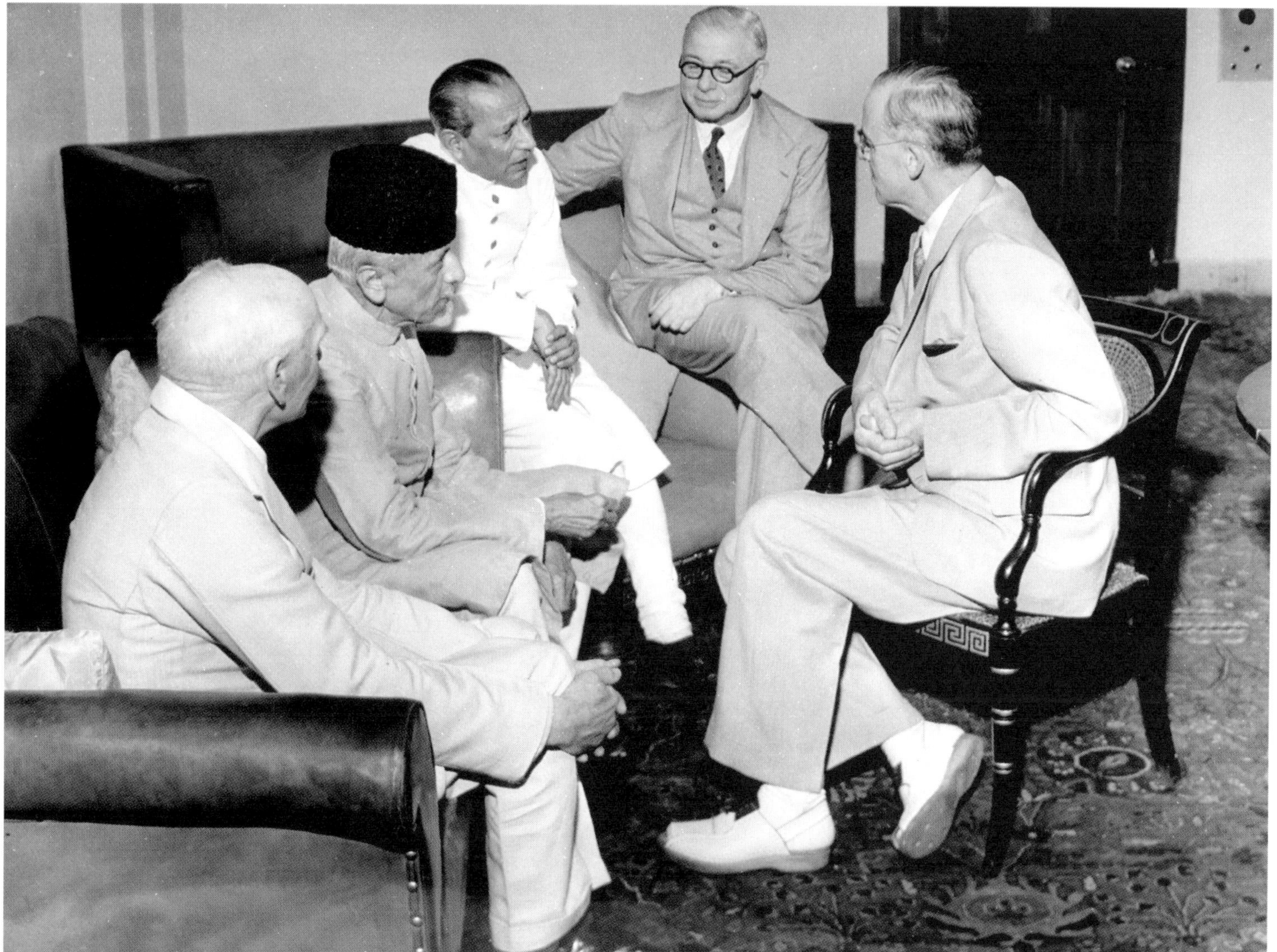

Left: Leading female member of the Indian Muslim League, Begum Mohammad Ali Johar, with Hussain Imam, Chaudhry Khaliq-uz Zaman, Sardar Aurengzeb, Mirza Abul Hasan Isphani, and Sardar Abdul Rab Nishtar.

Above: Members of the British Cabinet Mission, Lord Pethick-Lawrence (L), Sir Stafford Cripps (R), A.V. Alexander (2R) with Indian National Congress leader Maulana Abul Kalam Azad.

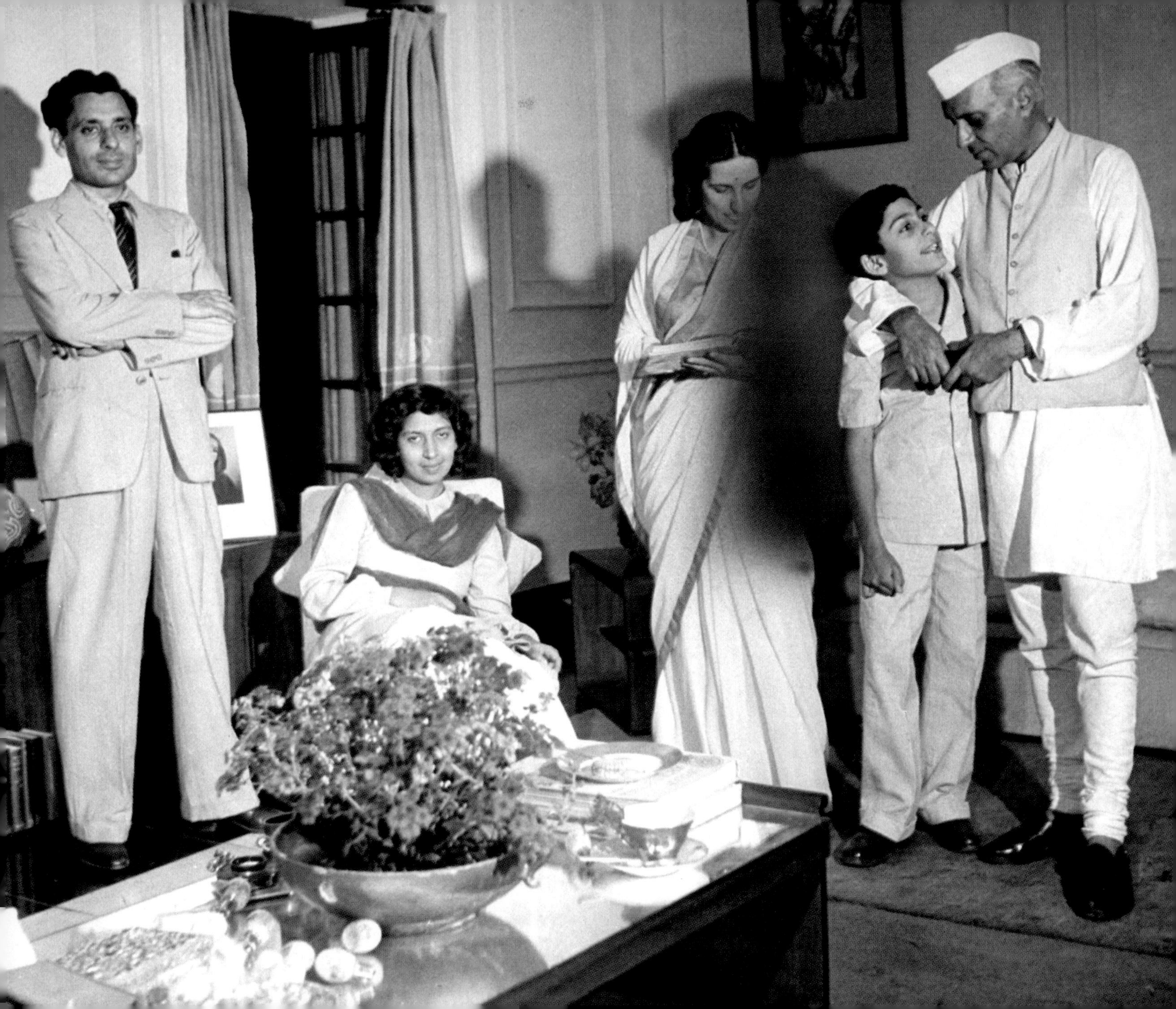

The first prime minister of independent India, Pandit Jawaharlal Nehru symbolized the overthrowing of European domination of Asia. Commanding respect from both the Eastern and Western worlds, Pandit Nehru's parting words to Margaret Bourke-White in 1948 were, '... the difference between the Indian and the Western mind [is that] the Indian would not ask what he should do, but what he should be.'

'The fact that independence had meant the birth of divided nations instead of a unified India, with bloodshed between them instead of peace and progress, had been a bitter blow for Nehru and the strain showed in his face. There was always a spiritual quality about Pandit Nehru's finely modeled face, and it seemed to me that suffering had increased that expression. Now that his aquiline features had grown thinner his eyes seemed all the more profound and glowing in their deepened setting....

'Pandit Nehru had just the words I needed to explain the efficacy of a Gandhi fast.

'"Voluntary suffering has great effect on the Indian mind." Nehru emphasized the word "voluntary". "Gandhi is a kind of sentinel who stands apart. He has felt great distress at the barriers growing up in India. He felt he must take this final step to direct people's minds, to divert them from wrong paths. The fast does two things. It introduces a sense of urgency to the problem and forces people to think out of the ruts – to think afresh. It produces a favourable psychological atmosphere. Then it is up to take advantage of this atmosphere....

'Speaking to people who had gathered at the prayer ground concerned about Gandhi's health during his last fast he said, "I saw the freedom of India as a vision. I had charted the future of Asia on my heart. We felt that India would be a great free country in this disturbed world. It was the aspiration of our youth. It was our pride. In the final analysis, countries do not attain freedom only on maps. The sentiment of freedom surges from the heart ... Thirty years ago Gandhiji arrived on the scene," Nehru was saying, "An odd-looking man. No art of dressing and no polish in his ways of speech. He did not indulge in high politics. He only said, 'Follow truth. If our goal is good, the path to it should also be righteous. If we want to be free, we must free each other first. Only a free people can lay the foundations of a free land.' These were the lessons of Gandhiji. He had warned us, if we swerve from the path of righteous behavior, we shall be ruined."'

Excerpted from *Halfway to Freedom* by Margaret Bourke-White

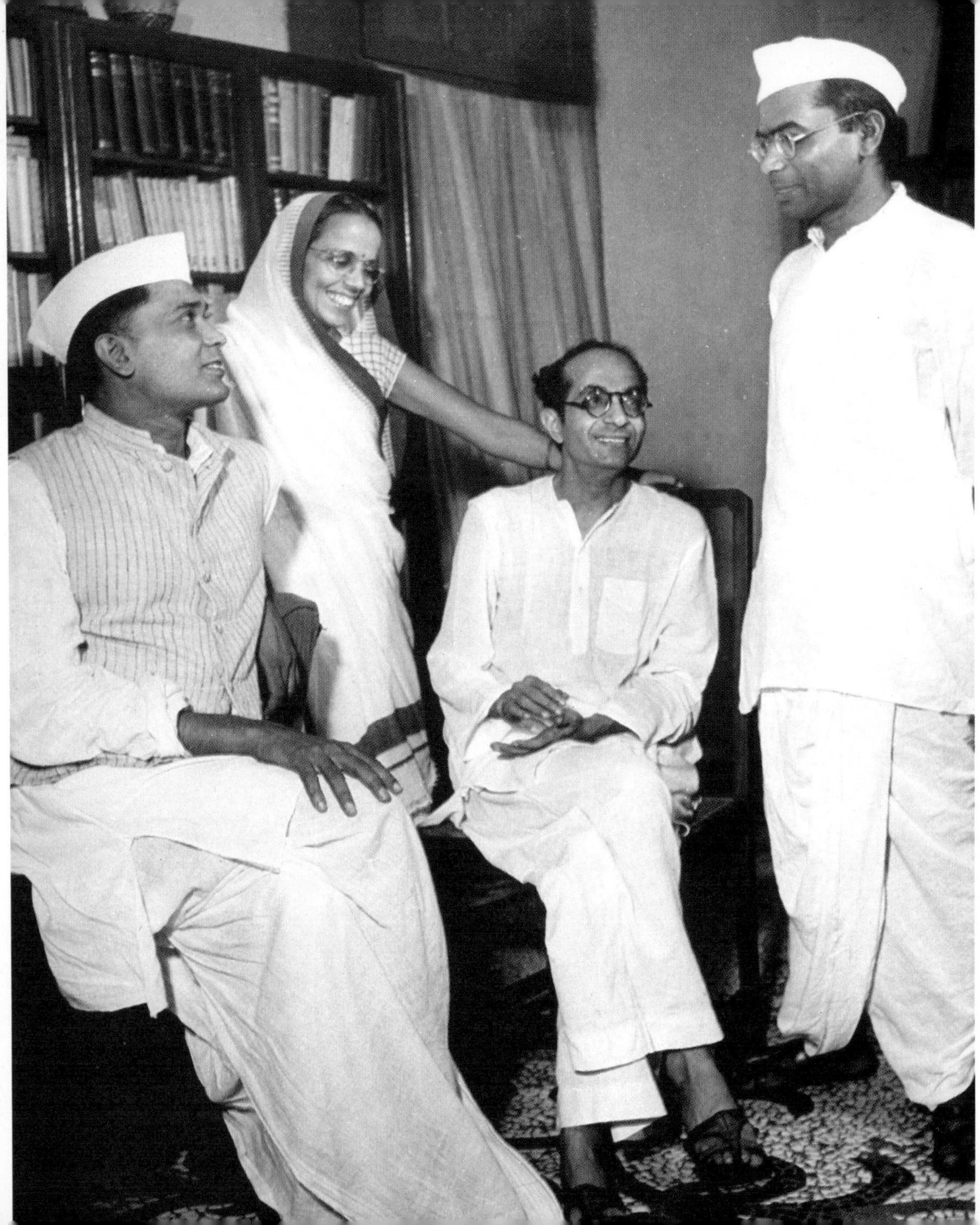

Left: Jayaprakash Narayan with wife Prabhawati; Yusuf Meherally, fellow socialist leader and former Mayor of Bombay and Dr Rammanohar Lohia, co-founder of Socialist Party.

Right: Sardar Vallabhbhai Patel with his 'inseparable' daughter Maniben.

'Part of the Congress for many years, the Socialist Party did break away from the ideology of Gandhi, Nehru and Patel with a large number of left-wing members. One of the founders of the Socialist Party, Jayaprakash Narayan, while explaining to me one of the reasons said, "Patel believes in patching up the old garment of our economy … We believe in making a completely new garment. As for Nehru, great a man as he is, he hesitates. He is waiting for the Congress to make up its mind. Government economic policy is hardly shaped by Nehru; Patel does the real shaping."'

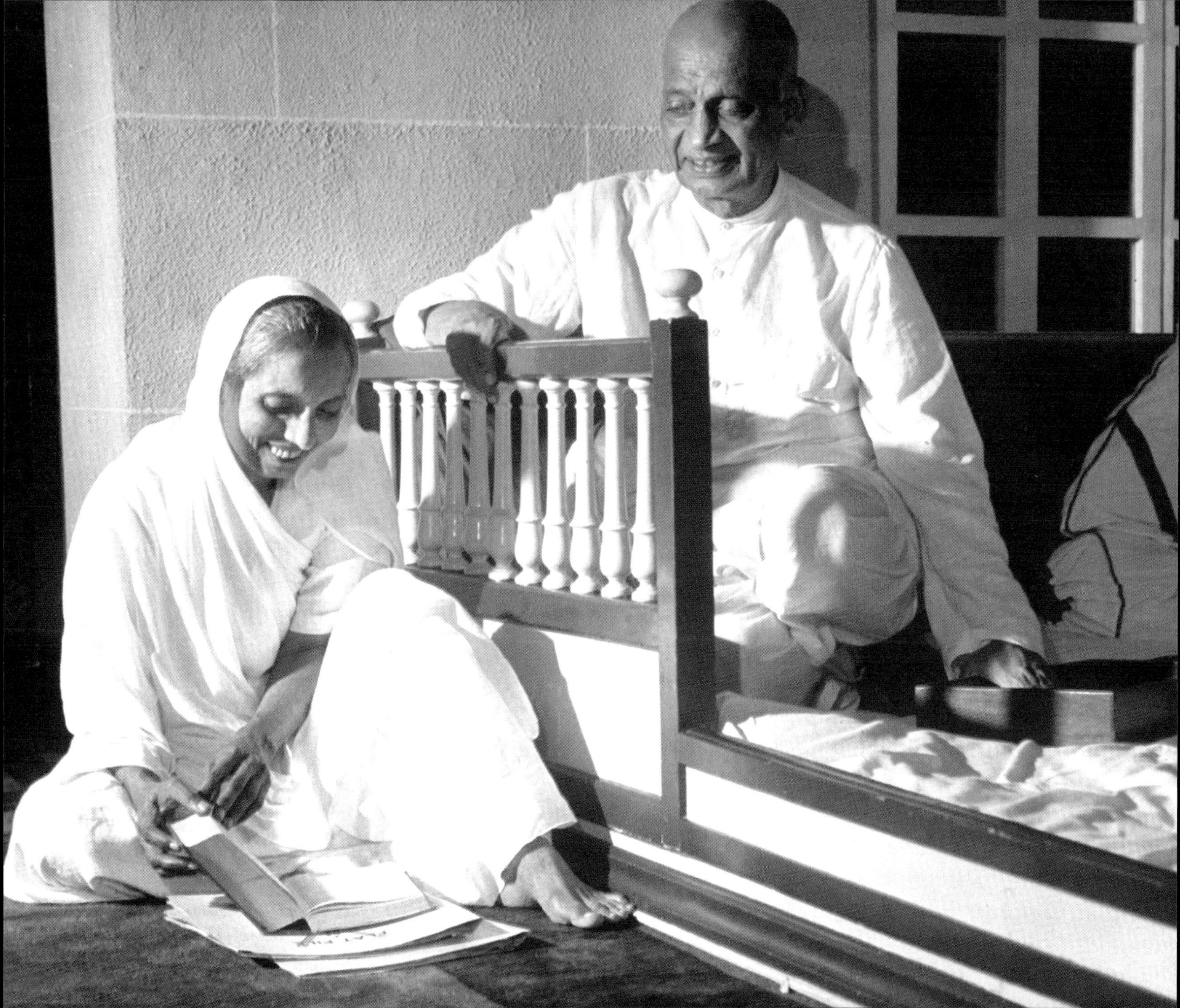

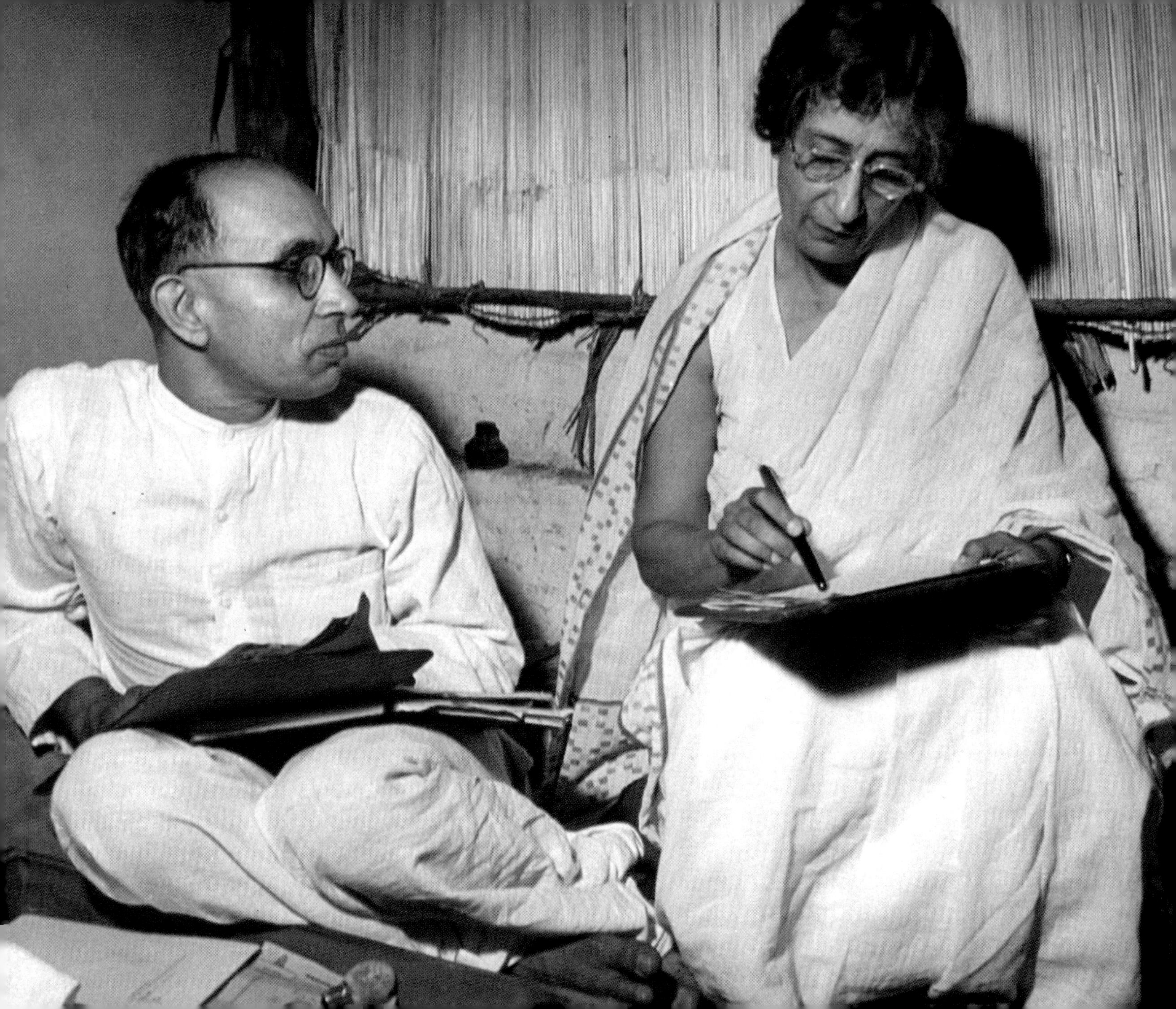

Left: Mahatma Gandhi's secretary Pyarelal working on an editorial in consultation with Rajkumari Amrit Kaur.

Right: Sarojini Naidu with the Maharani of Nabha and her daughter Kabula Devi.

'Sarojini Naidu was one of the great figures in India's fight for independence. She broke the trail into public life for women, was Governor of the United Provinces at the time of her death in March 1949. Witty and gracious, and widely known as a poet, she will always be remembered for her vital contribution to the emancipation of Indian women.'

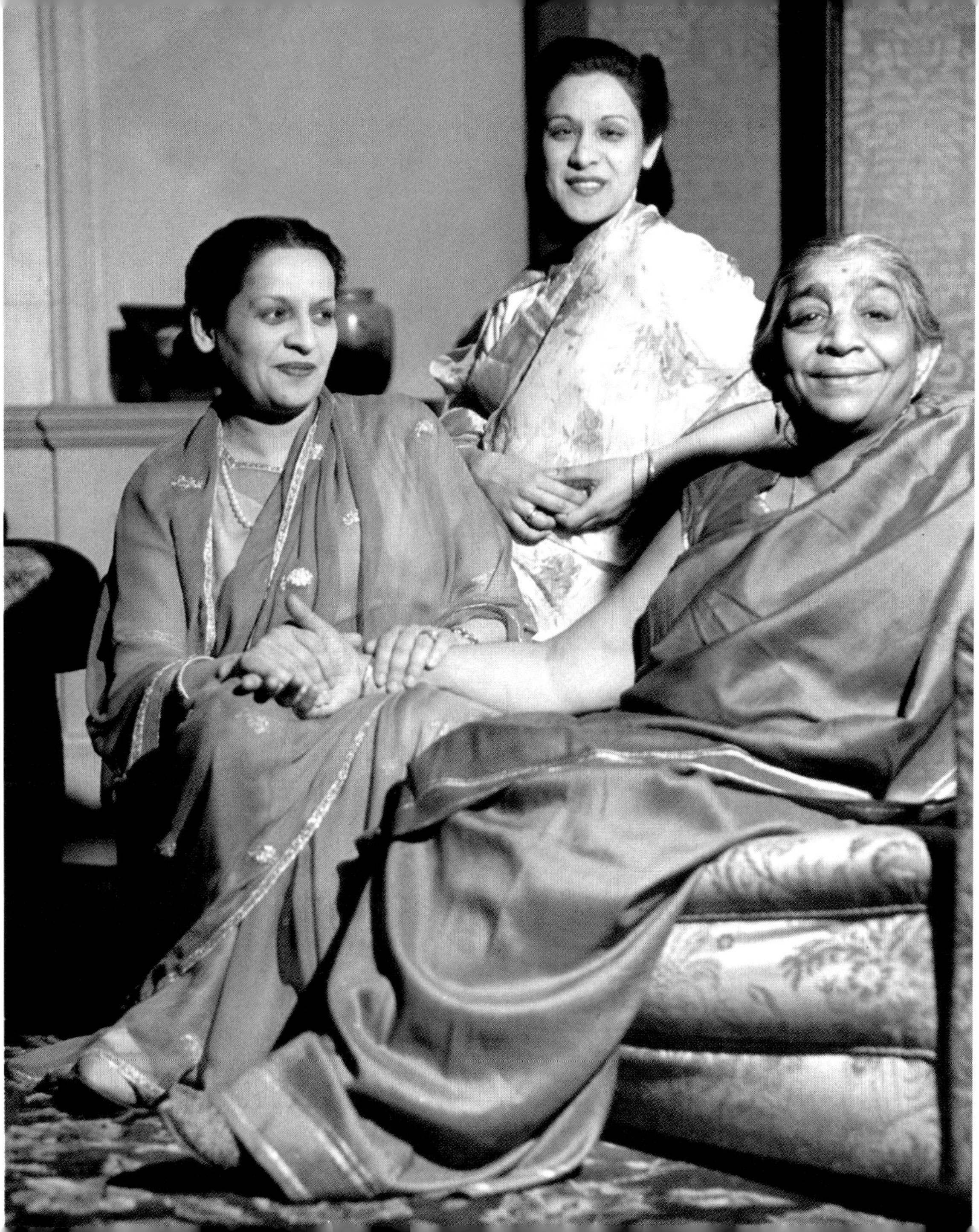

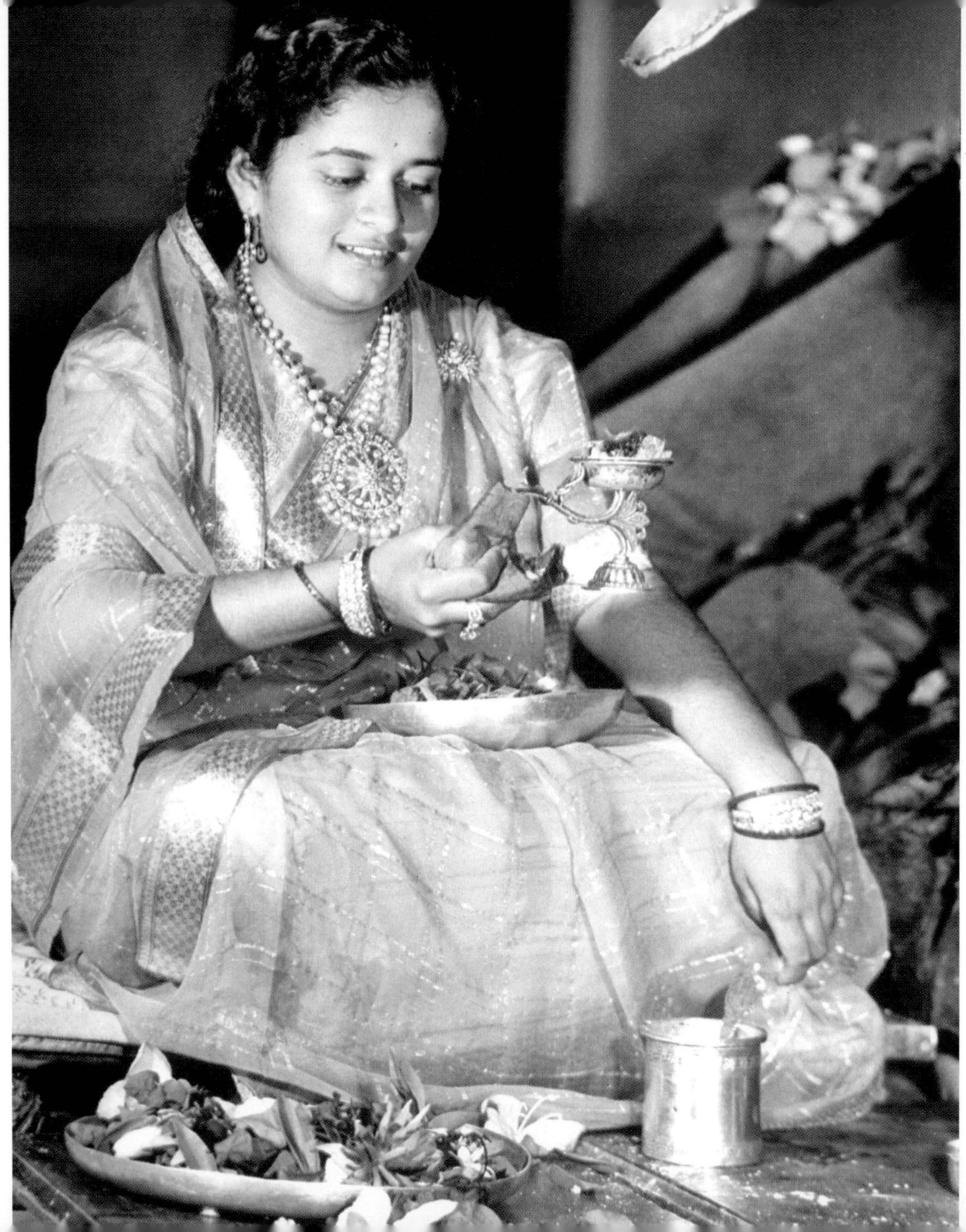

Left: Woman from a royal family.

Right: Maharaja of Mysore, Jaya Chamarajendra Wadiyar in royal finery.

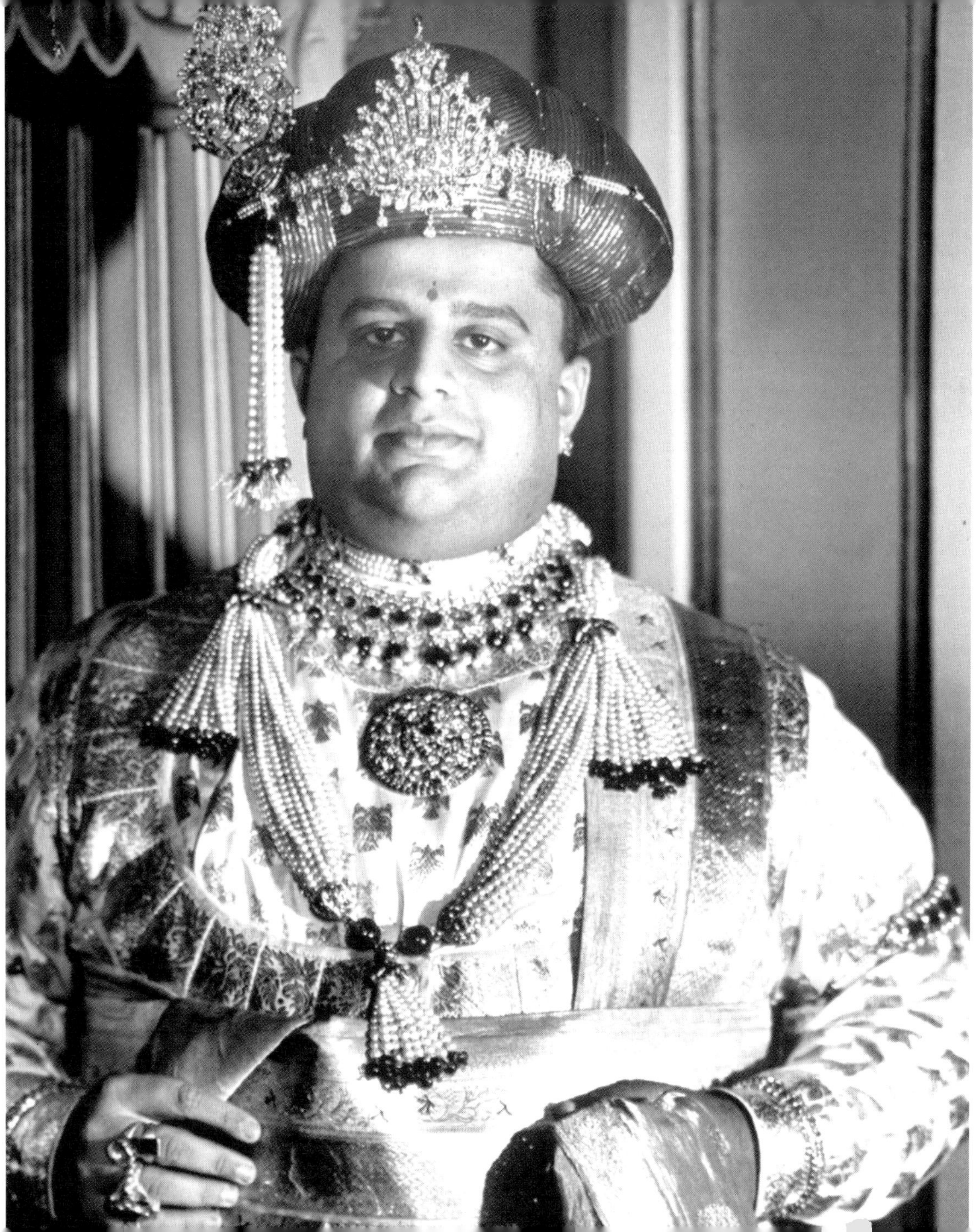

'At the time of the departure of the British, there was a surprisingly large number of princes – over five hundred maharajas, rajas, and nawabs, with their domains ranging from enormous Hyderabad to the size of a large farm.'

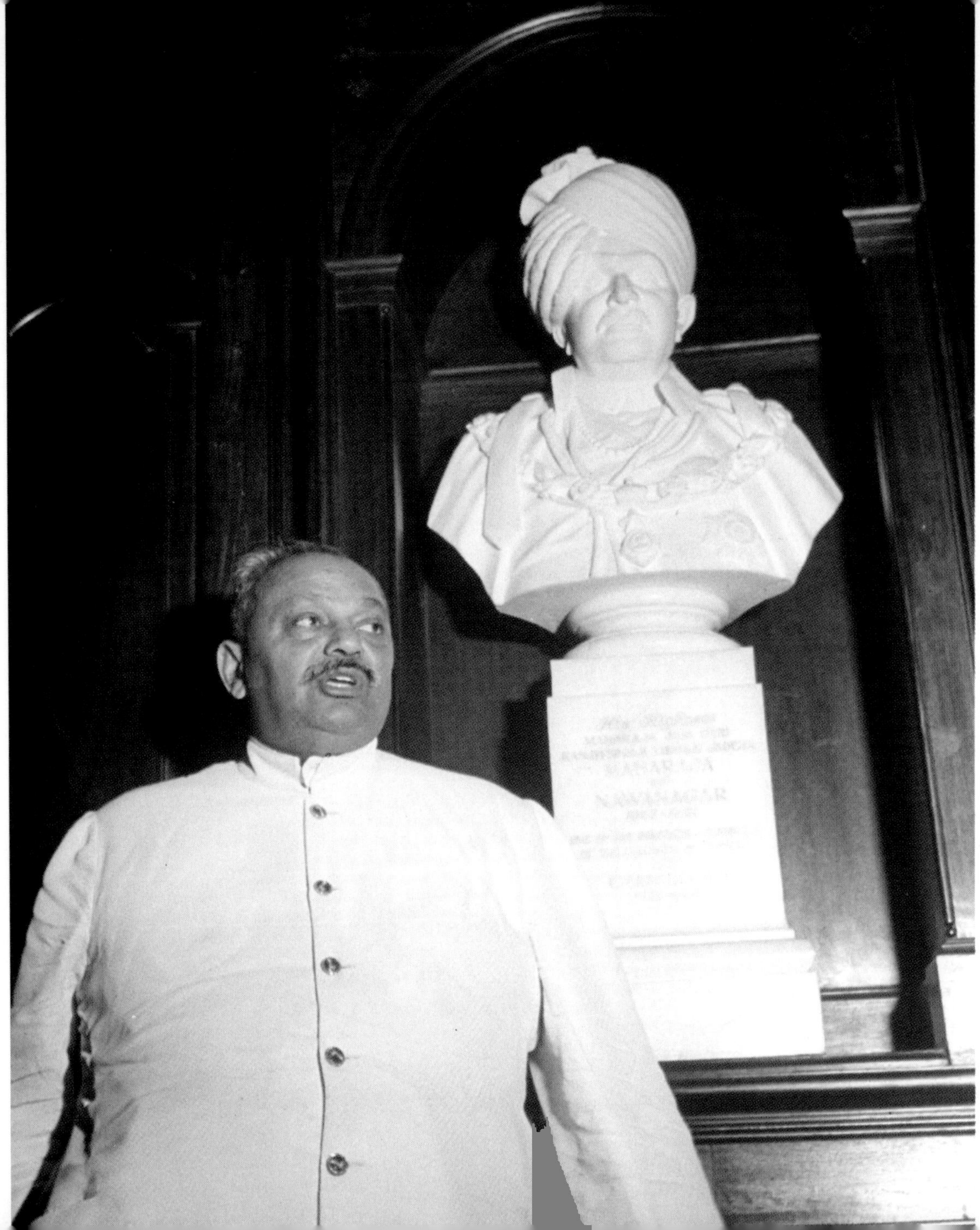

Left: His Highness Jam Sahab of Nawanagar in the Chamber of Princes standing next to the bust of Maharaja Ganga Singhji of Bikaner. Former Chancellor of the Chamber of Princes, Maharaja Jam Saheb had the reputation of being the best political brain among the maharajas.

Right: His Highness the Maharaja of Bikaner, Maharaja Sadul Singh in the Chamber of Princes. A great tiger hunter, the walls of his palace were covered with the skins of fifteen hundred tigers.

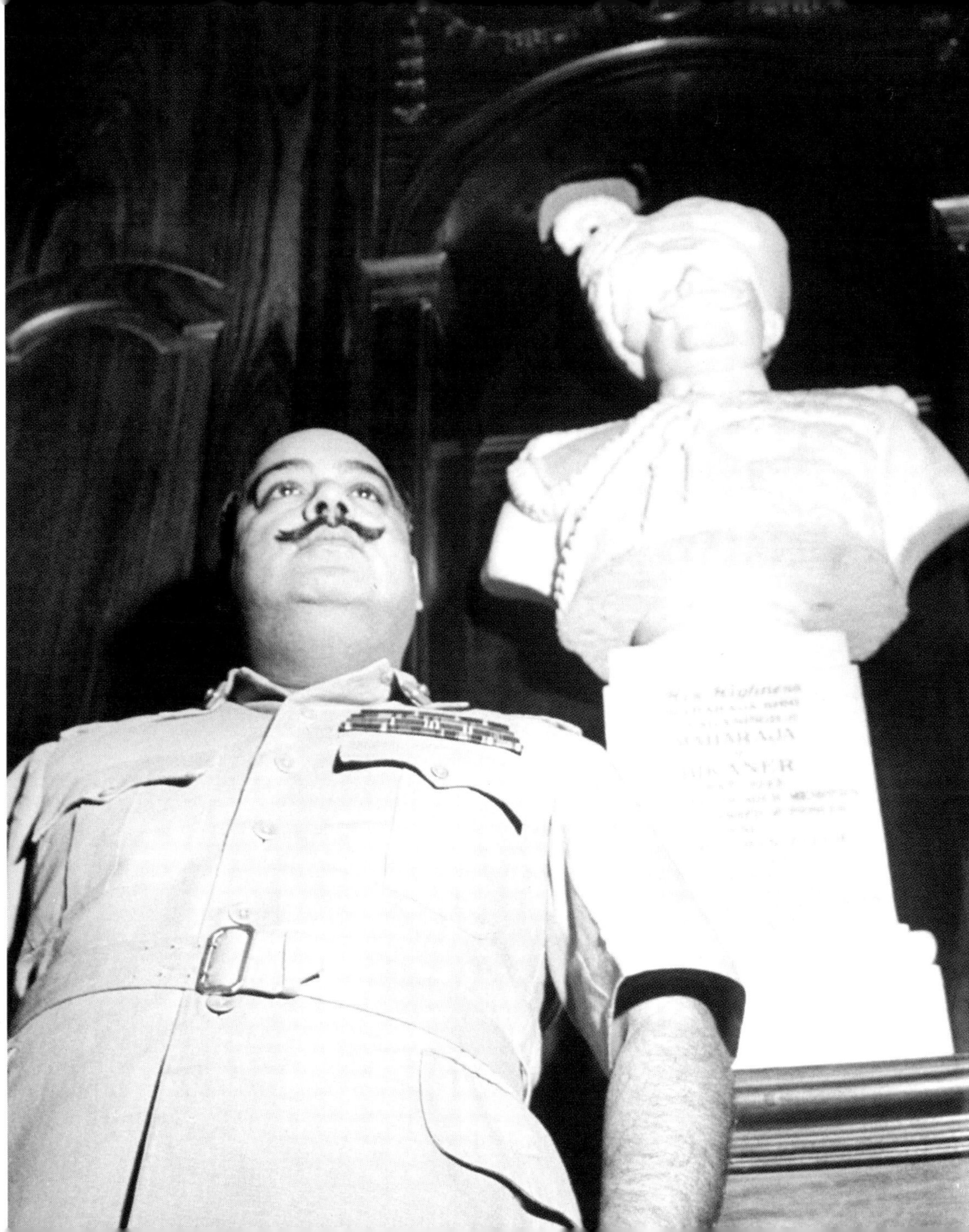

'The Viceroy is gone, and with him the British Political Agent. Left behind is a welter of maharajas and rajas, nizams and nawabs, mirs, walis, kahn sahebs, dewan, and state elephants. Without the support of the British Raj, the question is how long such feudalism will stand in the new Indian Union.'

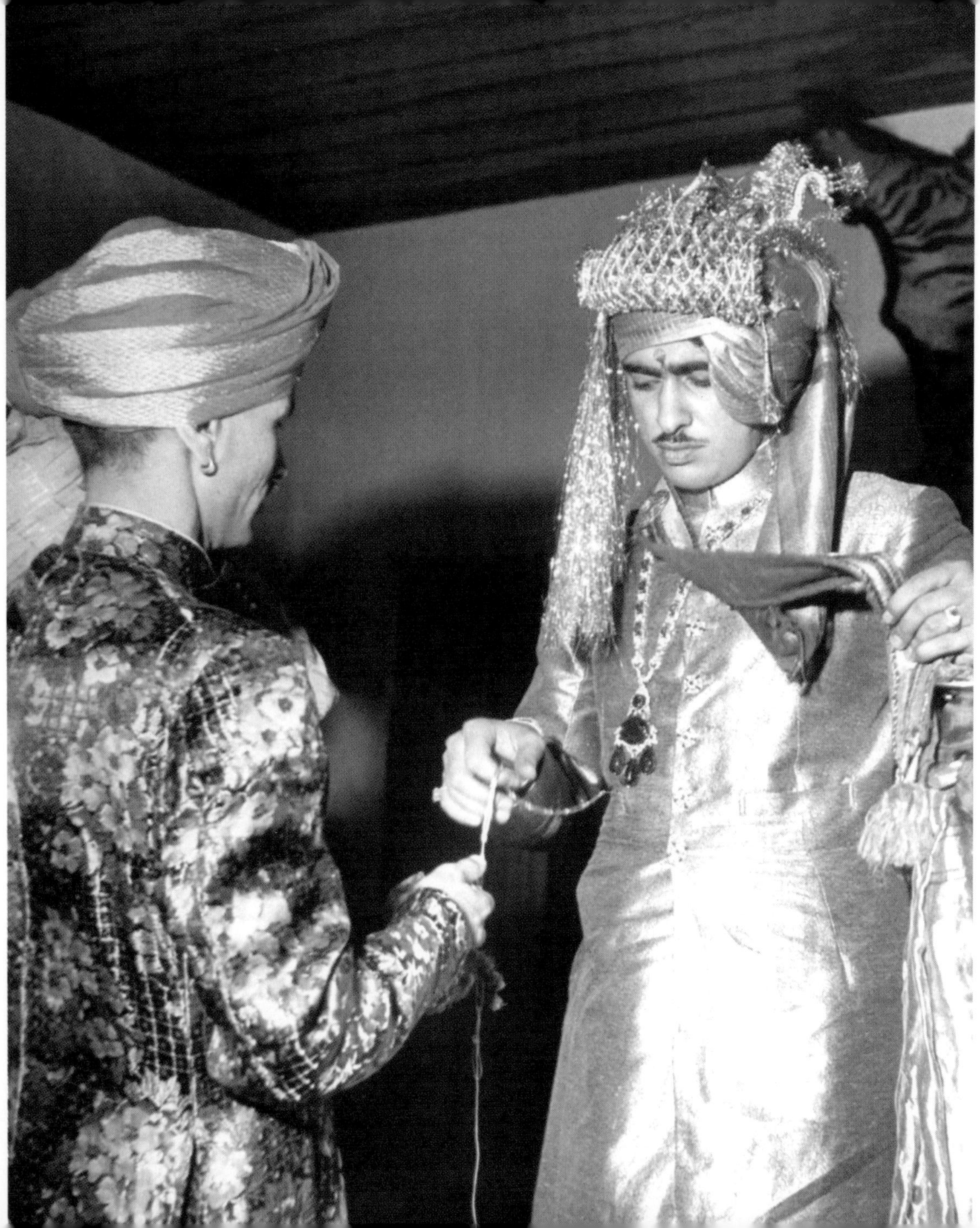

Left: A Rajput Prince of Mandi being presented a gift at the time of his wedding.

Right: Taking a break from the festivities and rituals of the elaborate wedding, the prince smokes a cigarette

'After the British boundary commission had drawn its line slicing off Pakistan from India, the princely states made up the enormous proportion of nearly

45 per cent of the territory within the Indian Union. Thus, the new India, with its government headed by Prime Minister Nehru and Home Minister Patel, and professing to be a democracy, found itself on Independence day with nearly half its land and more than one third of its population still under the rule of these "bejeweled, breathing fossils of feudalism," as one journalist called them.'

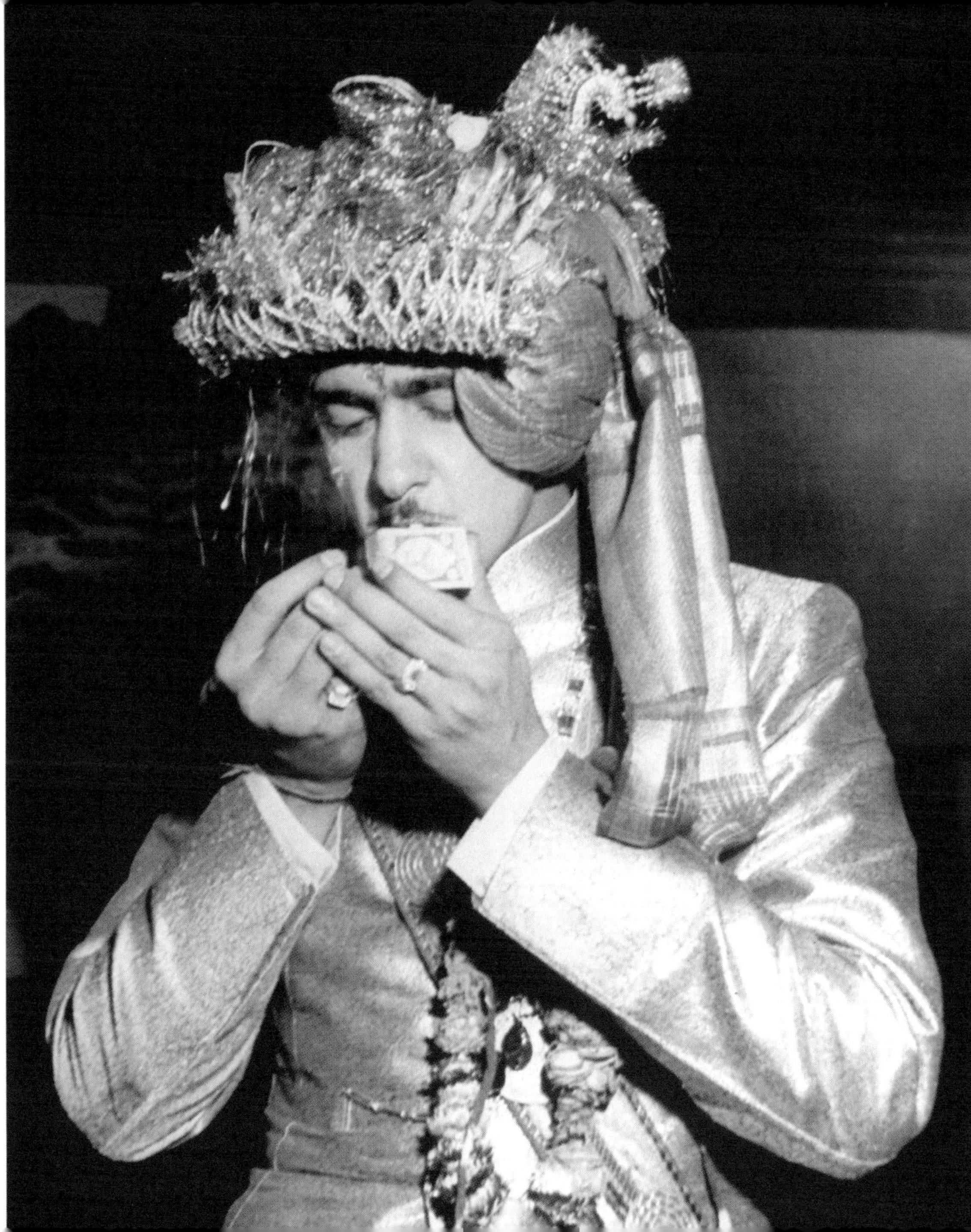

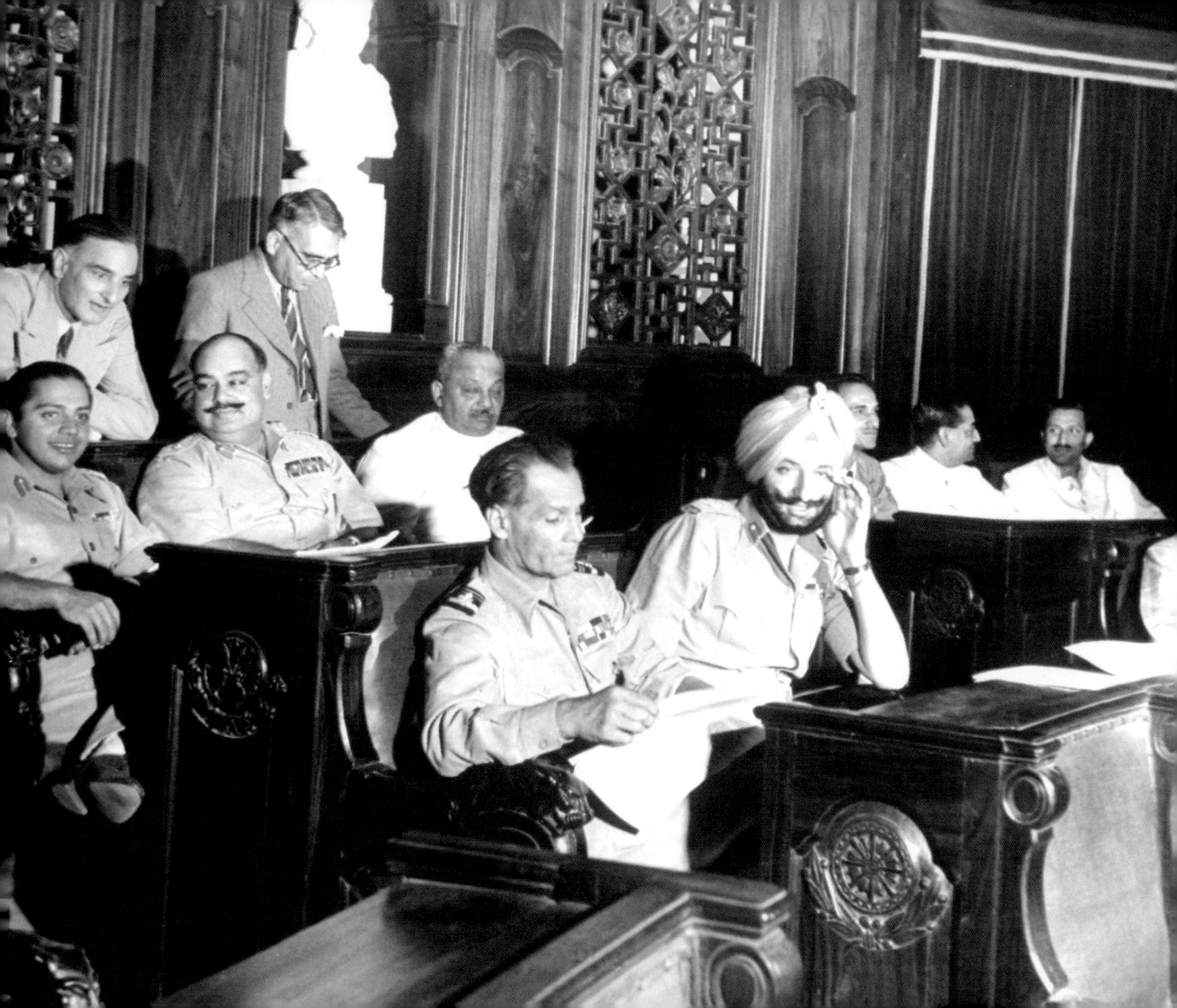

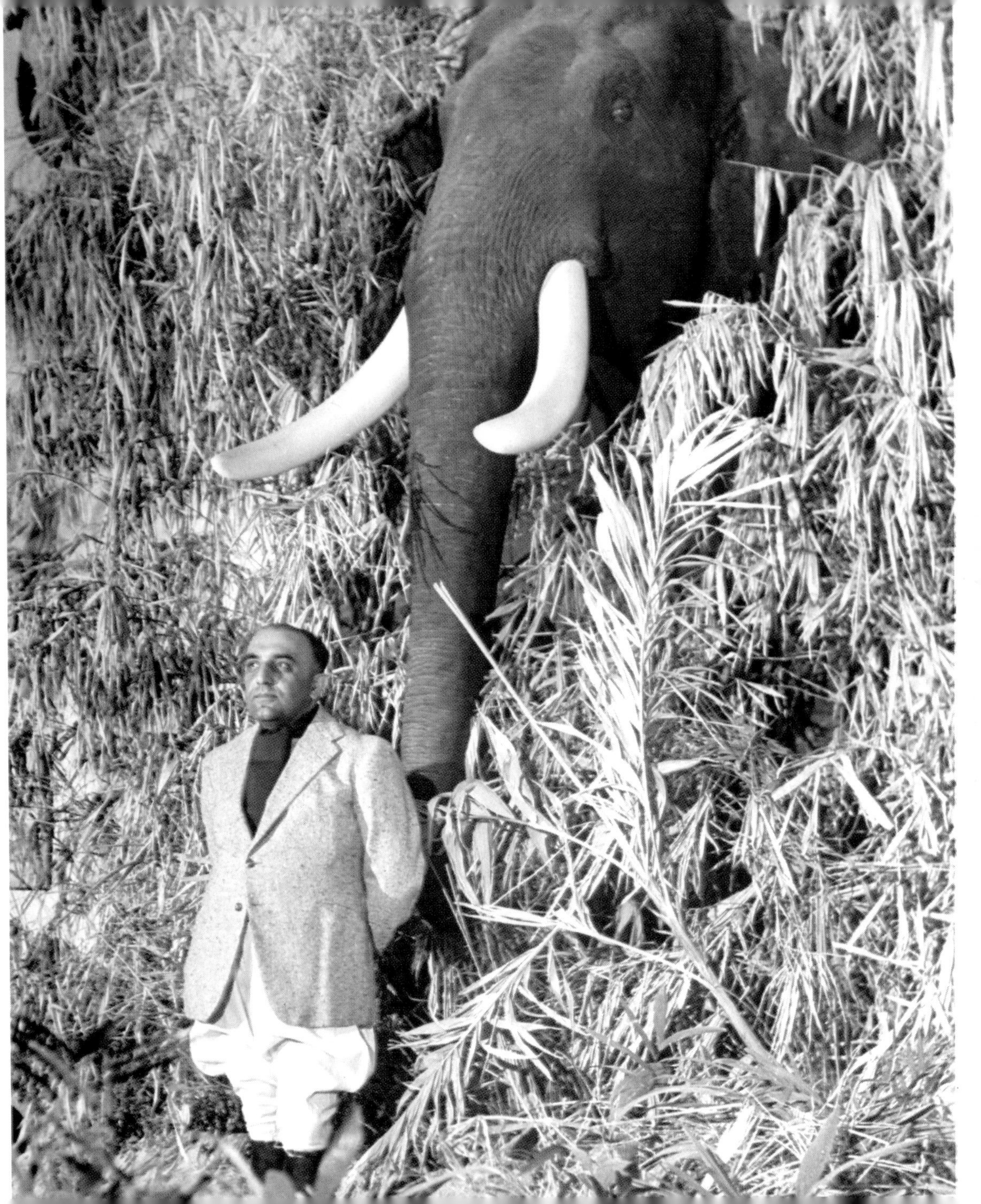

Left: Second row front (from L to R): Maharaja of Gwalior, Maharaja of Bikaner, Jam Sahab of Nawanagar, with the Nawab of Bhopal and Maharaja Yadavindra Singh of Patiala (first row) in the Chamber of Princes.

Right: Prince Azam Jah, heir to the throne of Hyderabad, posing next to taxidermic specimen of the elephant he shot in the game room of his palace.

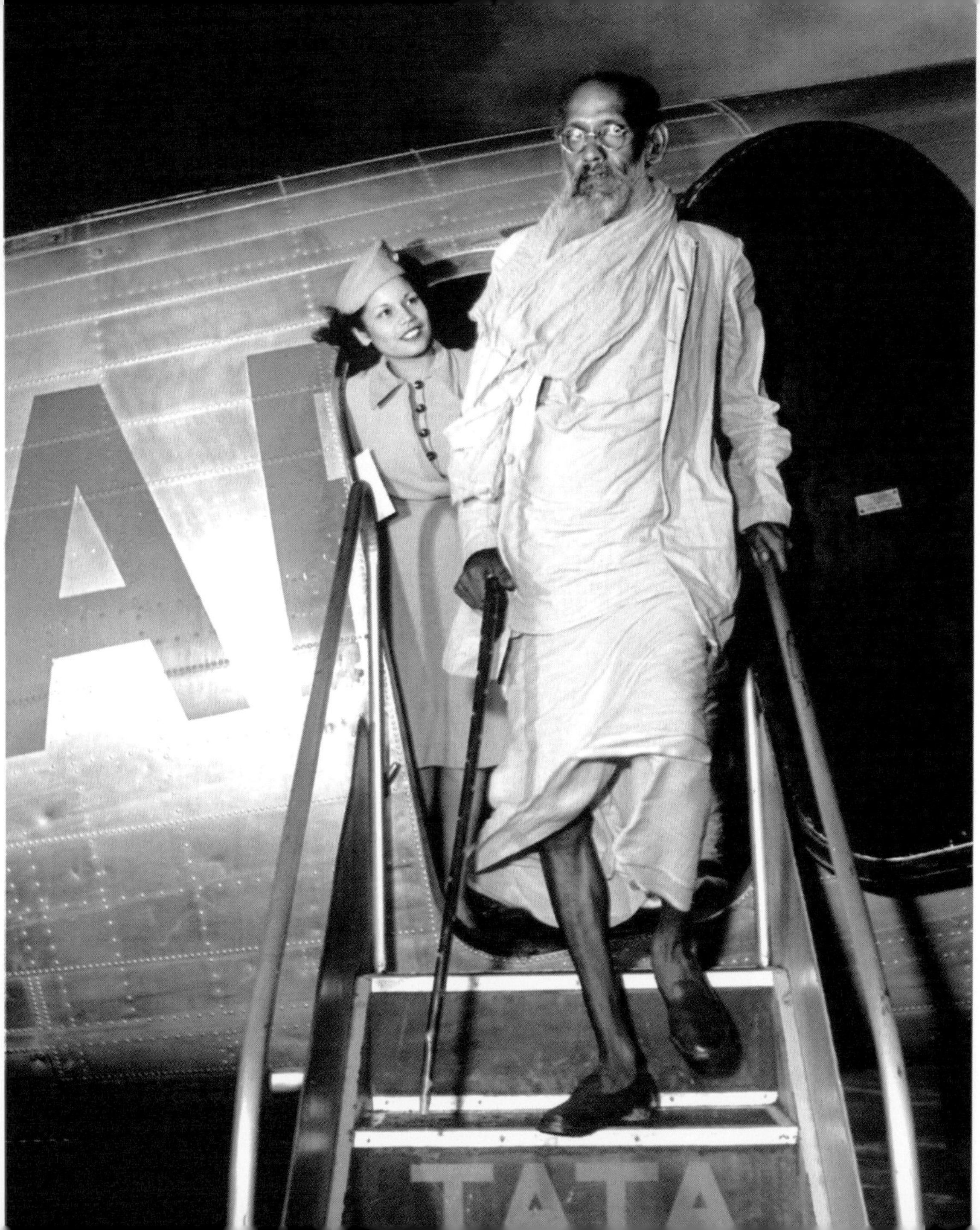

Left: Flight Attendant Avenell Divers bidding adieu to a sanyasi after a flight on Tata Airlines.

Right: Monica Gilbert showing the flight report to a Sikh passenger during a Delhi to Bombay flight.

'This sanyasi, an ascetic of great holiness, flew into Bombay from his remote retreat. Sanyasis have renounced the world to confine themselves to prayer and spiritual contemplation. Obviously this is something that can be done in an airplane. The pretty Tata hostess reported that the holy man conquered air-sickness with no difficulty.'

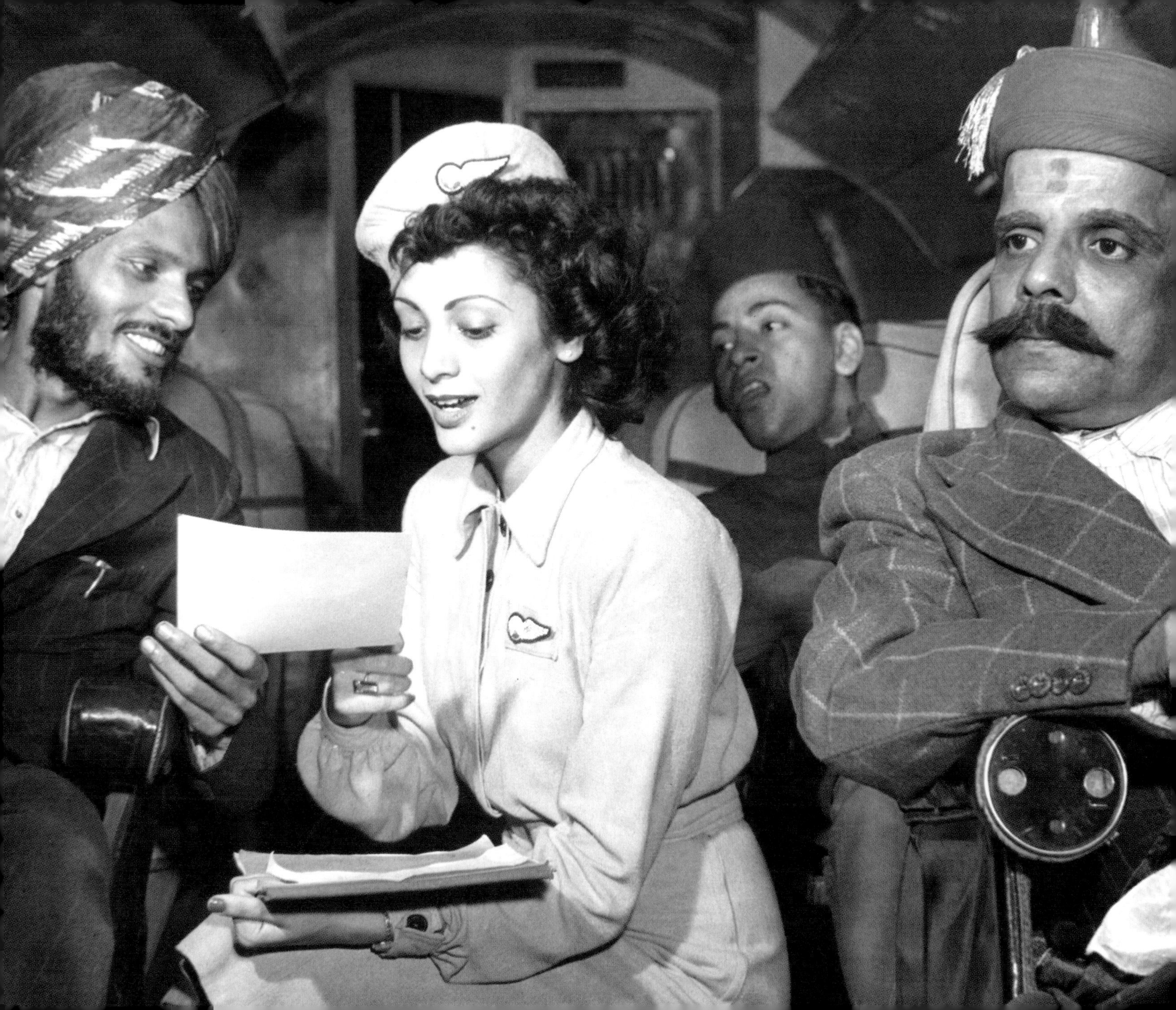

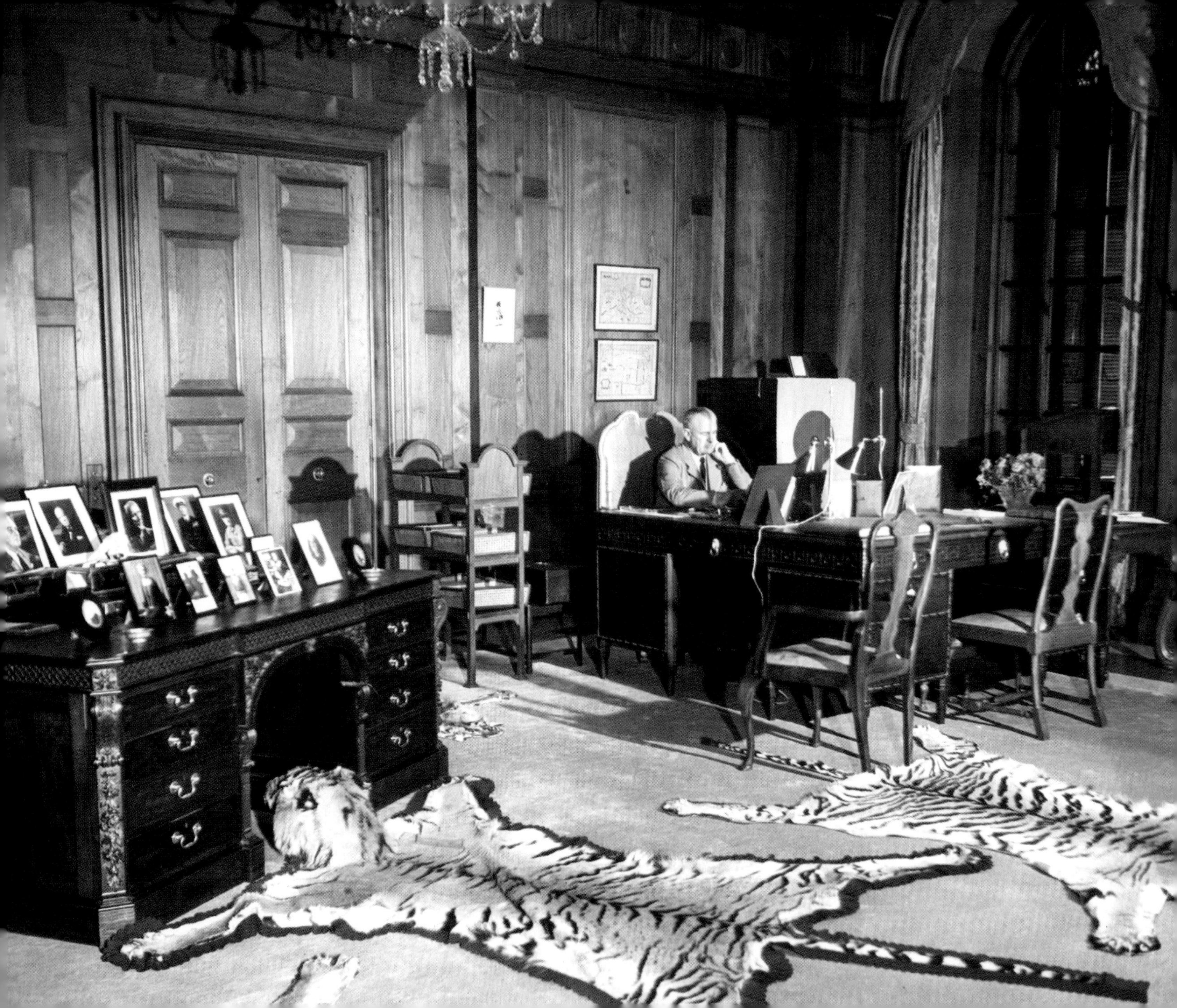

Left: Lord Archibald Wavell, Viceroy of India working at his desk at the Viceroy House, now Rashtrapati Bhawan.

Right: The Throne Room of the Lord Viceroy Archibald Wavell. At the centre of the main part of the palace, underneath the main dome, is the Durbar Hall, which was known as the Throne Room during the British rule when it had thrones for the Viceroy and his wife.

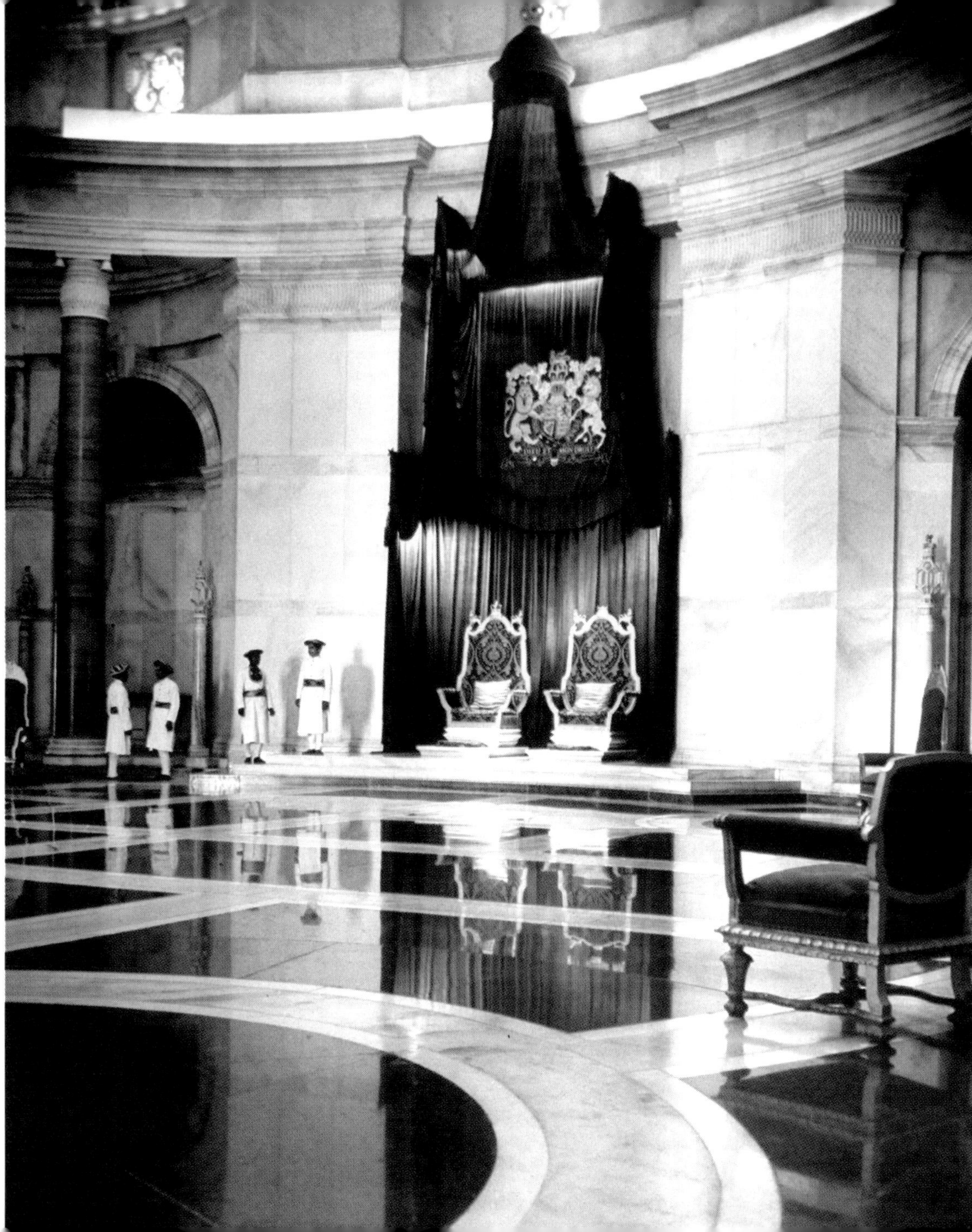

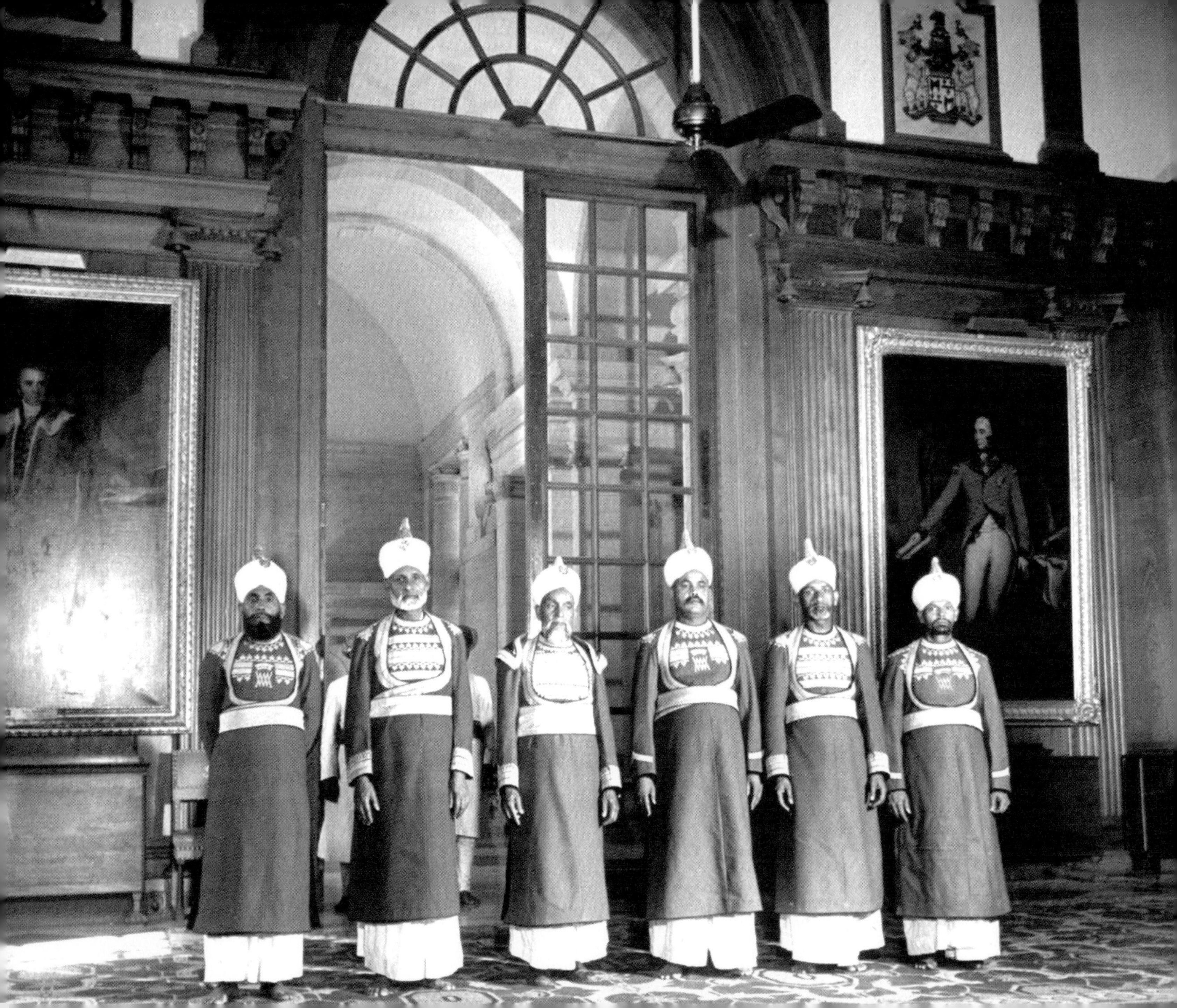

Left: Attendants waiting at the Viceroy House.

Right: Attendants cleaning chandelier in the Throne Room, Viceroy House.

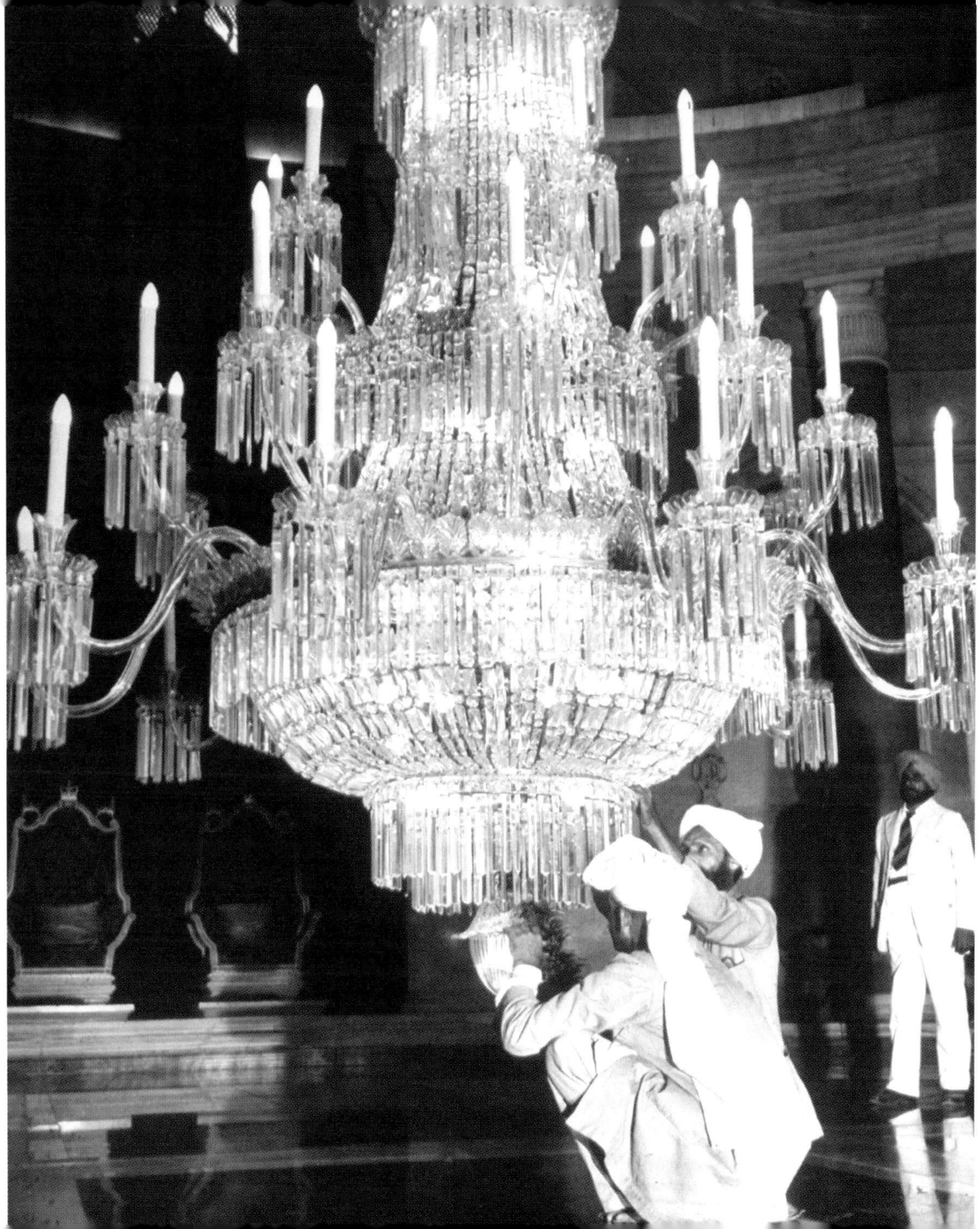

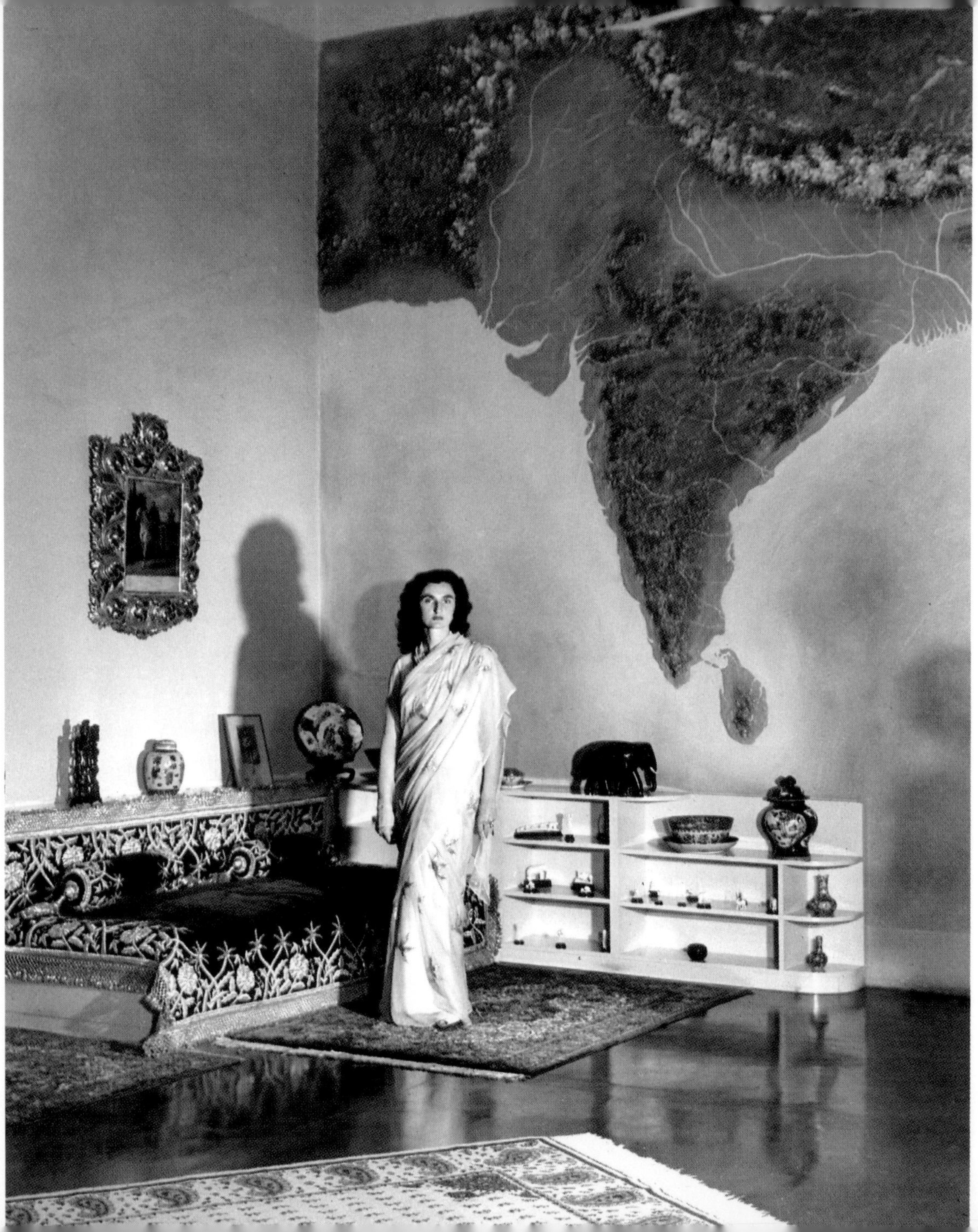

Princess of Berar, Durru Shevar, was the daughter of the Sultan Abdul Mejid Efendi of the Ottoman Empire, and married to Prince Azam Jah, the eldest son and heir to the last Nizam of Hyderabad state.

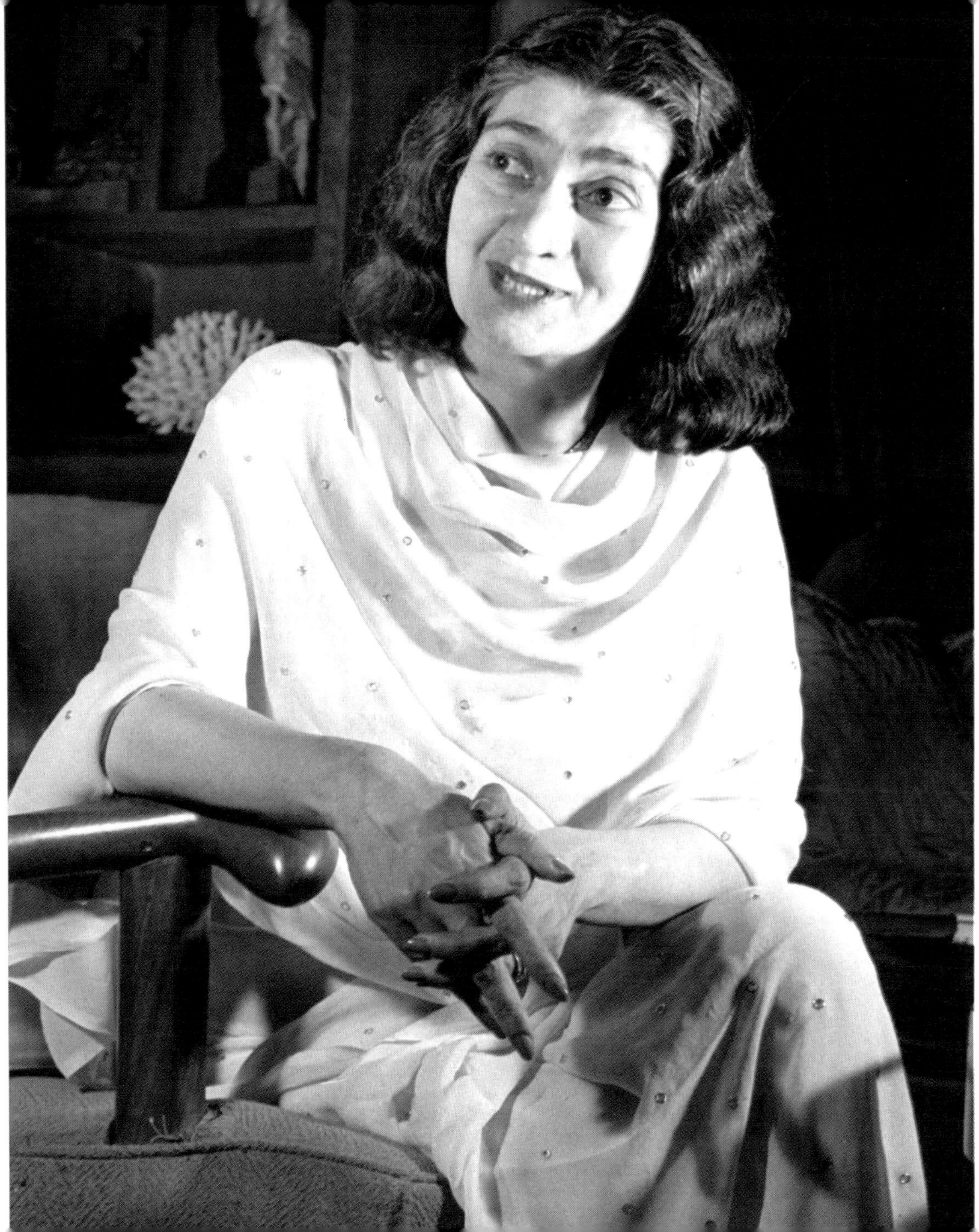

Mrs AJ Wadia, from one of the prominent families in Bombay, was member of the Indian delegation to the International Assembly of Women in New York.

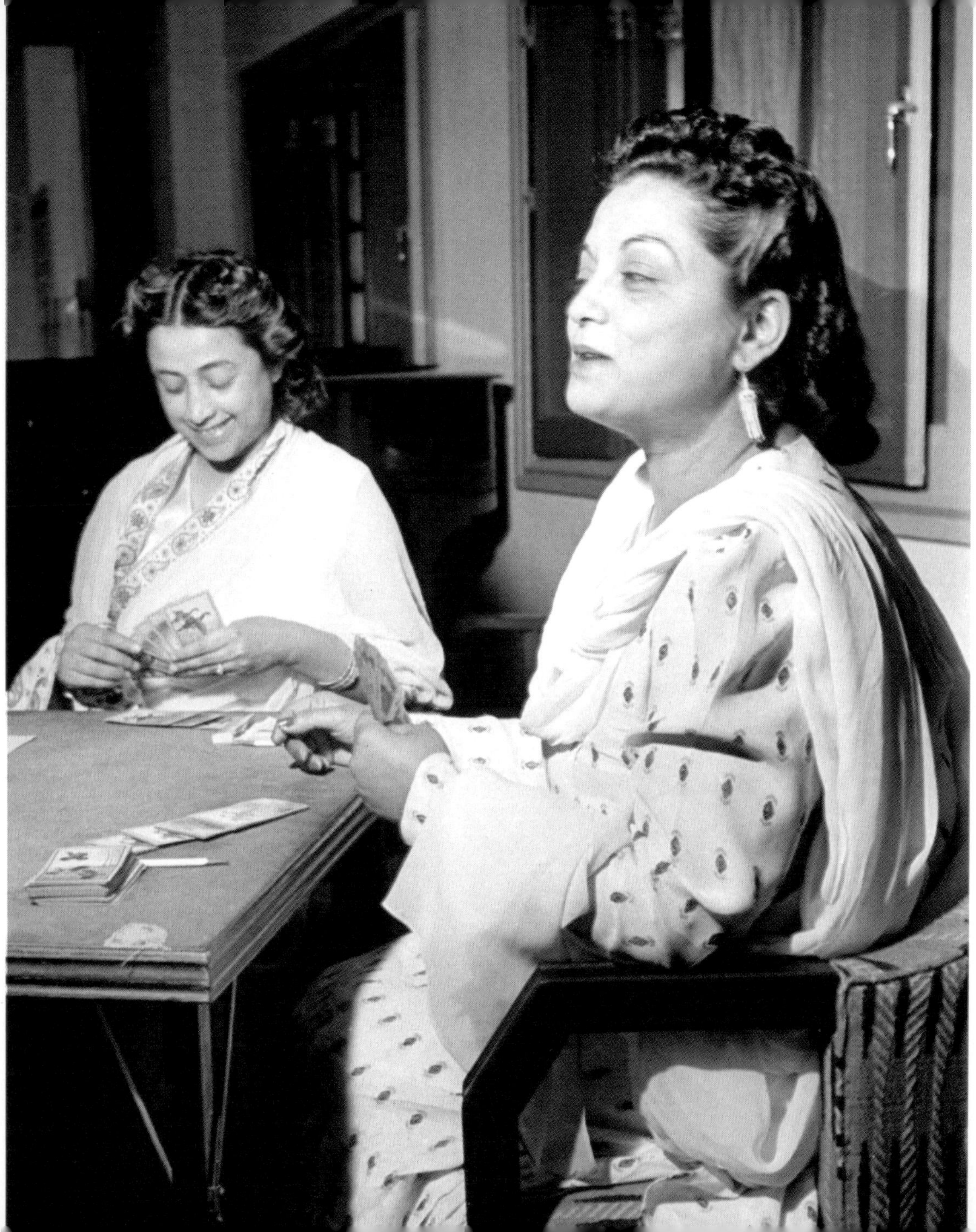

Begum Raana Liaquat Ali Khan (R) playing bridge with a lady friend. Wife of the first prime minister of Pakistan, Begum Raana also held important positions in the establishment. This included being the head of the All Pakistan Women's Organization and governor of Sindh in the 1970s under Zulfikar Ali Bhutto. This picture was taken at Liaquat Ali Khan's house in Delhi in May 1946. While the women played cards, Liaquat Ali Khan was meeting the Muslim Working Committee in the dining room.

With the Pakistan movement for independence gaining momentum, women's participation in the freedom struggle became necessary, both for increasing the Muslim vote bank and for displaying numerical strength at the Muslim League's political rallies. Some of the prominent figures in this movement were Begum Raana Liaquat Ali and Begum Fida Hussain. Coeduction and liberal attitude towards society and culture, especially amongst the Muslim elite, paved the way for women to come forward and take active interest in politics and also education of women. (Right) An unidentified woman Margaret met during her visit to Karachi in September 1947.

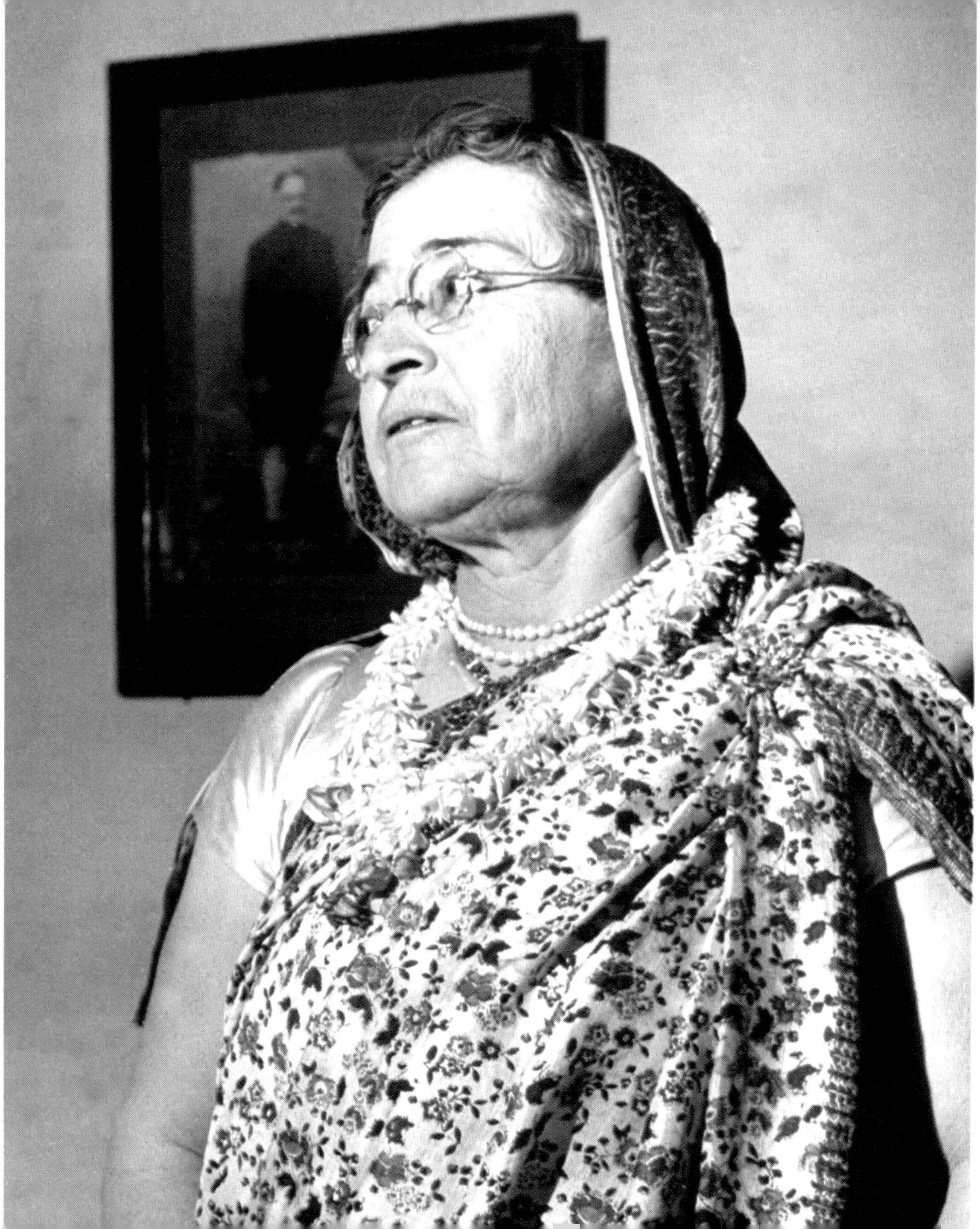

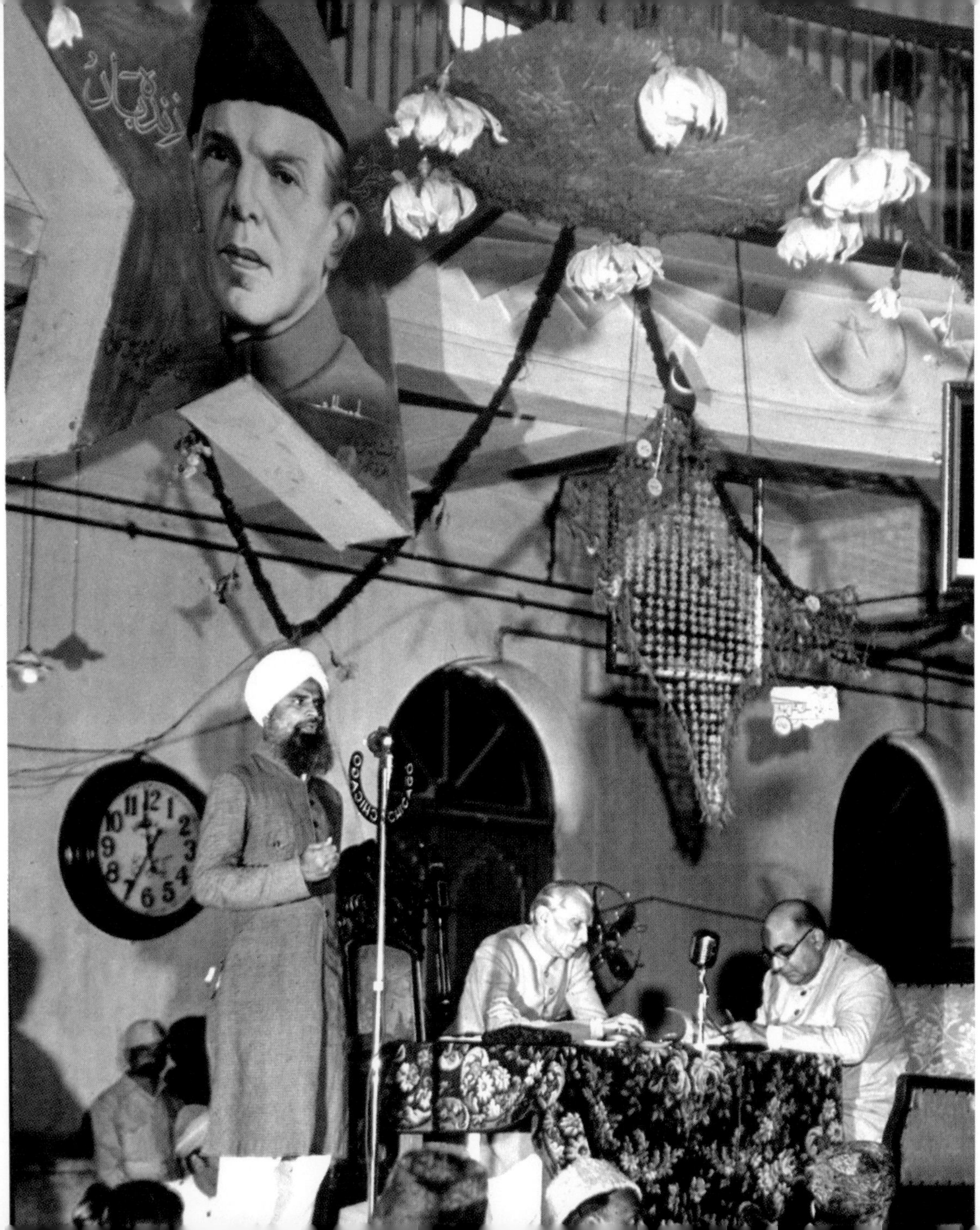

Left: Mohammed Ali Jinnah and Liaquat Ali Khan in the background at the table. Taken in Bombay in 1946, this picture is of a press conference renouncing Indian Cabinet Plan and declaring the intention to create Pakistan.

Right: Armed Pathan tribesmen waiting between Peshawar and Rawalpindi for their leader Batcha Gul of the Mohman tribe to arrive with trucks and extra ammunition, to lead them into battle in Kashmir. during their struggle for independence in 1947.

'Even after one month of Independence the Kashmir problem was unsolved. Their leader, Shiekh Abdullah wanted a people's government with equal rights and equal opportunities for all – irrespective of caste or creed. Though Pakistan was the first choice, the response from the Muslim League, lukewarm. Independence Day came, bringing with it partition, and the momentous question of accession to India or to Pakistan. From jail, Sheikh Abdullah raised the slogan: "Resposible government first and accession afterwards." His next act was to send emissaries of the All-Jammu and Kashmiri Nations State People's Conference to Pakistan to discuss accession. Jinnah did not bother to see these representatives … He might have had Kashmir with its three million Muslims if he had been willing to recognize popular rule. But it is not surprising that Jinnah should have shuddered at the very idea of a people's "joint government of the Hindus, the Sikhs, and the Muslims".'

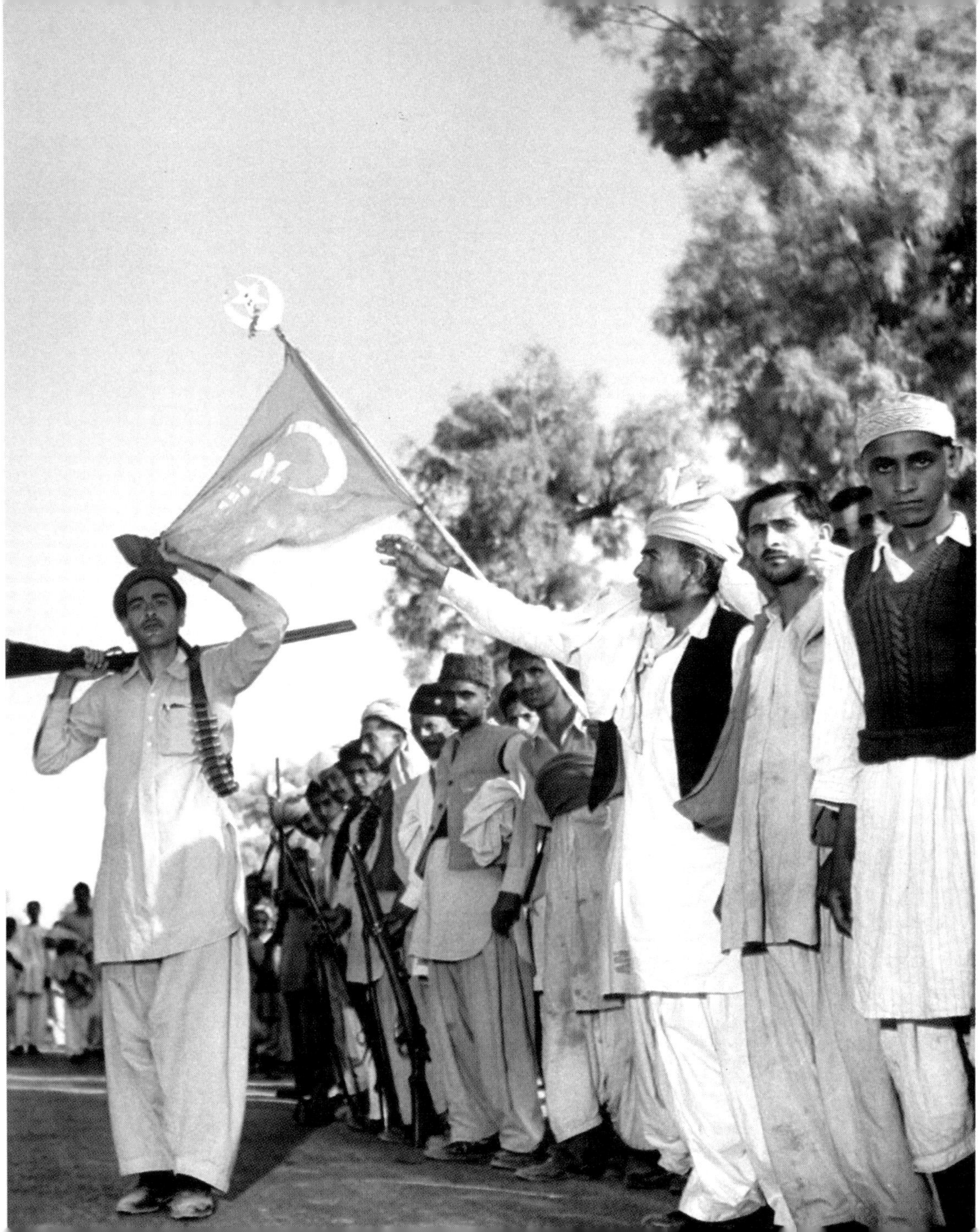

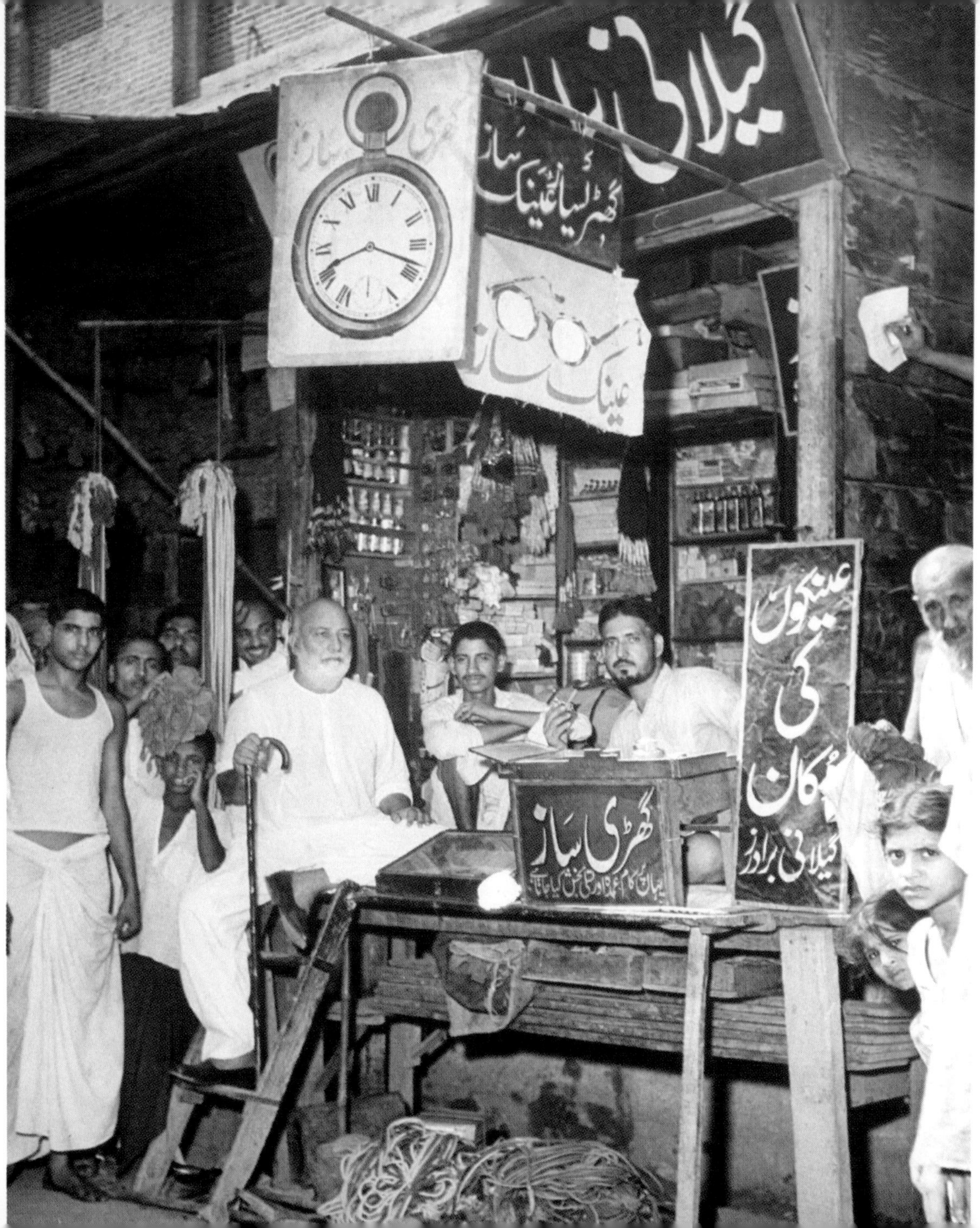

Left: Shopkeepers at their stores in Lahore.

Right: Rear view of Hindu men announcing prayer time 6.30 pm lined up along wall looking down into the Gandhi Colony.

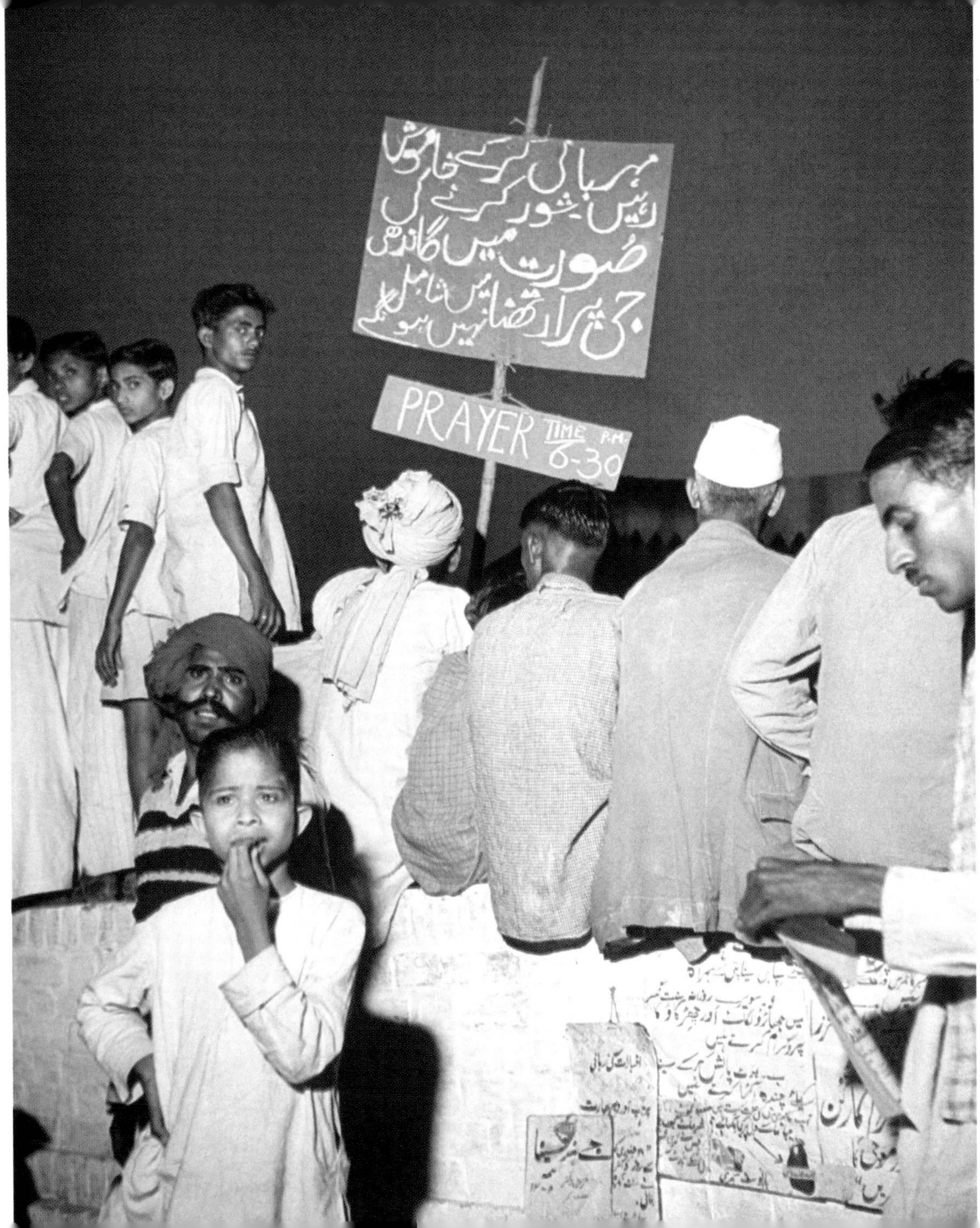

'… despite calamities great enough to rock a stronger nation to its foundations, Pakistan came through its first year better than expected, with a balanced budget, a favourable trade balance, and a bright program for industrial development.'

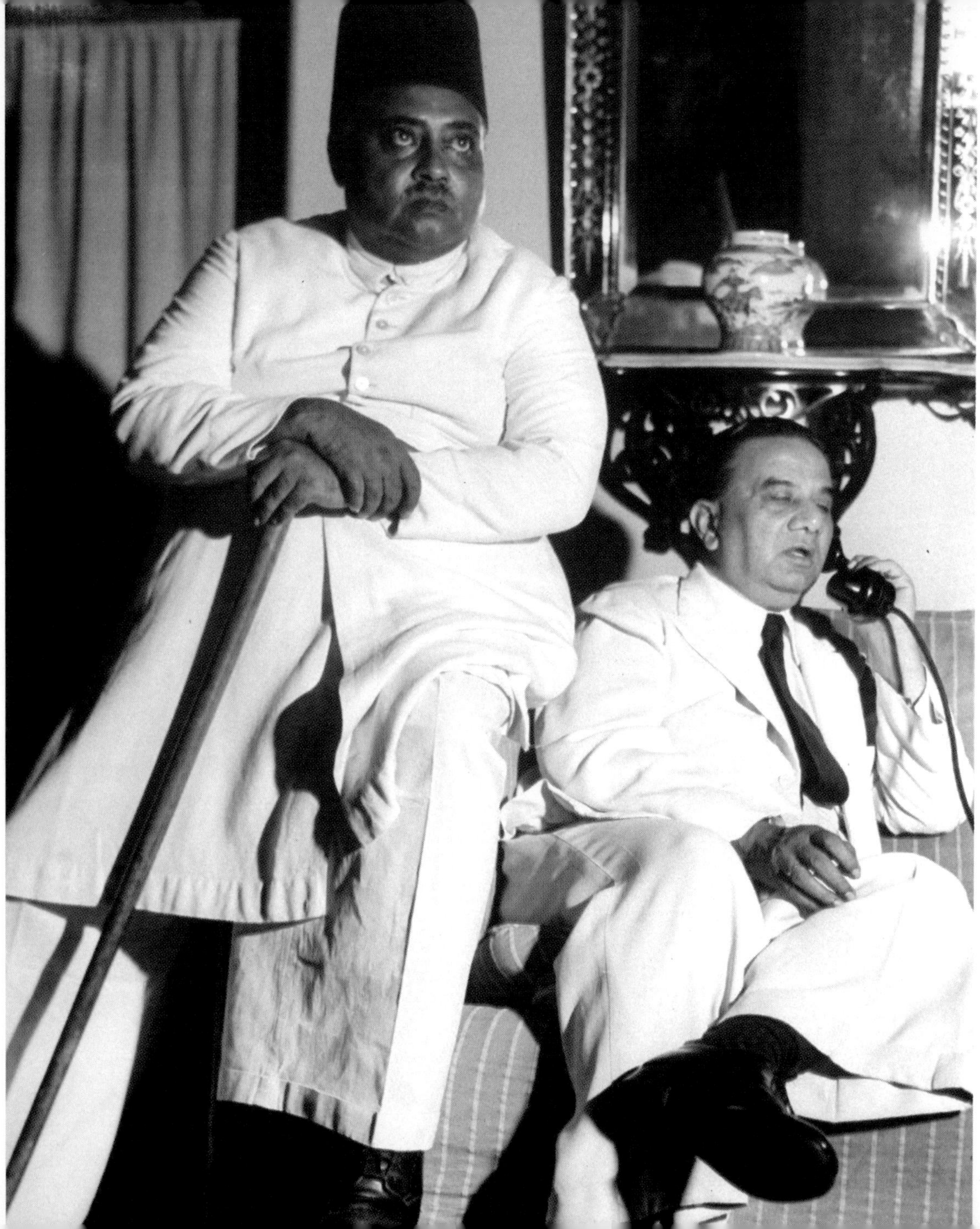

Hussein Shaheed Suhrawardy (R), chief minister of Bengal in undivided India, with Khwaja Nizamuddin. Suhrawardy, a leader of the Muslim League, played a crucial role in the Direct Action Day in Calcutta. Khwaja Nizamuddin came from the Nawab of Dhaka's family.

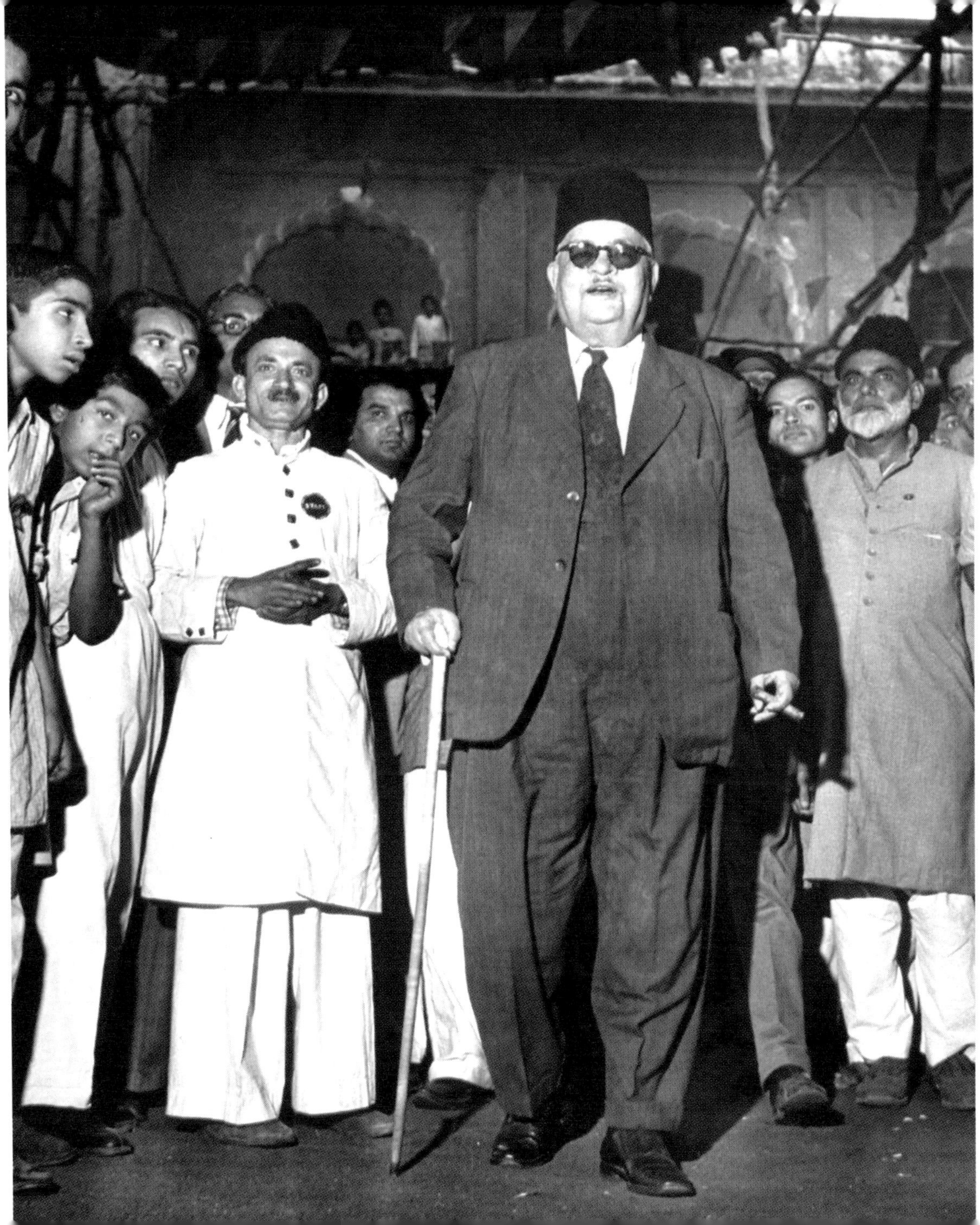

Sir Ghulam Hussein Hidayatullah, was the chief minister of Sindh from 1937 to 1938 and again from 1941 to 1947 and the governor of Sindh from 1947 to 1948.

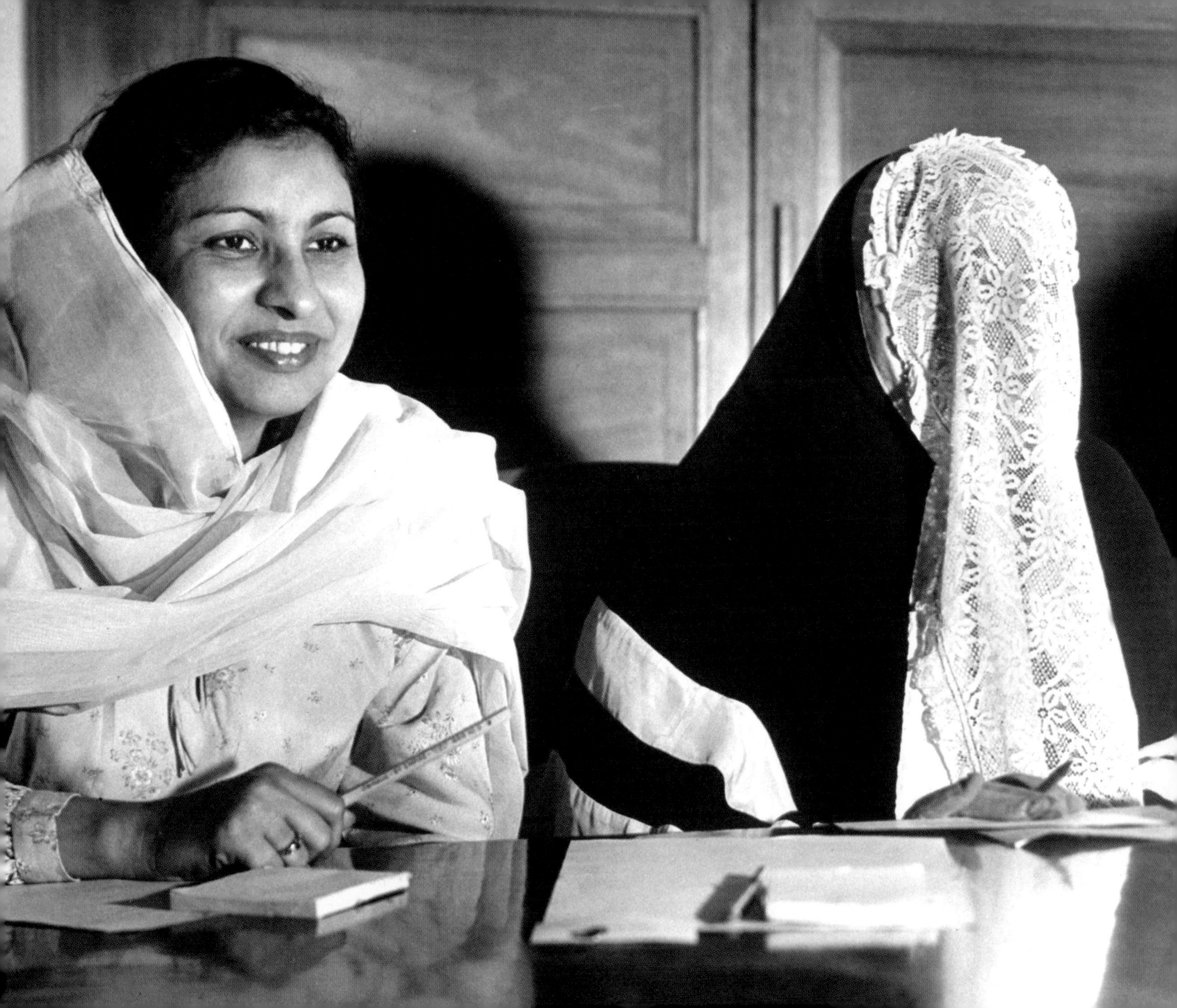

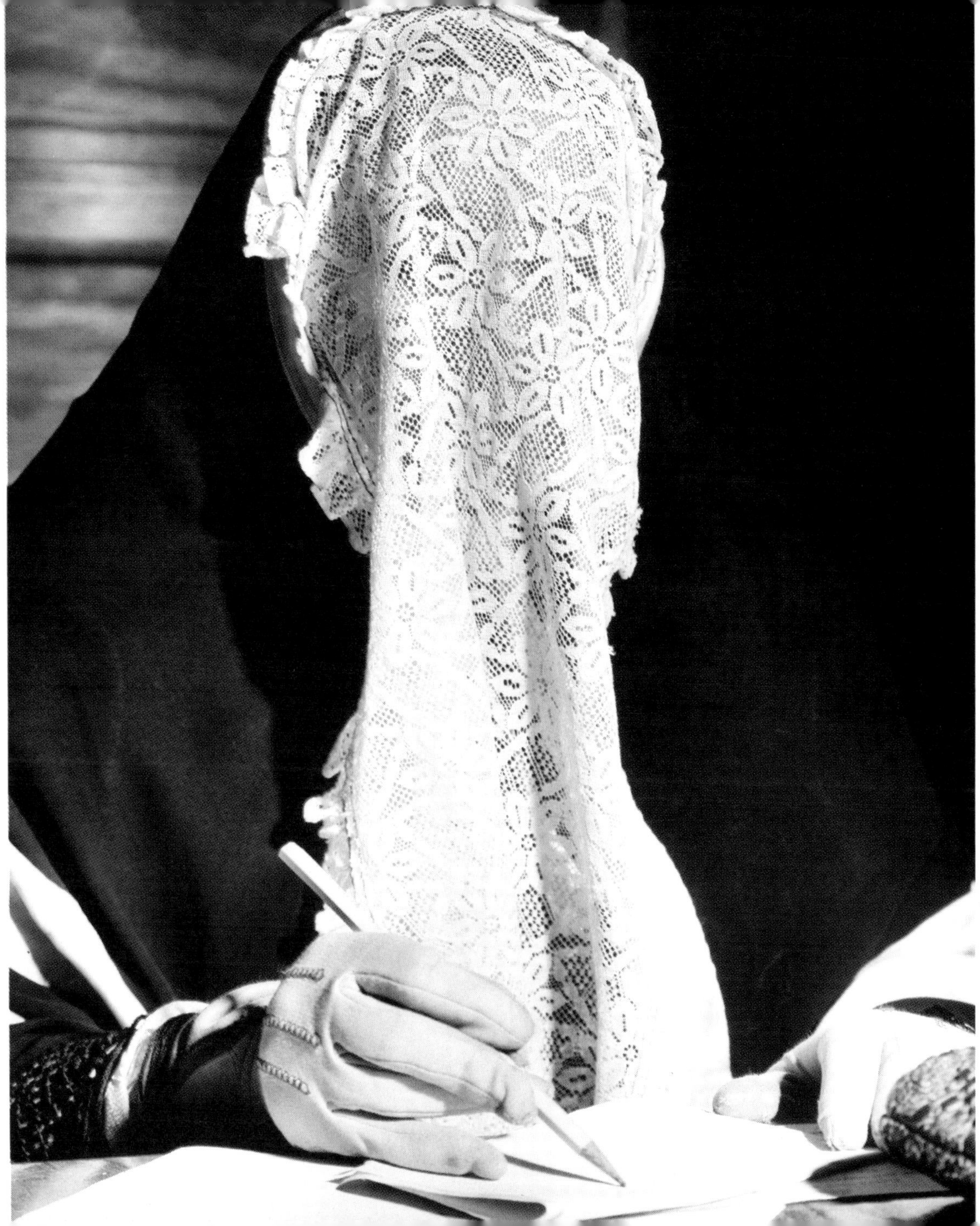

Left: The woman in burqa is Khadeeja Feroze Ud-din, a depupty directress of education and public instruction with Begum Sofia Ahmed, the daughter of the governor of Sindh at the women's education conference in Karachi in 1947.

'Khadeeja Feroze Ud-din veils face and hides hands in the presence of me. That she opposes coeducation is not surprising. A dual system of schools will be an expensive tribute for the hard-pressed state to pay to an archaic orthodoxy.'

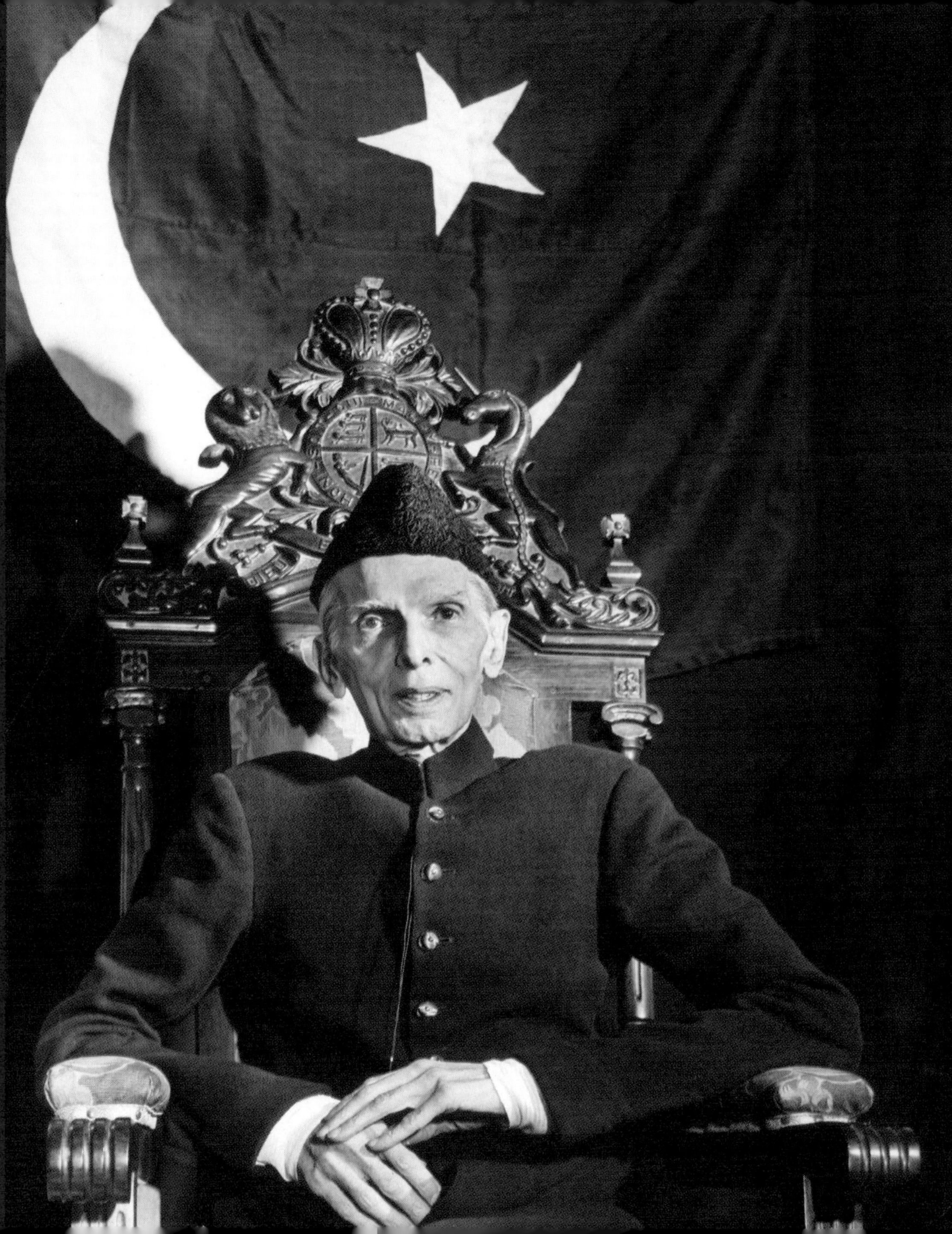

PAKISTAN'S QUAID-I-AZAM: MOHAMMED ALI JINNAH

The youngest Indian to be called to the Bar in England, Mohammed Ali Jinnah, the first Governor-General of Pakistan rose to prominence as a young leader of the Indian National Congress with a faith in Hindu-Muslim unity. But it cannot be denied that he was 'out of place in the Gandhian-led movements and averse to Nehru's socialist republic'. About her visit to Karachi in October 1948 to take his photograph for the cover of Life *magazine, she writes:*

'During this period, when Jinnah was not seeing even his ministers and when his intimidated palace staff and aide-de-camp dreaded crossing him in the smallest matter, Miss Fatima – after repeated and baffling postponements – won his consent to be photographed. He finally agreed, I suspect, because the Quaid-i-Azam, even at seventy-two, was still dramatically handsome and as fond as any good-looking man of having his picture taken. …

'Miss Fatima and I planned the picture very carefully. As a fitting background for the Father of the Nation, we would hang the national flag on the wall. But at the last minute we made the disconcerting discovery that there was not a single Pakistan flag in Government House, only the Quaid-i-Azam's personal banner. The Muslim Women's National Guard finaly came to our rescue with a huge Pakistan flag … Miss Fatima and I congratulated ourselves on the pleasant contrast of the dark green with the light-toned clothes we had selected for her brother … he was to put on his pale cream Muslim sherwani … and his fez of light gray astrakhan – the famous "Jinnah cap".

'But the Quaid-i-Azam took us both by surprise and appeared for the sitting in a costume of his own design, a dark maroon sherwani and matching fur fez, the first piece of maroon fur I had ever seen. While it was no doubt a dyer's masterpiece, the choice was photographically unfortunate against the dark green flag. But my dismay at the dyed fur was dwarfed by my shock at Jinnah's changed appearance – the unsteady step, listless eyes, the white-knuckled, nervously clenched hands. As I went ahead with my pictures, Miss Fatima, … slipped up before each shot and tried gently to uncurl the desperately clenched hands. He came to life only once while I was working, when his sister, as disappointed as I over the dark blob of maroon, hurried up with a gret armful of light-toned Jinnah caps.

'The Quaid-i-Azam waved them away with one word: "No".'

Excerpted from *Halfway to Freedom* by Margaret Bourke-White

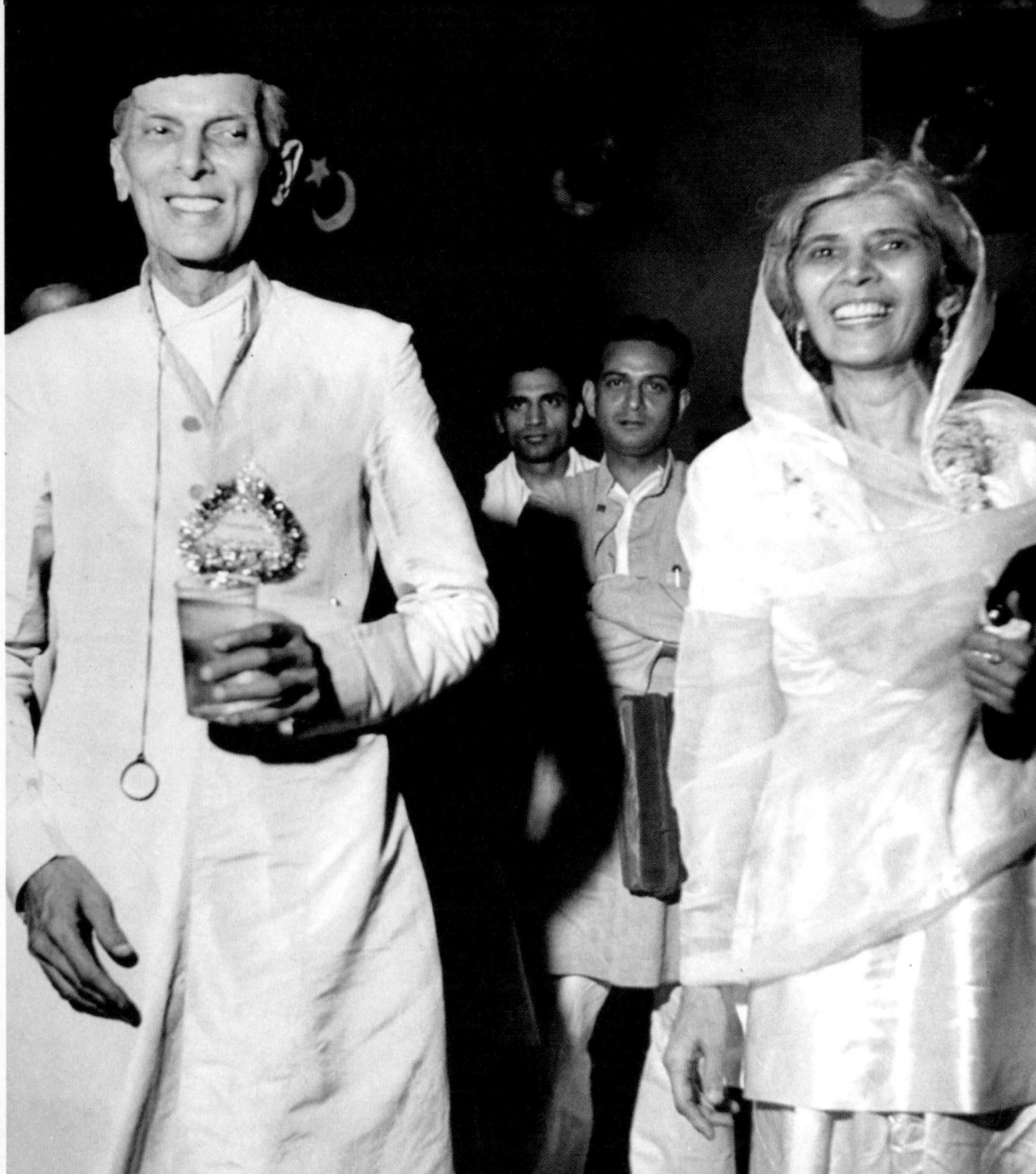

Left: Mohammed Ali Jinnah with his sister Fatima Jinnah.

Right: Mohammed Ali Jinnah, immaculately dressed in a Western outfit.

Margaret Bourke-White went to Karachi in September 1947, a month after the creation of Pakistan. Karachi was its mushrooming capital with the new Governor-General staying in the red sandstone Government House with his sister, Fatima, as hostess.

'Mr Jinnah had put on what his critics called his "triple crown": he had made himself Governor-General; he was retaining the presidency of the Muslim League – now Pakistan's only political party; and he was president of the country's lawmaking body, the Constituent Assembly.... "We never expected to get it so soon," Miss Fatima said when I called. "We never expected to get it in our lifetime." If Fatima's reaction was a glow of family pride, her brother's was a fever of ecstasy. Jinnah's deep-sunk eyes were pinpoints of excitement.'

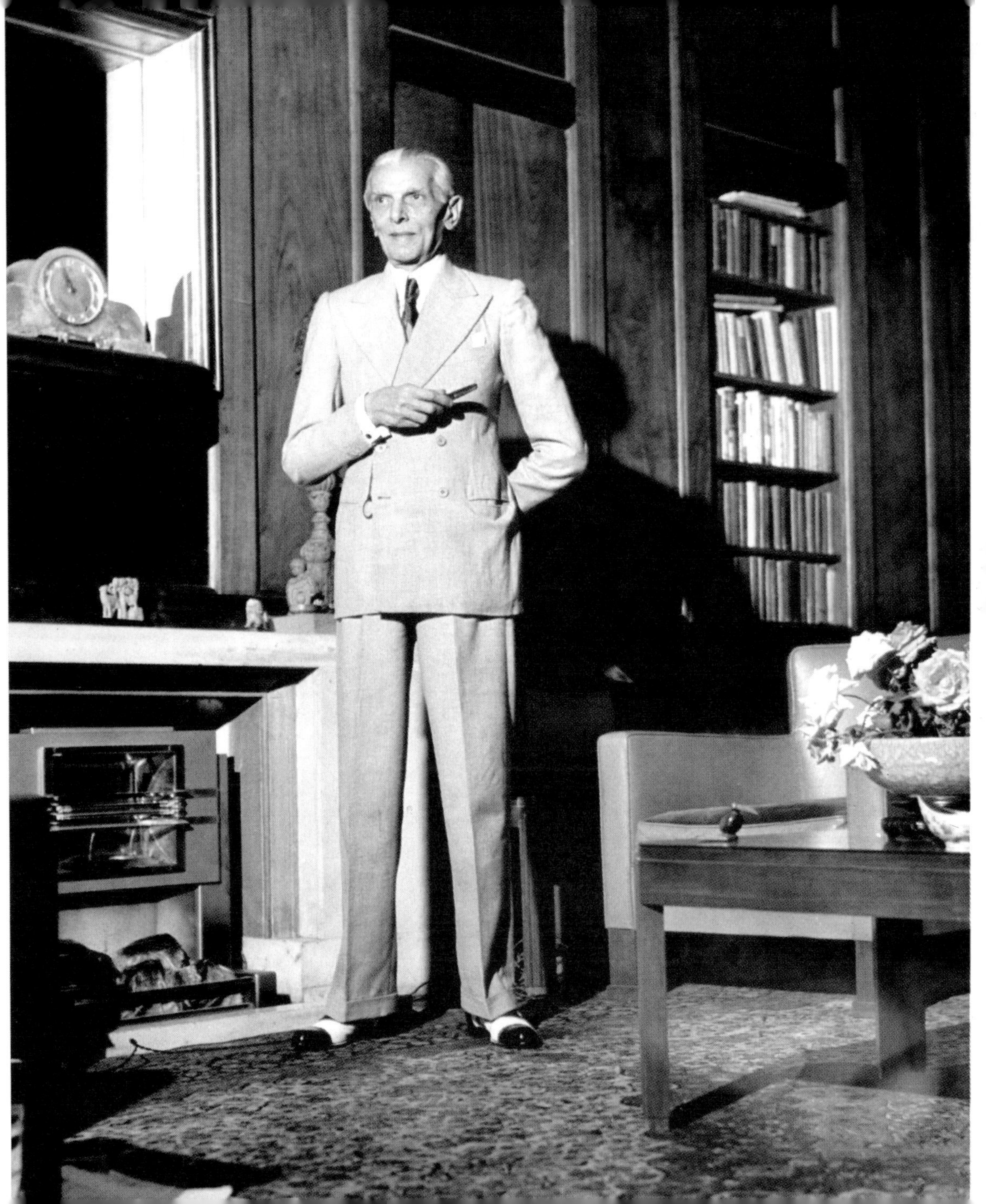

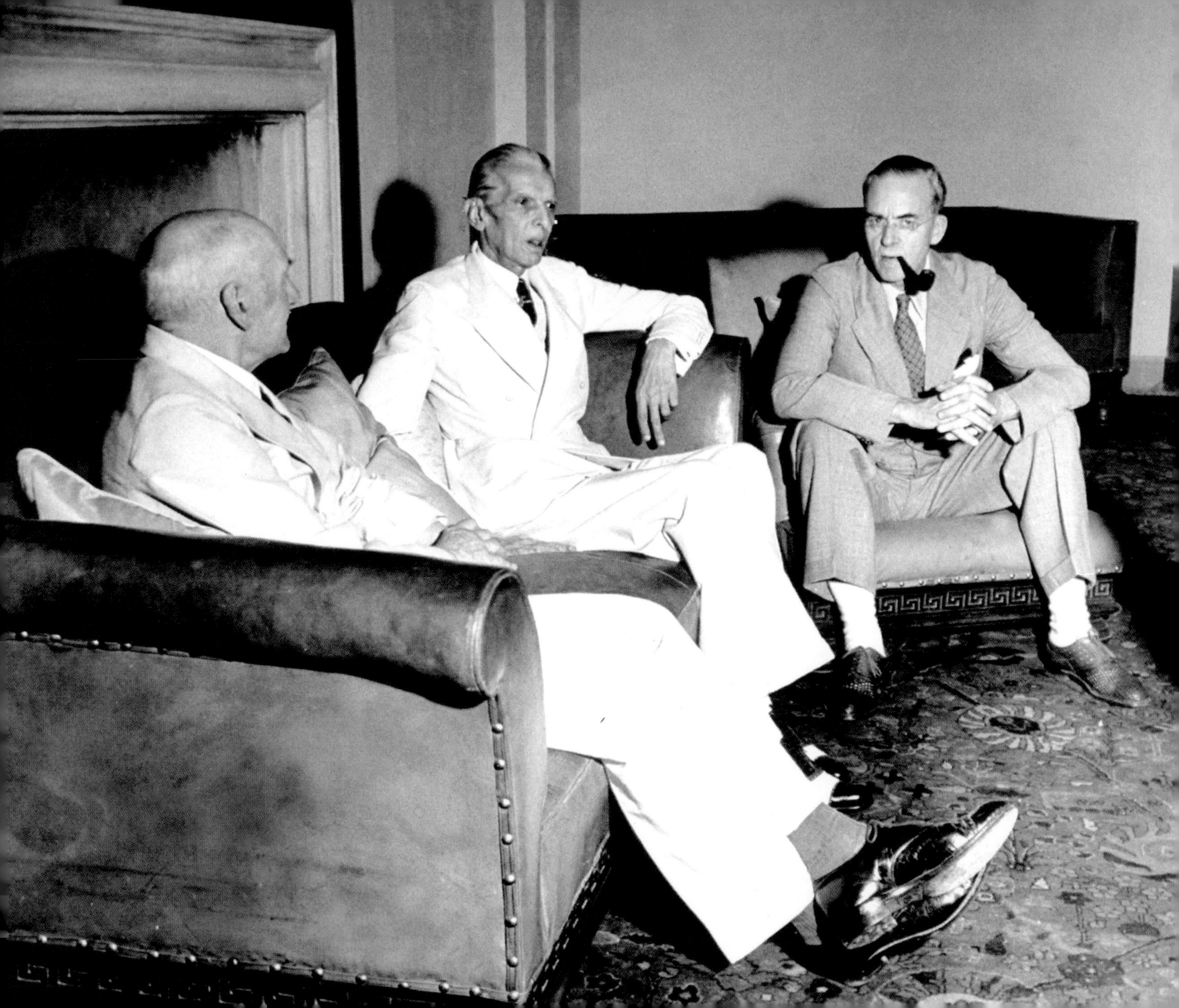

Left: British Cabinet Commission members Frederick William Pethick Lawrence (L) and Sir Stafford Cripps in discussion with Jinnah at the Viceregal Lodge, Shimla, in 1946. It had always surprised Margaret Bourke-White that,

'… the determination to establish a separate Islamic state came not from some Muslim divine in archaic robes, but from a thoroughly Westernized, English-educated attorney-at-law with a clean shaven face and razor sharp mind … leader of the Muslim League and architect of Pakistan, had for many years worked at the side of Nehru and Gandhi for a free, united India, until in the evening of his life he broke sharply with his past to achieve a separate Pakistan.'

Right: Mohammed Ali Jinnah with Liaquat Ali Khan at his residence, 10 Aurengzeb Road, Delhi.

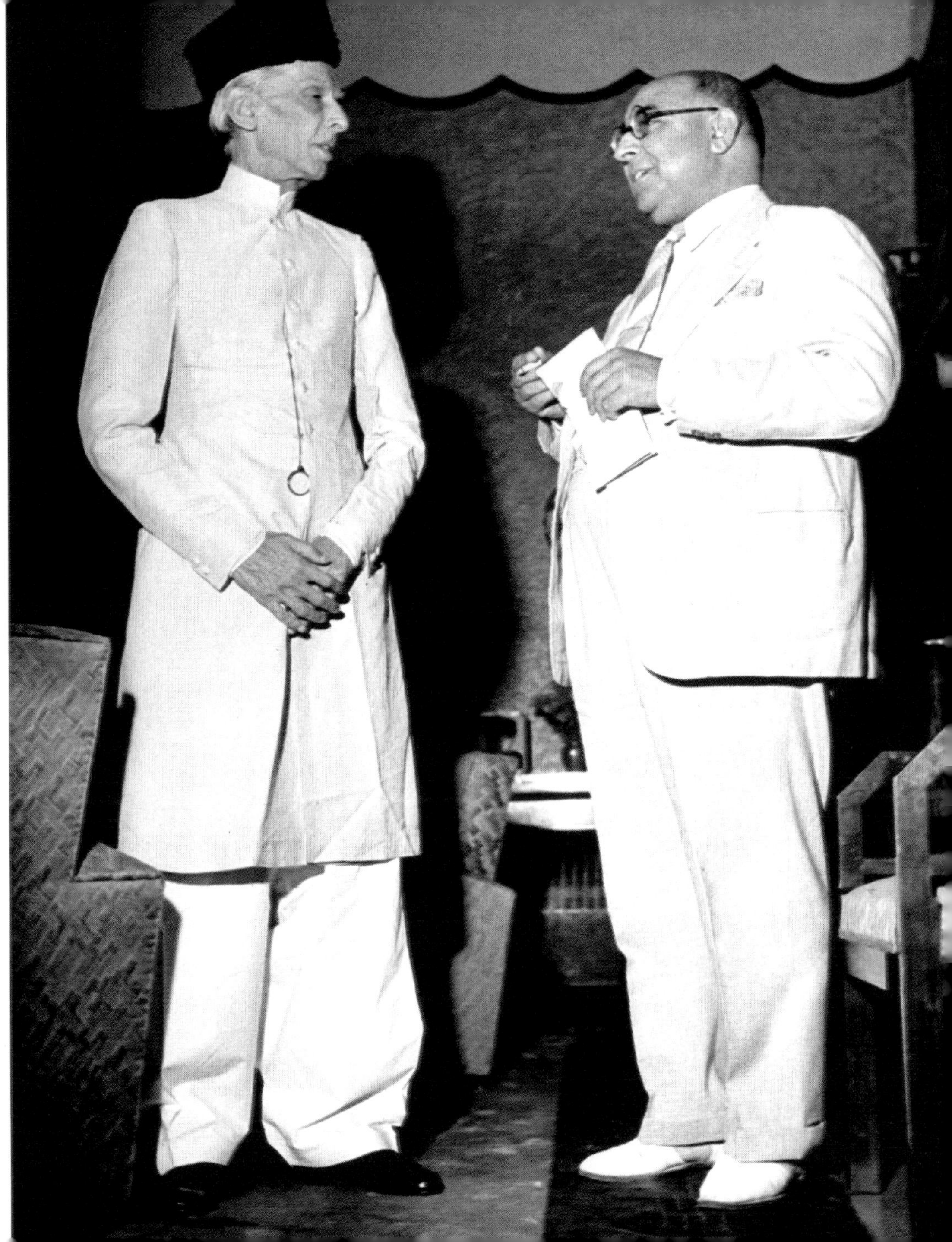

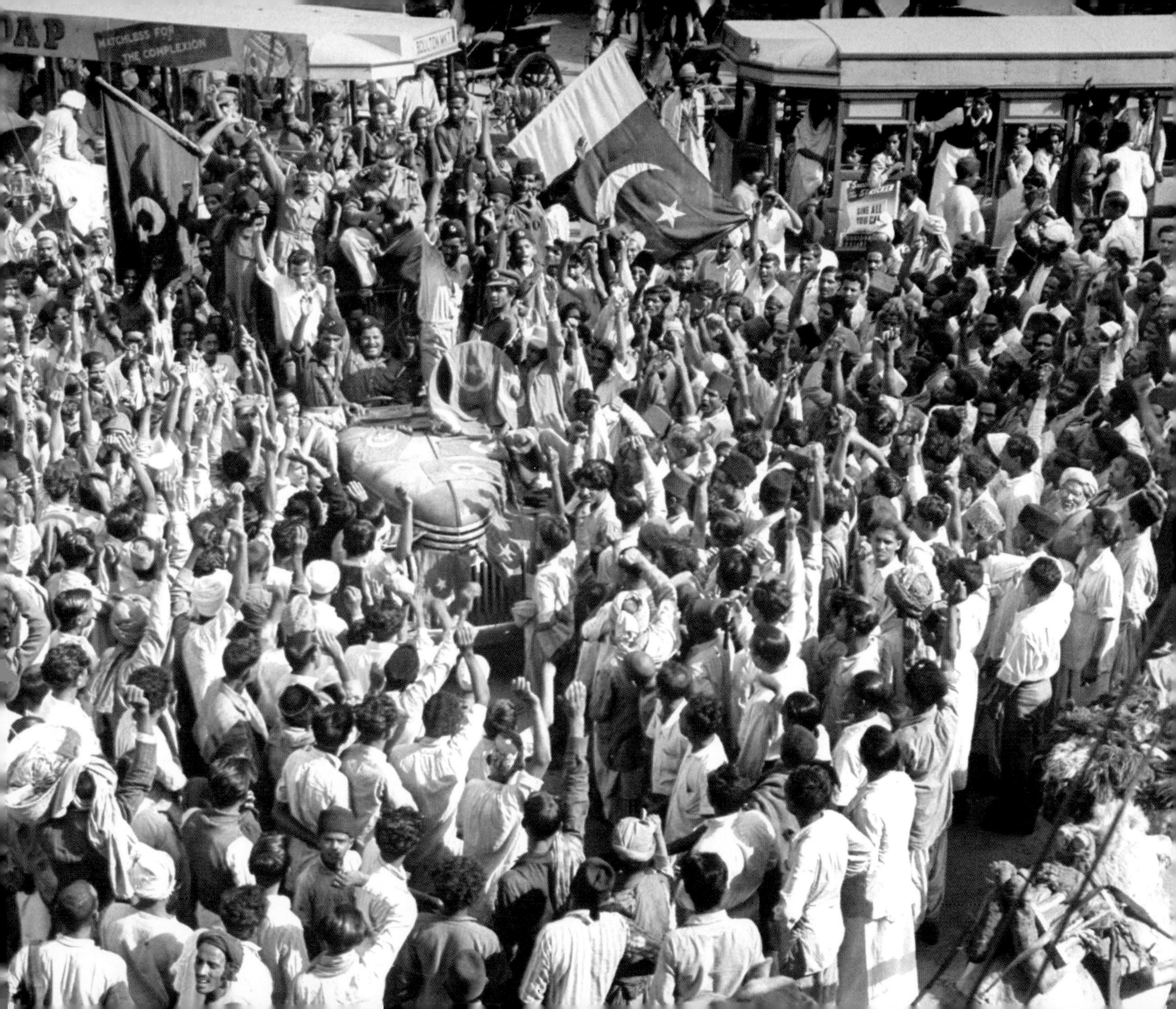
MATCHLESS FOR
THE COMPLEXION

Left: December 1947, Karachi, Muslim League guardsmen chanting 'Free Kashmir' on a truck they ride through crowd at Boulton Bazaar.

Right: Saeed Abdullah Haroon haranguing a Young Muslim League meeting in a frantic style popular with zealots. Youngest son of Haji Abdullah Haroon, Saeed Haroon was one of the closest associates of Jinnah. He had the distinction of being a 'Salar' in the National Guards and serving as ADC to Jinnah. This picture appeared in the 5 November 1948 issue of the Life *magazine.*

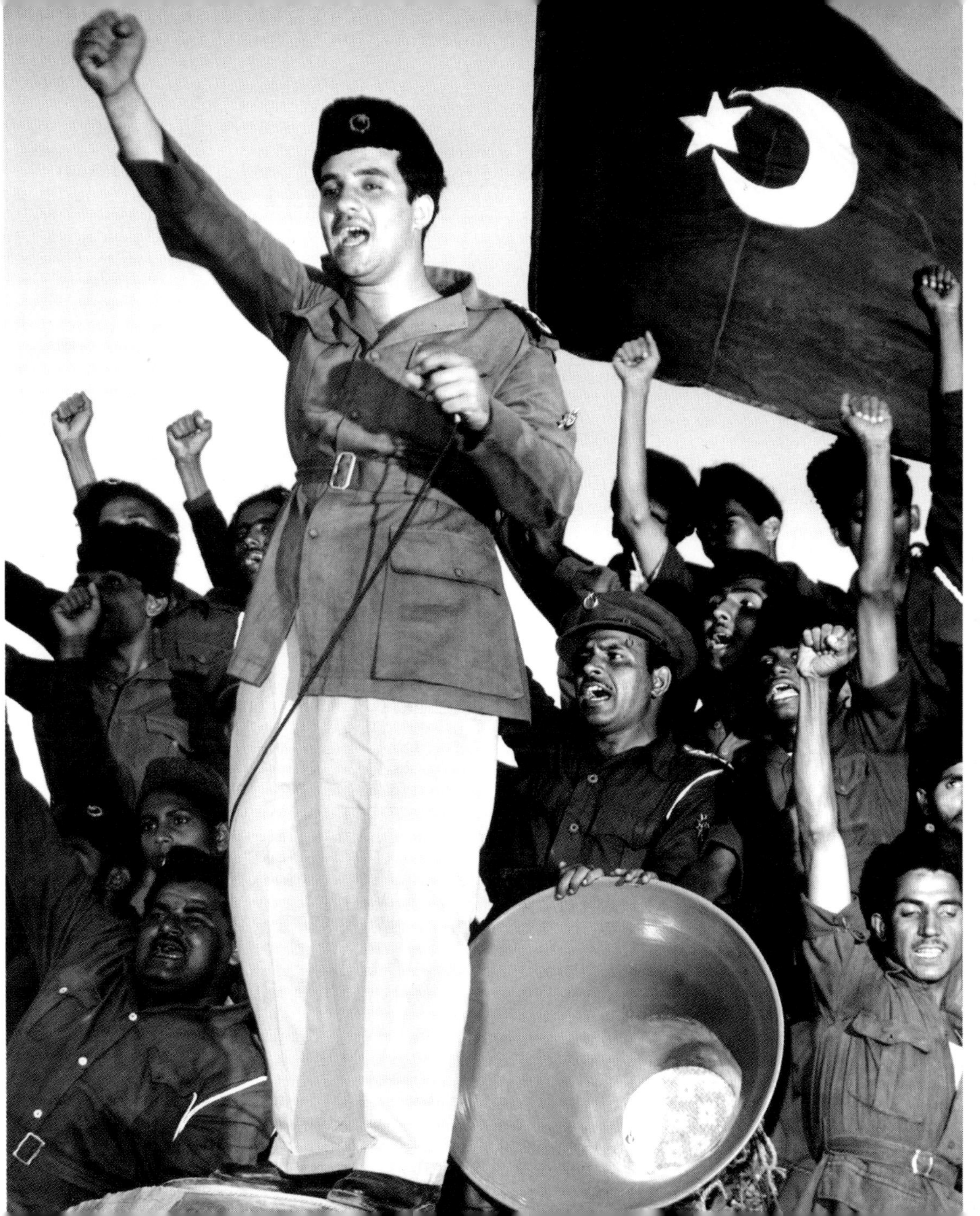

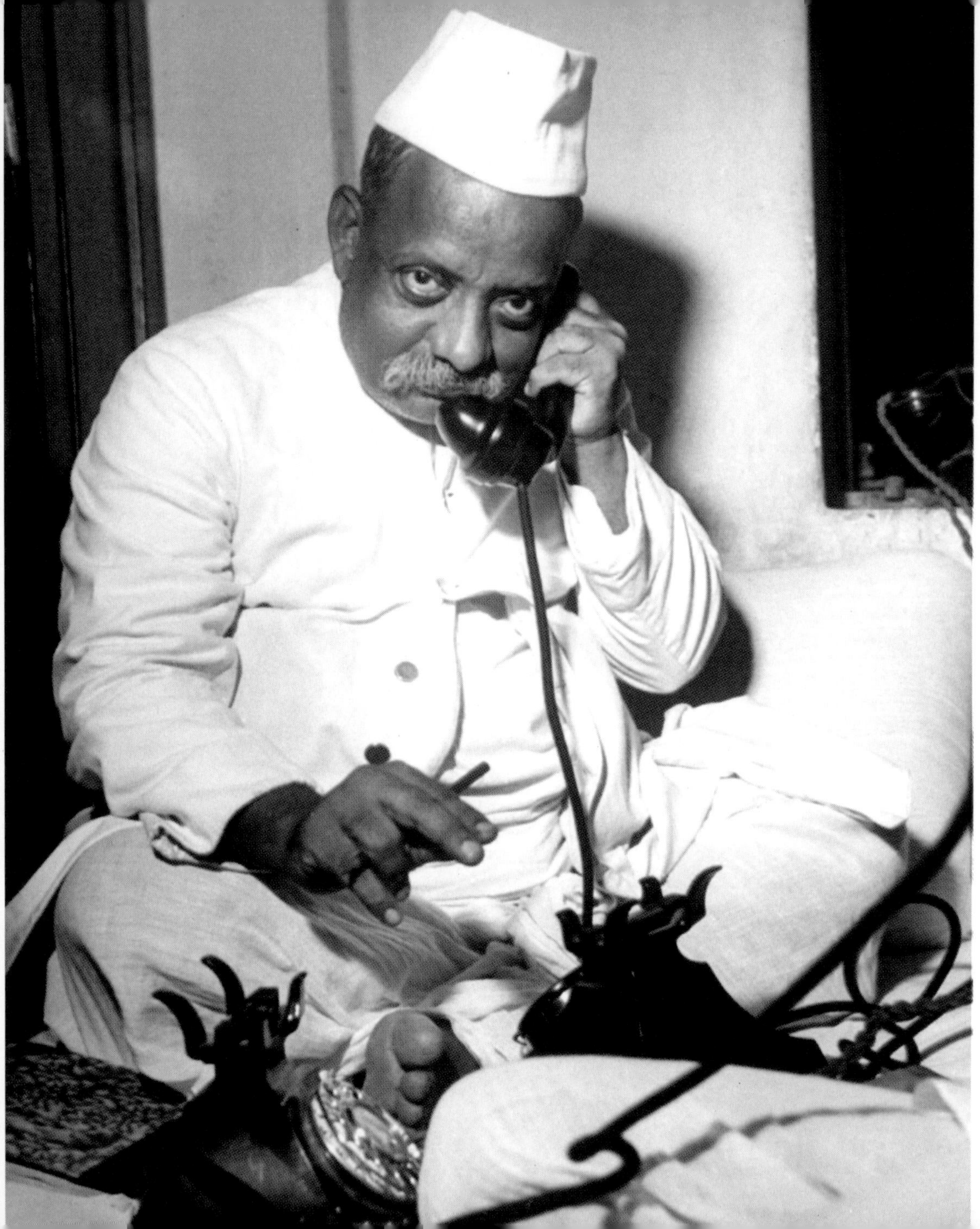

Brokers of Bombay Cotton Exchange busy in their dealings.

'Bhuleshwar Corner in Bombay is the busiest with the building of the Cotton Exchange and also buildings on either side packed with tiny brokers' and traders' offices. Further up this street are the Bullion Exchange and many banks. Brokers in India consult astrologers, who find market advice in heavenly signs, but complain that "the bazaar isn't what it used to be two thousand years ago".'

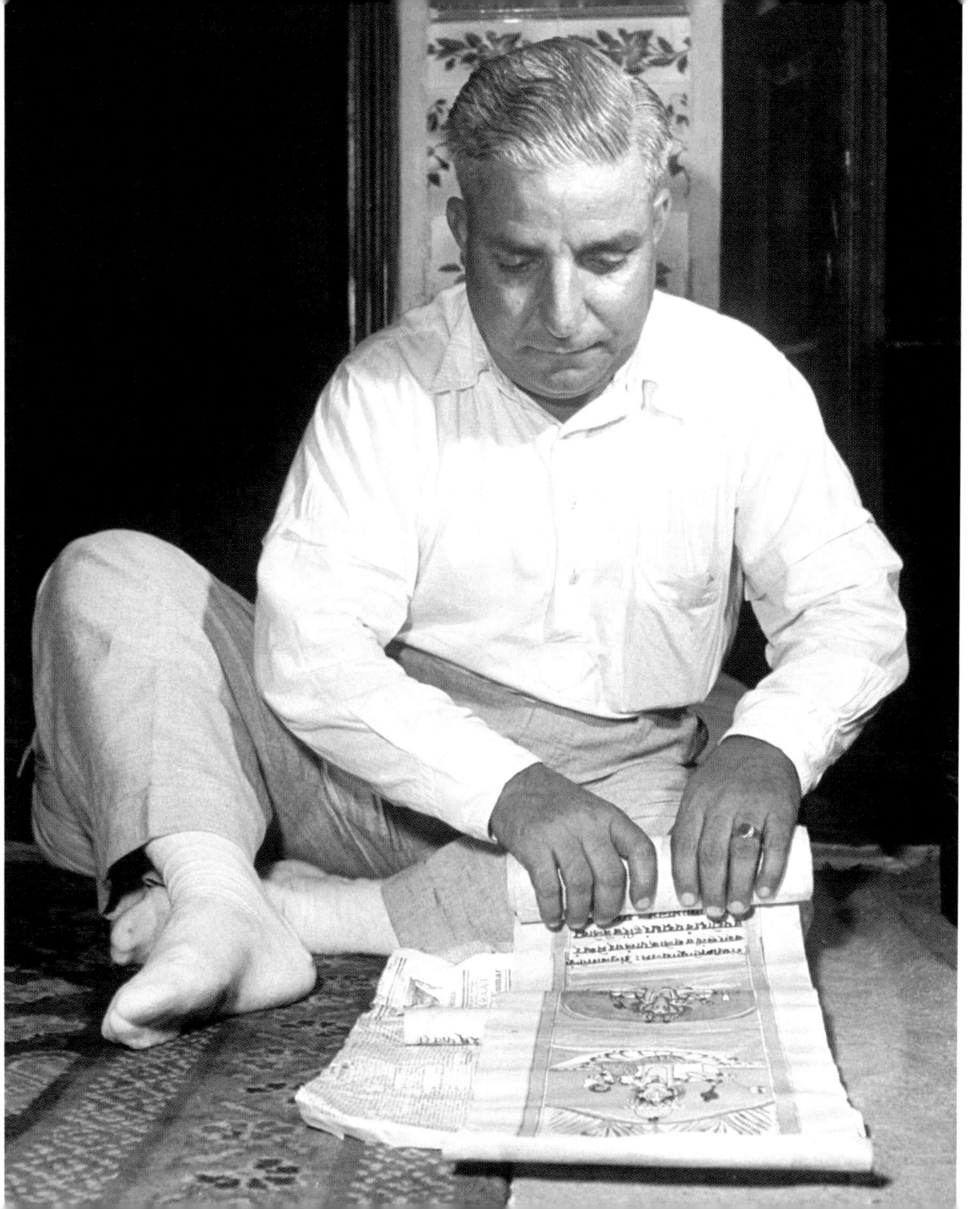

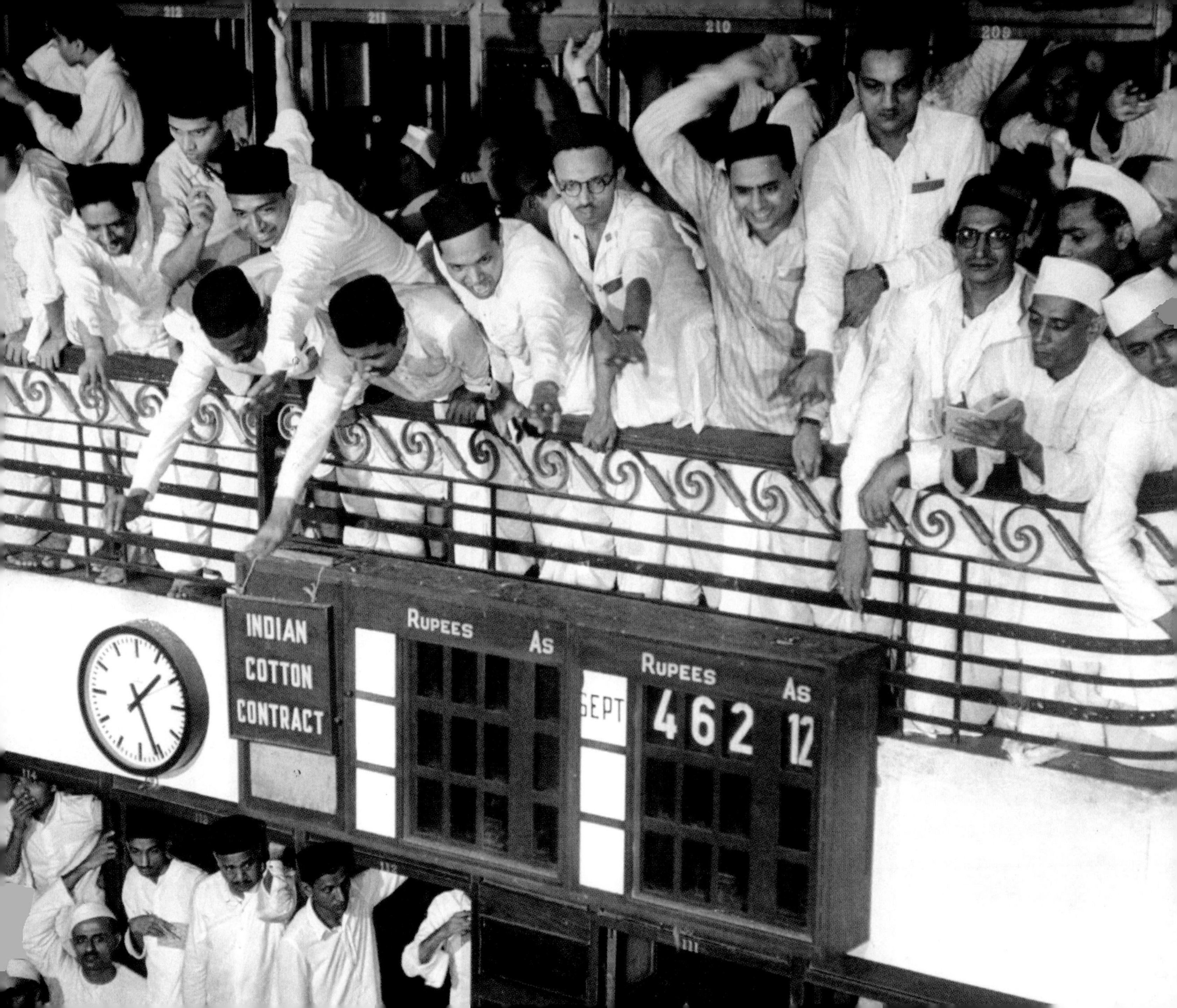
INDIAN
COTTON
CONTRACT
RUPEES
As
RUPEES
As
SEPT
462
12

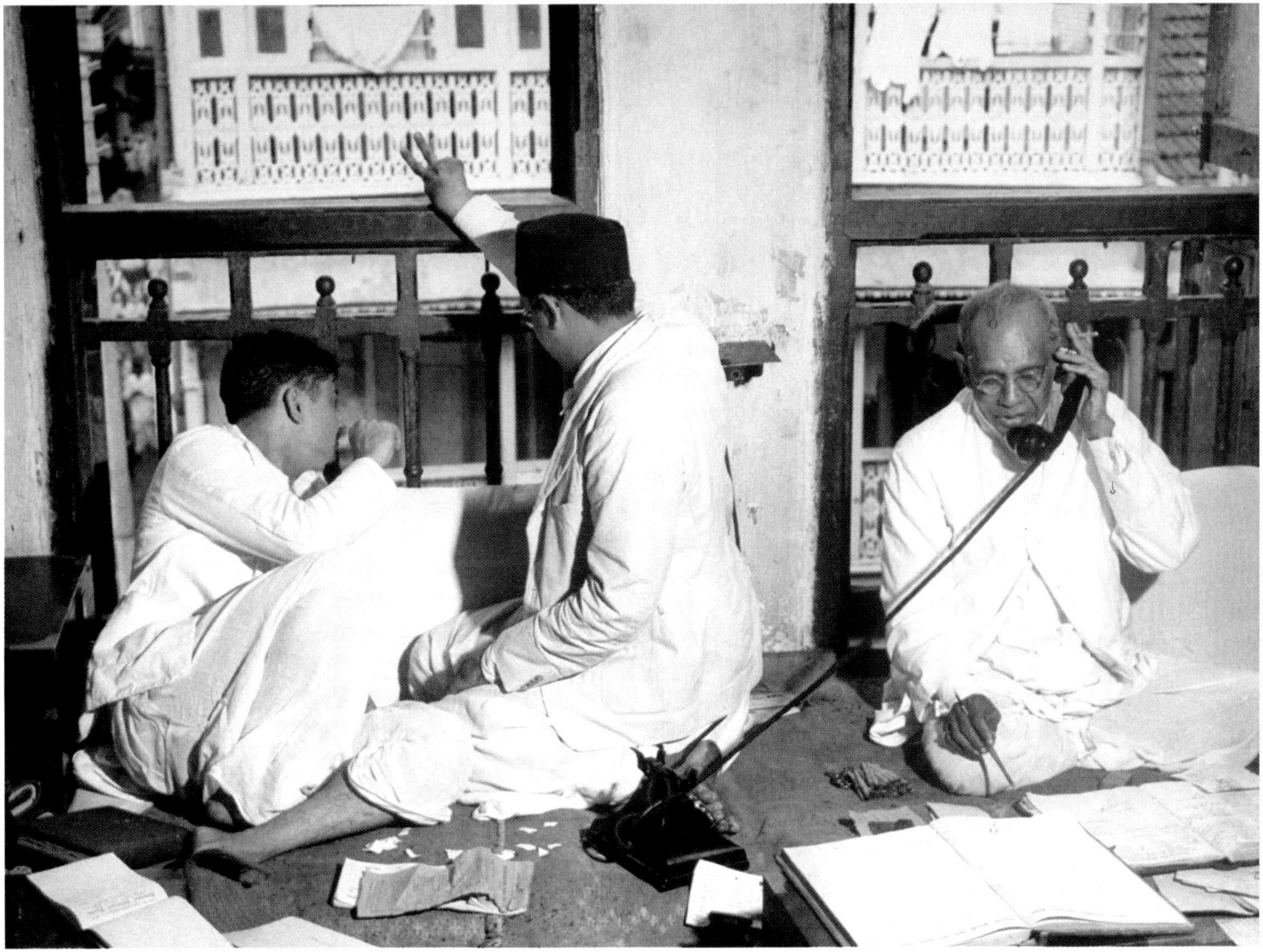

'Inside the Cotton Exchange is wild, organized bedlam, [it is] so crowded that traders must cling to straps on the wall to keep their footing. Biggest operators in Bombay speculations are pink-turbaned Marwadis. Many traders are of the numerically small Parsi sect.'

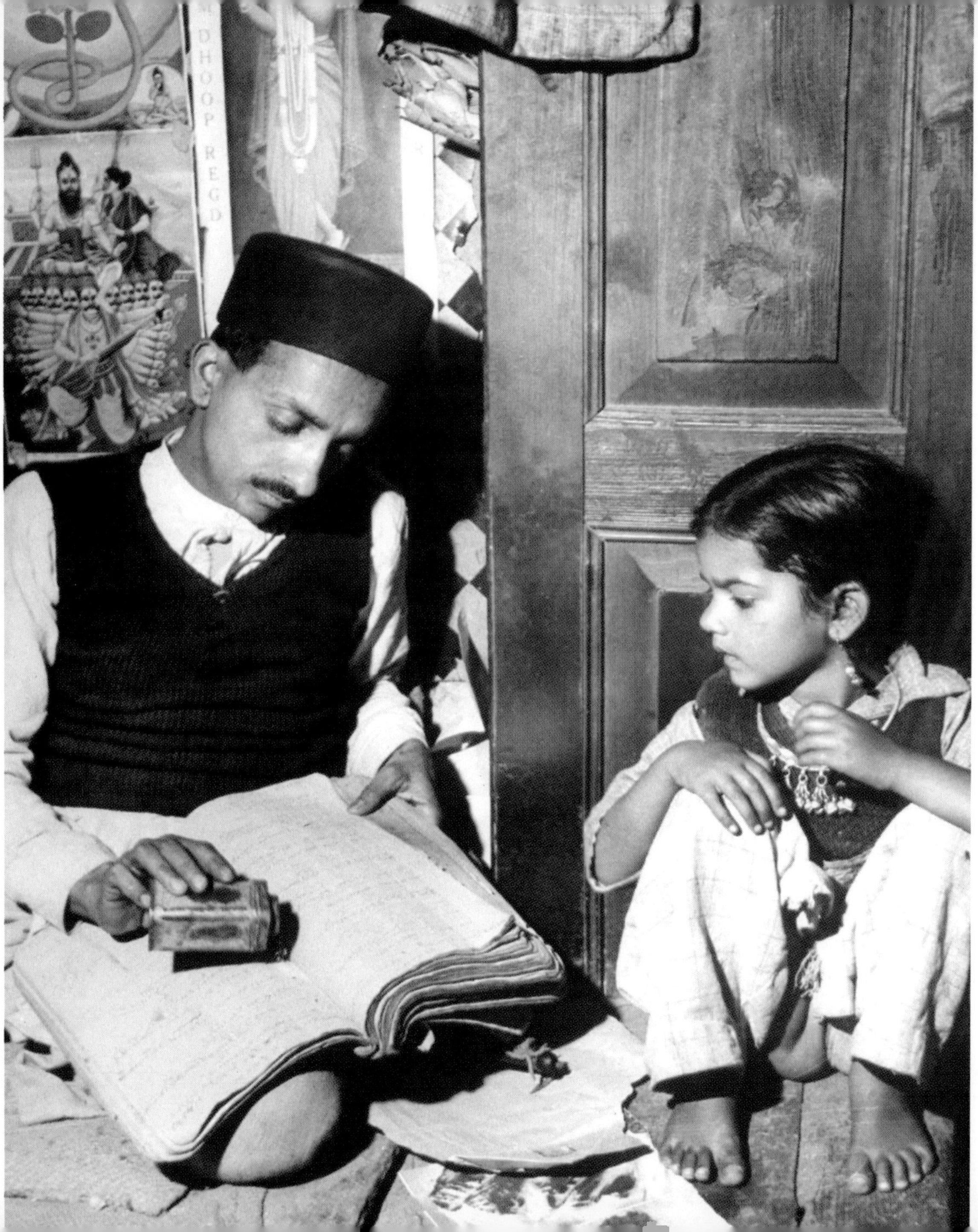

Left: Indian moneylender working on his money ledger under the watchful eye of his young daughter.

Right: Sita Ram, a Hindu priest, washing hands as his young daughters, clad in sarees, look on.

'Through her travels to various parts of India, it was not just the political developments Margaret Bourke-White was concentrating on. She was equally interested in the intricacies of the Indian social and cultural life, the division on the lines of caste and creed as well as problems the new nation was facing.'

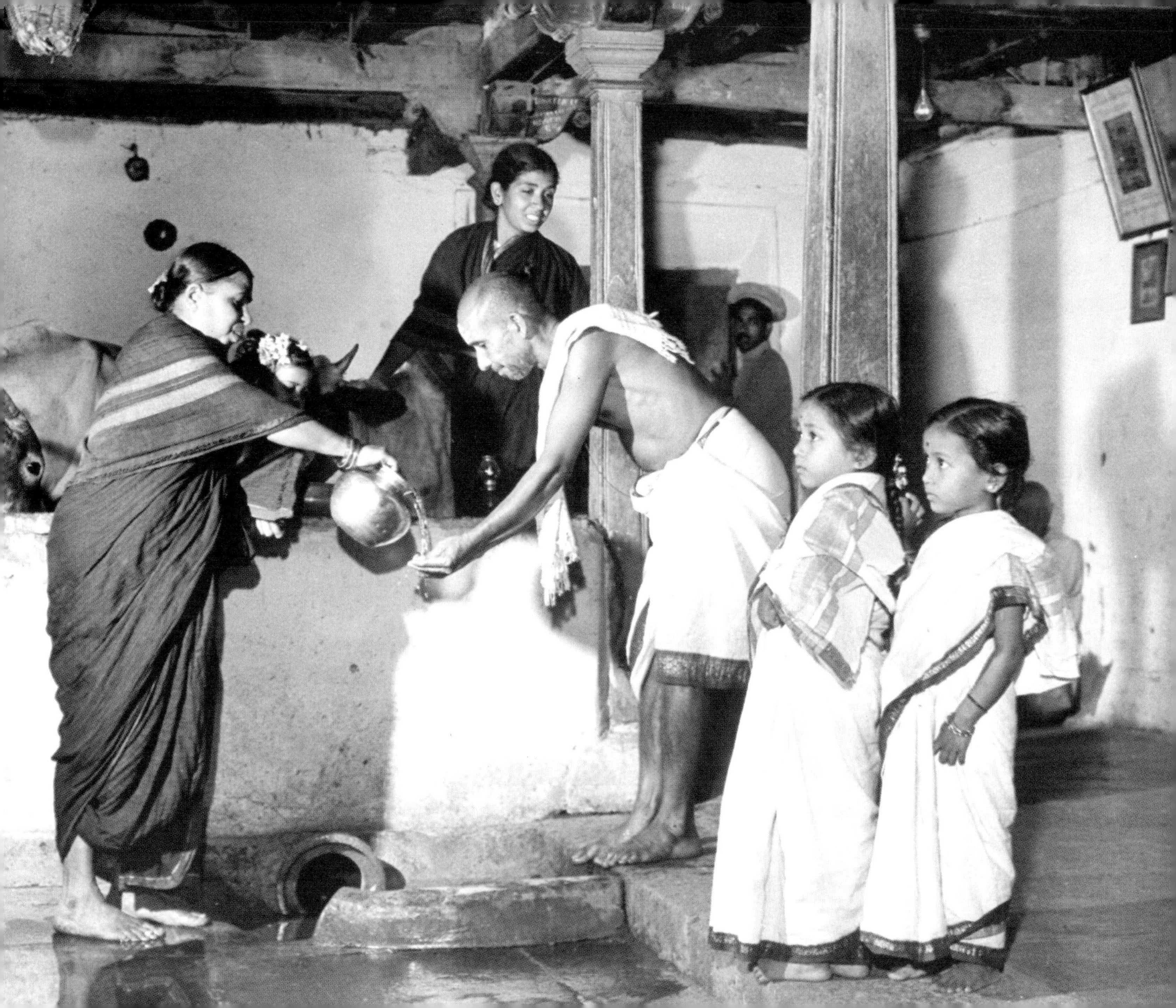

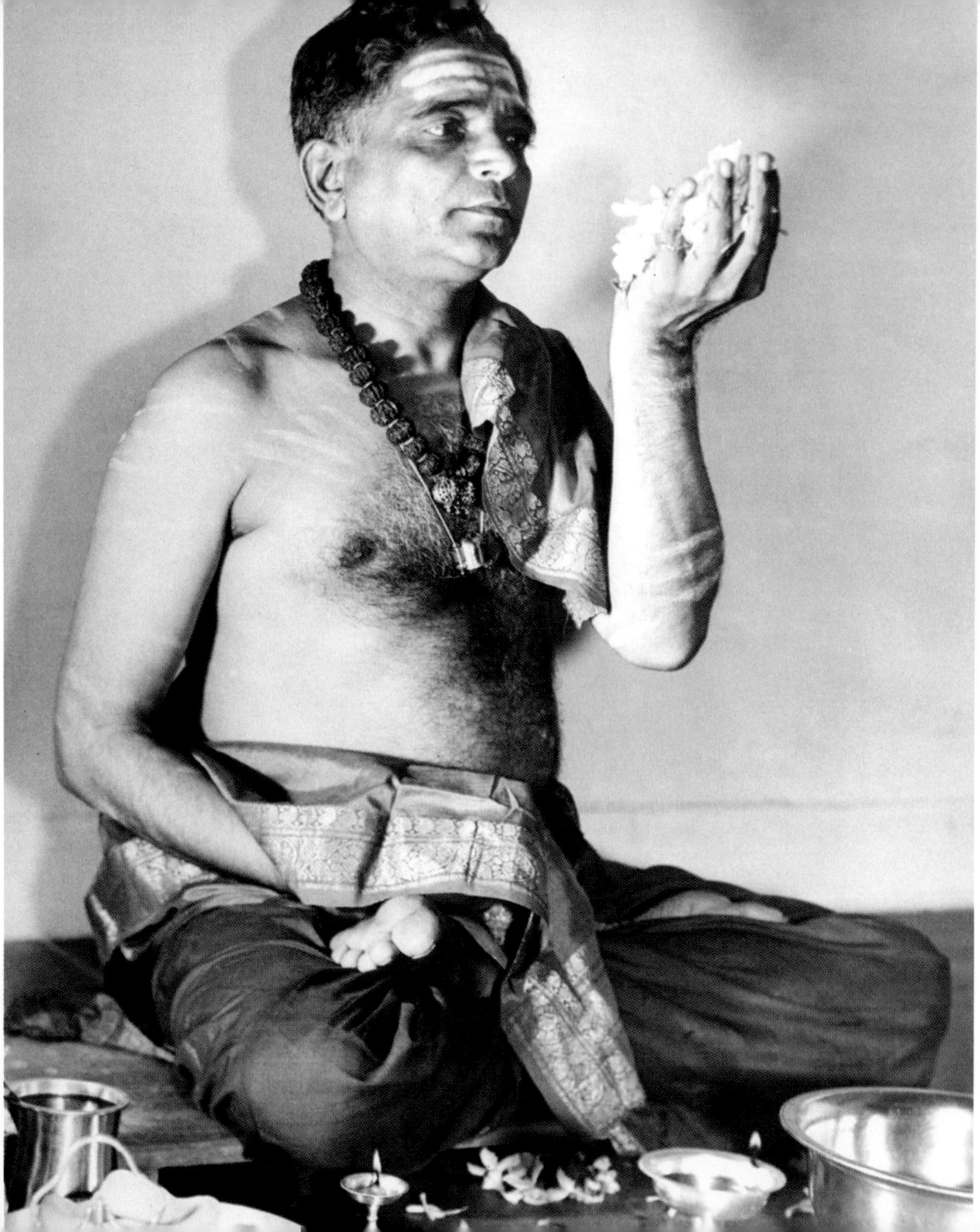

It was not always easy for Margaret Bourke-White to make friends in the villages and start talking to people around for their reactions. But wherever she went she was always asked by people rich and poor to share their food with them.

'I learned to like this dramatic sequence of flavors – although I never quite accustomed myself to some of the flaming concoctions I had to eat for breakfast – but stubbornly as I tried, I never learned to sit on the floor and eat with my fingers. To get the better of a platter of cereal grains swimming in soupy sauces by the skill of your hand alone is, I decided, an art which needs cultivation from babyhood. Finally I gave up trying to eat like an Asian and carried a fork and spoon at all times in my handbag, bringing them out at mealtime to the great amusement of the Indian families I visited.'

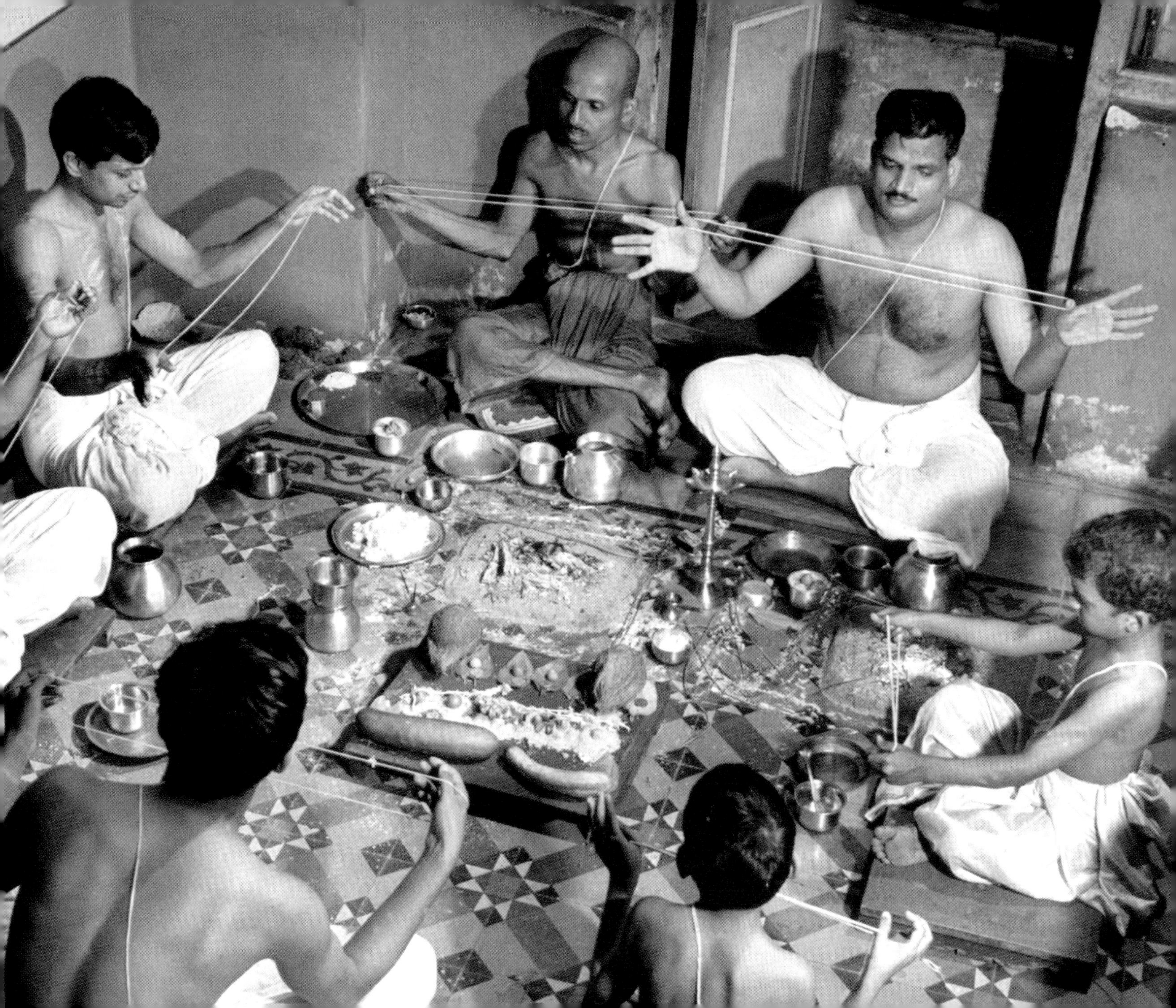

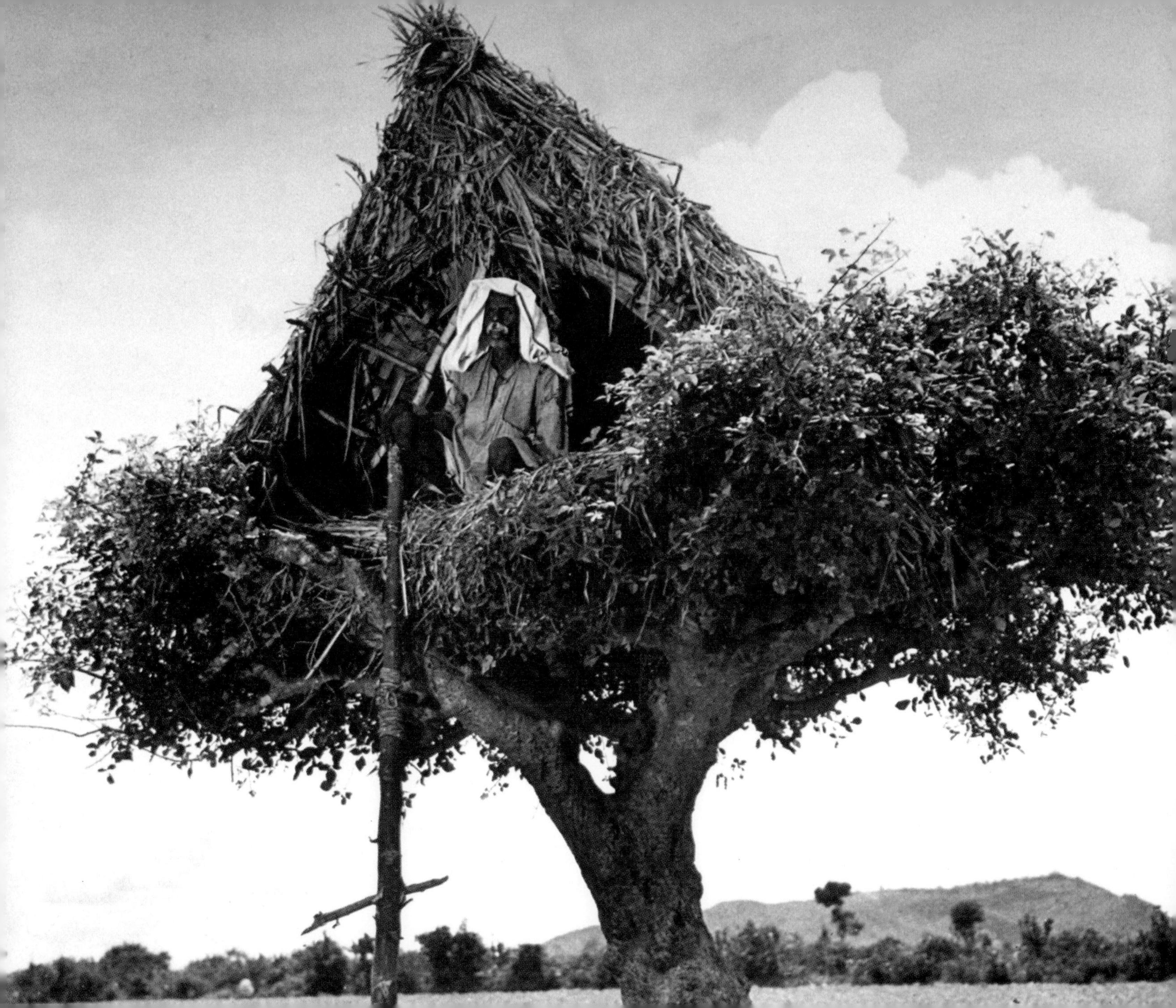

Left: An old man who spends his days perched on a tree as scarecrow to keep his fields free from birds and animals.

Right: The wedding regalia is traditional, and is usually handed down in families.

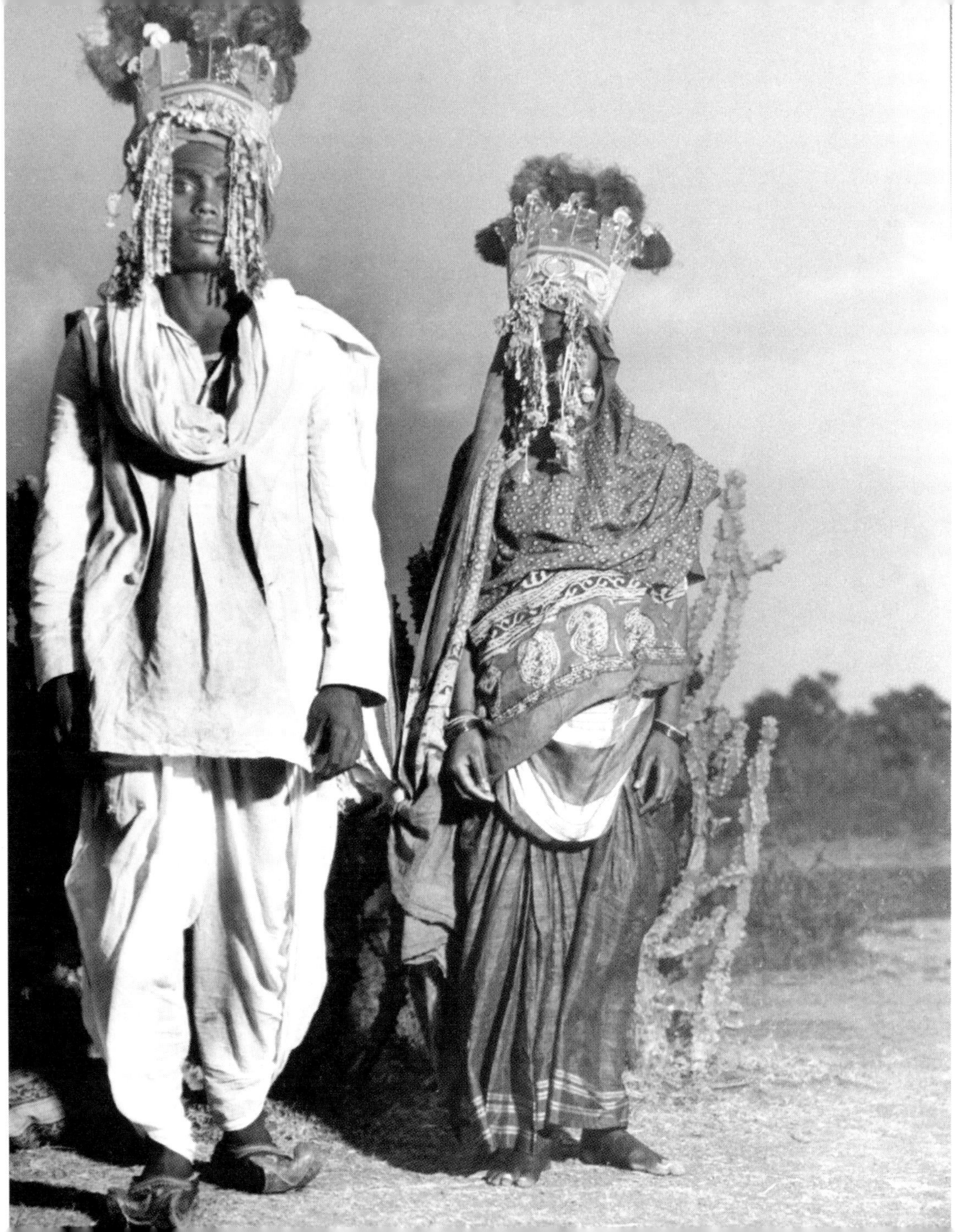

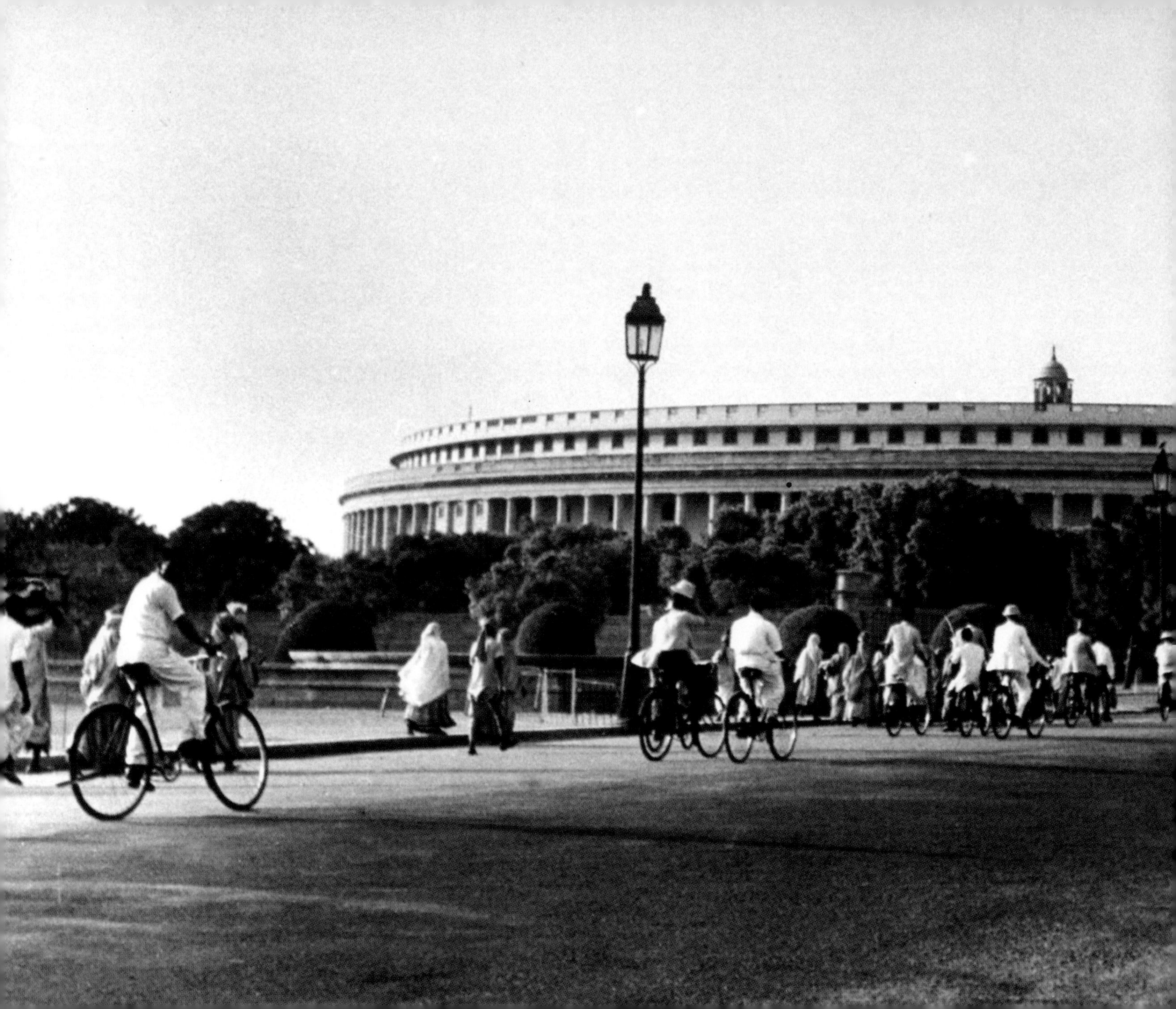

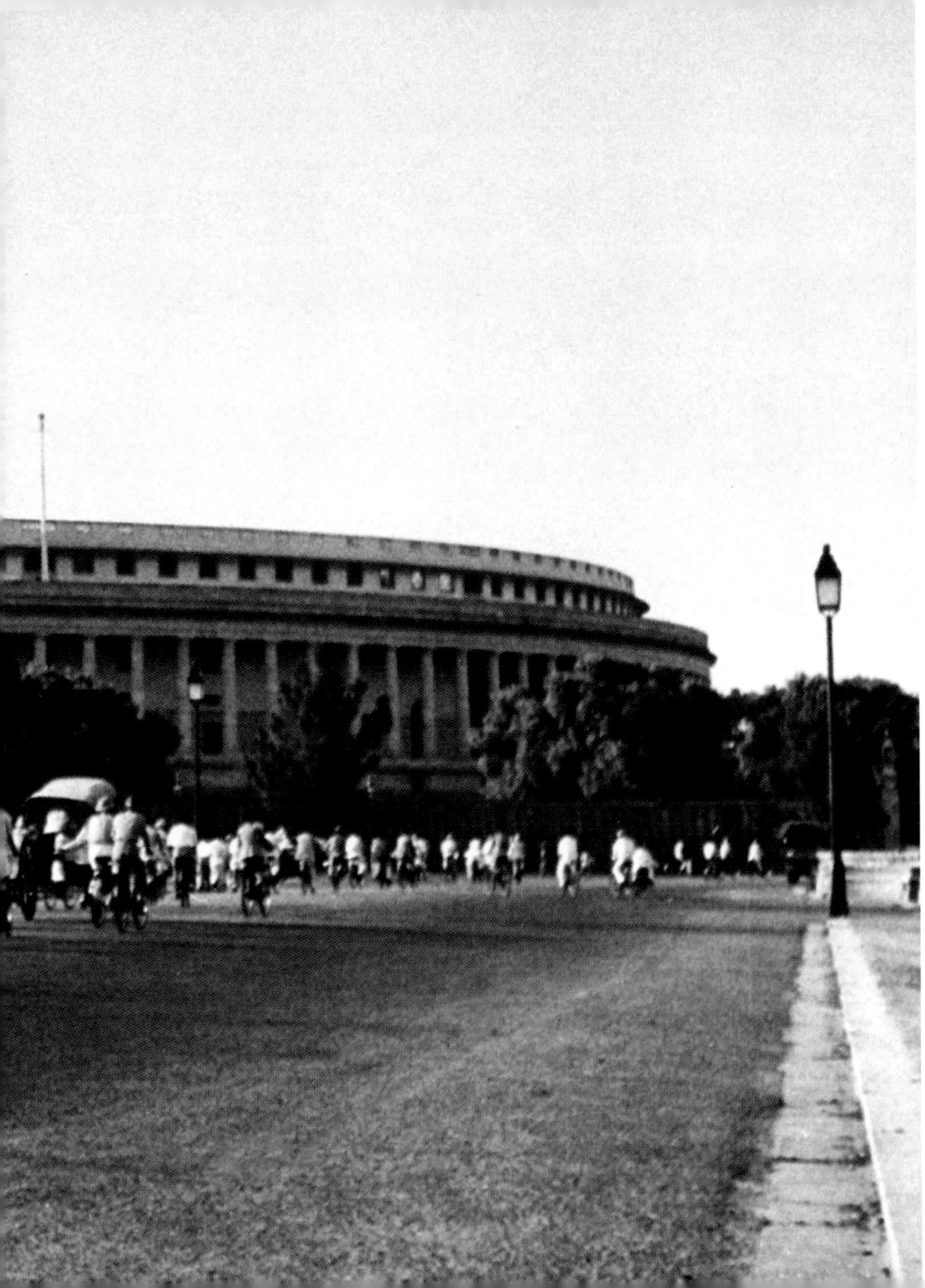

The Indian Parliament: Government employees riding past the Indian assembly building.

'The seething conflicts, the ferment and growth, the powers of medievalism clinging to ancient privilege while the people struggle upward to reach the light – this to me was the drama of India. When new nations rise from the debris of an outworn order and begin drawing up democratic laws, it marks an important step not only for them but for the whole forward march of the world. India and Pakistan are far from realizing complete "freedom"; new constitutions do not automatically dissolve old inequities … But to an American, the whole charter of liberty for the Indian people is illuminated by its first five words. "We the People of India …," it begins.'

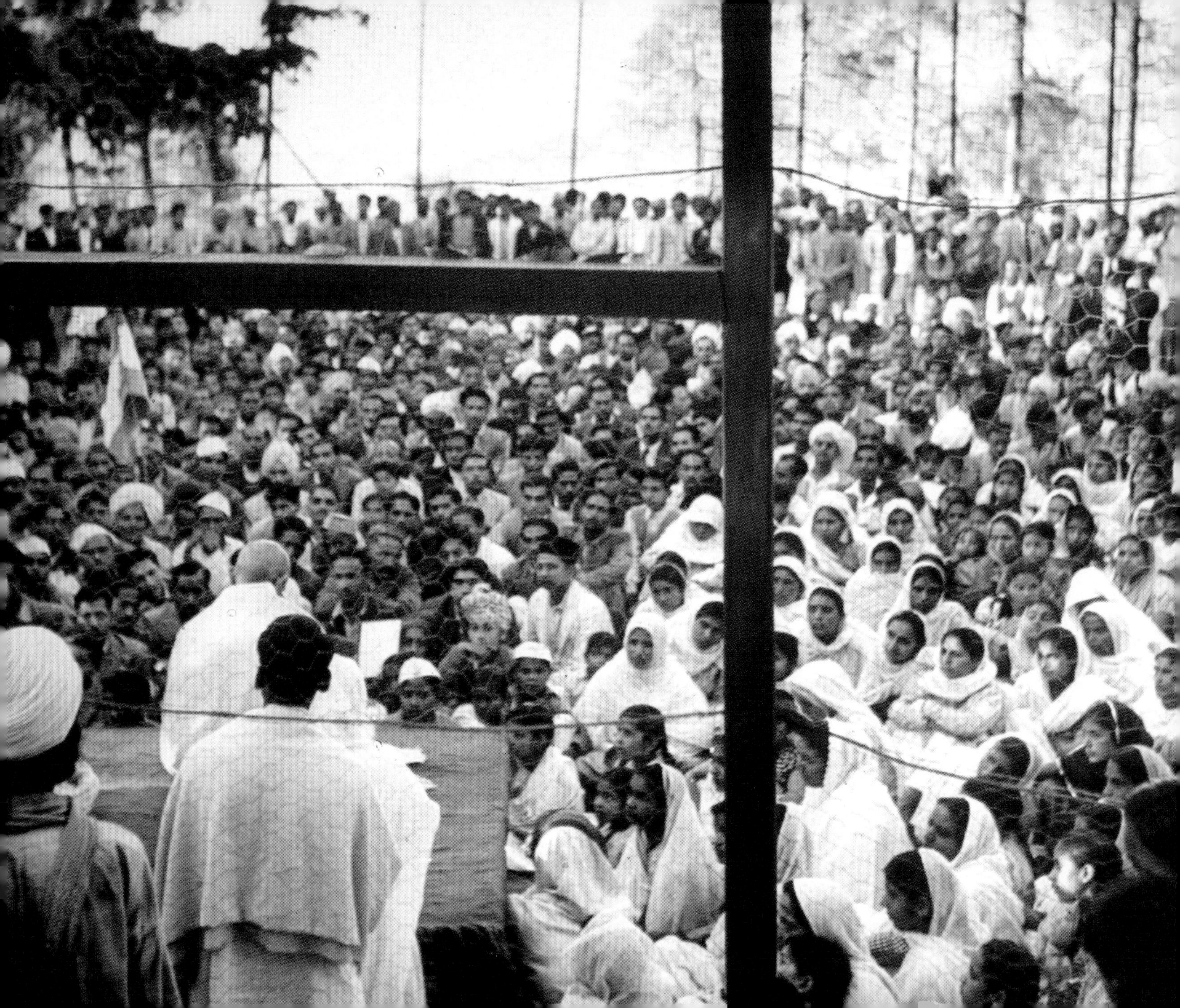

Minutes after Margaret Bourke-White came out of the Birla House on 30 January 1948 after meeting the Mahatma, she heard the news. A Hindu fanatic had killed the apostle of peace and non-violence. She rushed back to the Birla House and saw multitudes of people rushing to see the Mahatma. Though no photographers were allowed in, she was permitted to enter the room where his body lay. She pulled out her concealed camera and set off the flash, but before long someone seized her camera and the film was destroyed. In Halfway to Freedom *she desribes her surrelistic experience.*

'Gandhiji's clear, compelling voice of tolerance – that most powerful single voice in the nation – had to be stilled if the forces of intolerance were to survive. It was no accident that Gandhi was done away with by a fellow Hindu – one of those who stood for all that was worst and most rabid in the religion, just as Gandhi stood for all that was broadcast and best in Hinduism....

'By dawn the lawns and gardens of Birla House and all surrounding houses, Albuquerque Road and all streets leading into it, were flooded with people. By the tens of thousands they swirled through the Birla gates, until they crushed in an indivisible mass against the house. And still they came, beating against the walls of the house in surging waves of mourning humanity. I doubt that there has ever been a scene like it; certainly there has been none in my experience. The house, with its rising terraces, was like a rocky island holding its precious burden high above this sea of grief. Laid out on the roof of terrace was the figure of Gandhi, tranquil and serene, where all could see and receive his last darshan....

'For the first time in many months the Muslims of the city came in large numbers, to follow with heavy hearts the body of the man who had championed their rights to peace and security as a minority. "The Muslims in India have lost their father," people were saying. Not since the spontaneous and short-lived joy of Independence Day, exactly five and half months earlier, had the Muslims of Delhi mixed with Sikhs and Hindus so fearlessly and openly....

'The flames had risen high into the sky now, and the million people seemed to have sunk into a low bowl of darkness. All through the night most of them would continue to watch until the flames burned low, until at dawn Nehru, more lonely looking than ever, would speak a few sad words over the ashes, saying, "We have failed to protect our greatest treasure."

Excerpted from *Halfway to Freedom* by Margaret Bourke-White

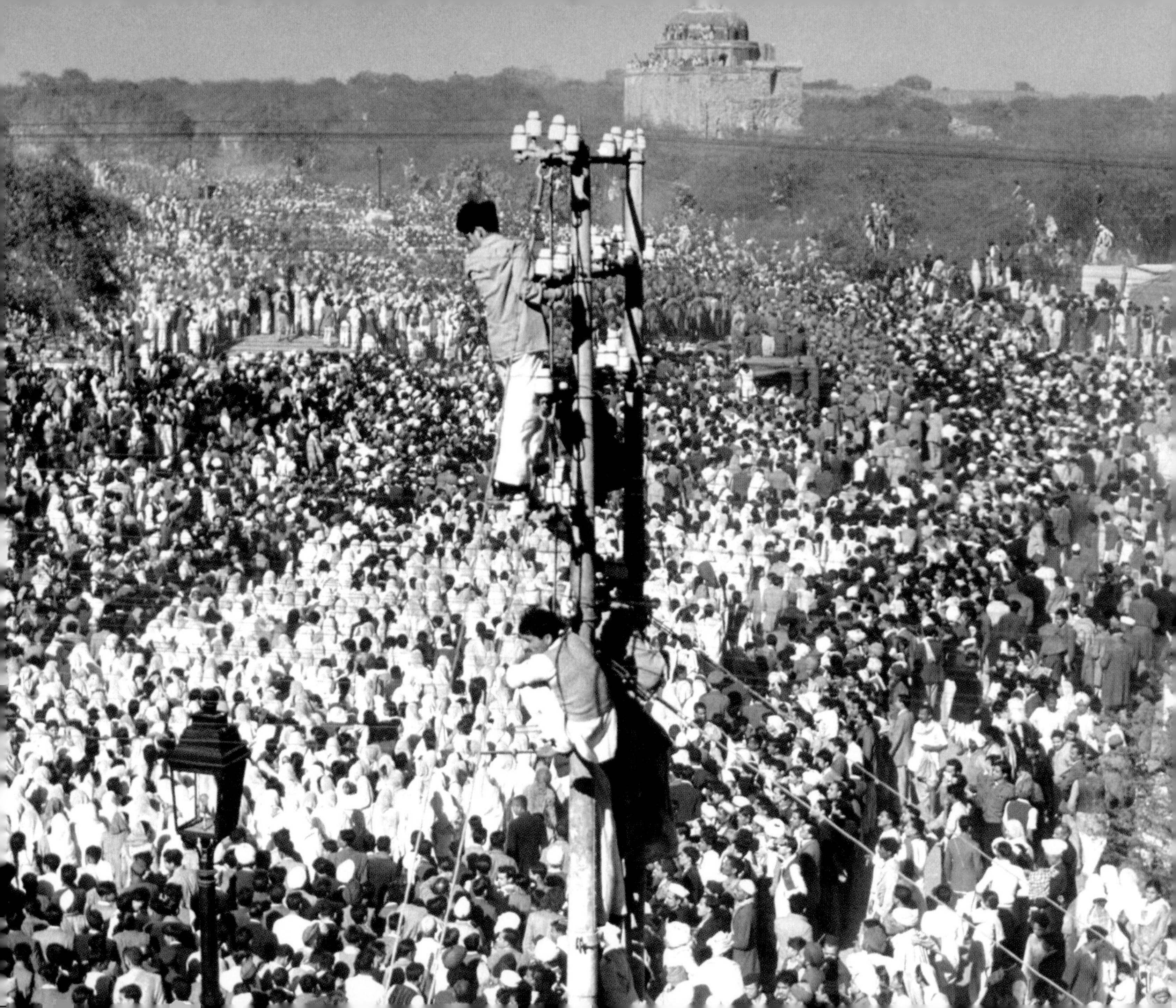

Margaret Bourke-White was probably the last journalist to interview and photograph him on 29 January 1948. About this special and memorable day, she writes:

'Since this momentous day, many people have asked me whether one knew in Gandhi's presence that there was an extraordinary man. The answer is yes. One knew! And never had I felt it more strongly than on this day, when the inconsistencies that had so troubled me dropped away and Gandhi began to reach forward and probe into that dreadful problem which has overwhelmed all of us. Nehru has said of Gandhi that he was "obviously not of the world's ordinary coinage; he was minted of a different and rare variety," and during these last moments of our talk I felt, as Nehru has expressed it, that sometimes "the unknown stared at us through his eyes."'

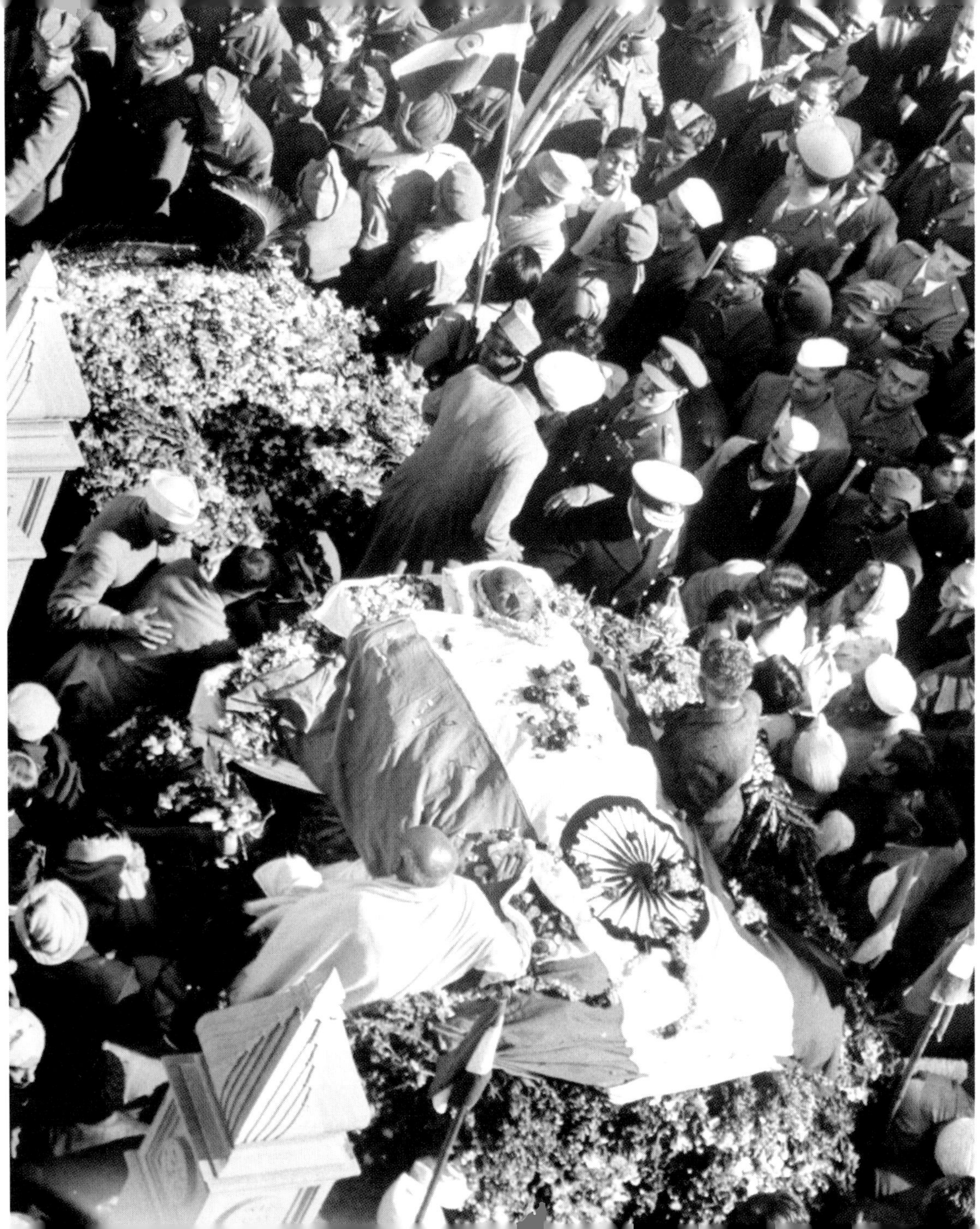

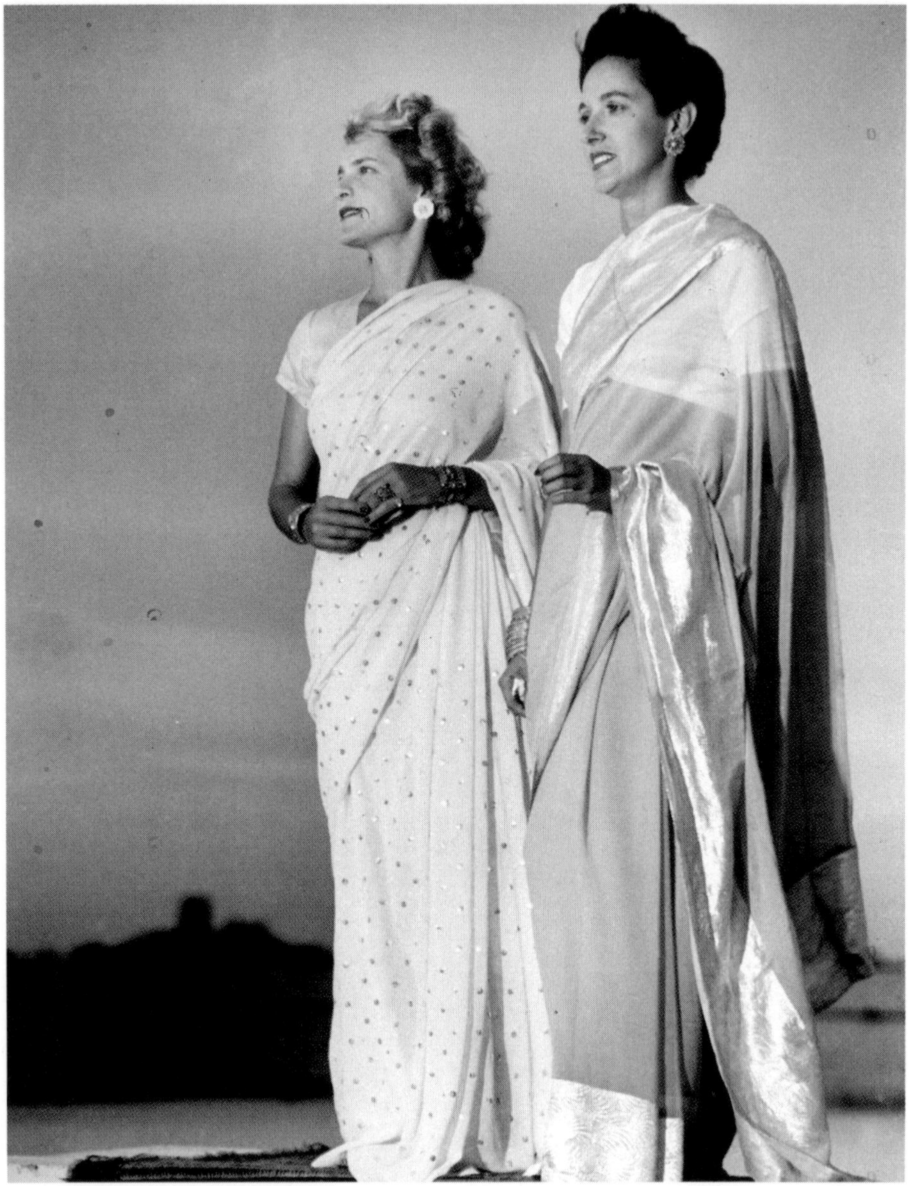

Left: Margaret Bourke-White with Lee Eitingon, a reporter with Life *magazine.*

At age forty-seven, Margaret discovered she had Parkinson's. Determined not to allow the disease to take over her life, she staved off its debilitating effects through exercise, medication, even a controversial surgery. For twenty years, Margaret soldiered on, taking photographs, travelling. Things became progressively difficult, yet her zeal for life and her work was irrepressible, as Vicki Goldberg writes:

'She was transformed by her struggle into a battered shell that housed a surprising radiance, as if her fabled physical energy had been condensed into some kind of inner electricity. She seemed to shrink, but her eyes grew more alive and piercing.... As the odds against Margaret grew higher and her options narrowed, her courage burst all bounds. She seemed no longer to know fear. She laughed at life the very moment it struck her down.'